157-160

W9-BKB-400

Mathematics In Our World

Third Edition

Robert E. Eicholz

Phares G. O'Daffer

Charles R. Fleenor

Contributing Writer
Randall I. Charles

▲ Addison-Wesley Publishing Company
Menlo Park, California · Reading, Massachusetts · London · Amsterdam · Don Mills, Ontario · Sydney

Illustration Acknowledgments

David Broad: 23, 38, 45, 58-59, 72-73, 76-77, 103, 108-109, 115, 132-133, 141, 197, 200-201, 220-221, 262-263;

Dick Cole: 1, 12-13, 30-31, 128-129, 163, 166-167, 178-179, 222-223, 244, 257, 276-277, 282-283;

Susan Jaekel: 207, 218-219;

Heather King: 320-321;

Pat Maloney: 20-21, 42-43, 45, 48, 56-57, 93, 105, 110-111, 122-123, 150-152, 168-169, 202-203, 232-233, 242, 264-265, 298-299, 302;

Pat Marshall: 319A-319B

Sharleen Pederson: 18, 28-29, 138, 148-149, 163, 172, 192-193, 238-239, 284-285, 310-311;

Bob Tamura: 6-7, 26-27, 40-41, 45, 50, 74-75, 90-91, 96-97, 121, 142, 186, 212-213, 229, 240-241, 250-251, 254, 257, 266, 286-287, 297, 308-309, 312, 316A-316B, 318

Cynthia Swann-Brodie: 341, 342, 343, 344, 345, 346, 347, 348

Photograph Acknowledgments

Elihu Blotnick*: 1 top right, center, bottom left and bottom right, 2 top, 4, 5, 11 both, 16, 34-35 top, 36 all, 45 top left and bottom right, 46 all, 47 all, 48, 50 all, 52 all, 54 all, 55 top, 56, 60, 61, 67, 68, 70 both, 70-71 center, 81 all, 82, 84-85, 94 top right, 99, 100 all, 101 all, 102 top right and bottom center right, 105 top and bottom right, 106 top, 116-117 top, 130 top right, 134-135 top center, 144, 145, 150, 154 top, 163 top left, top right, bottom left and bottom right, 164 top, 166-167 top center, 170 all, 173, 174 top, 175 both, 180, 188-189 all, 198, 199, 202-203, 207 top left, top right, center and bottom left, 208-209 all, 215, 216-217 top, 224-225 all, 230, 234 both, 235, 250, 255, 257 top right, center left and bottom right, 258 top, 259, 274-275, 281 top, 290, 291 top and bottom, 294 top left, center left and bottom left, 295 top center, 298, 300 left, 301 left, 304;

George B. Fry III*: 24, 45 bottom left, 89 right, 226-227;

George Hall*: 102 top center left;

Bil Plummer*: 102 bottom left;

William Rosenthal*: 291 center;

Nikolay Zurek*: cover

Mark Tuschman*: 98 top, 270–271

*Photographs provided expressly for the publisher. All other illustrations and photographs by Addison-Wesley staff.

Acknowledgments

Pachisi by Whitman, copyright © 1967 by Western Publishing Company, Inc., p. 88;

The Title Deed Cards and Playing Pieces are trademarks identified with MONOPOLY® real estate trading game equipment of Parker Brothers Division General Mills Fun Group, © 1935, 1946, 1961 and are used by its permission, p. 110-111;

Scrabble brand word tiles used with the permission of Selchow & Righter Co. Scrabble is the registered trademark of Selchow & Righter Co. for its word games and entertainment services, p. 111

Copyright © 1983, 1981, 1978 by Addison-Wesley Publishing Company, Inc. All rights reserved. No part of this publication may be reproduced, stored in a retrieval system, or transmitted, in any form or by any means, electronic, mechanical, photocopying, recording, or otherwise, without the prior written permission of the publisher. Printed in the United States of America. Published simultaneously in Canada.

ISBN 0-201-18130-4

ABCDEFGHIJKL-DO-8765432

Contents

Contents

Level 11

Addition and Subtraction to 10
Addition and Subtraction to 18
Problem Solving—Using Your Skills
Geometry 1

Addition and Subtraction to 10

Getting started

Which equation goes with which picture?

A $4 - 1 = 3$ B $3 + 2 = 5$ C $4 + 3 = 7$ D $5 - 2 = 3$

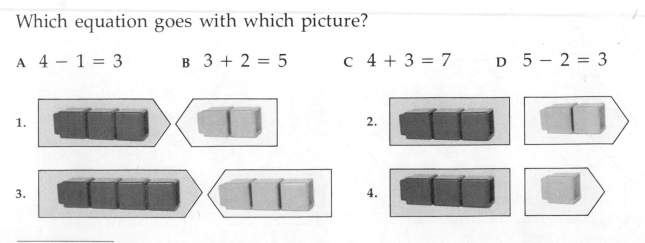

1.

2.

3.

4.

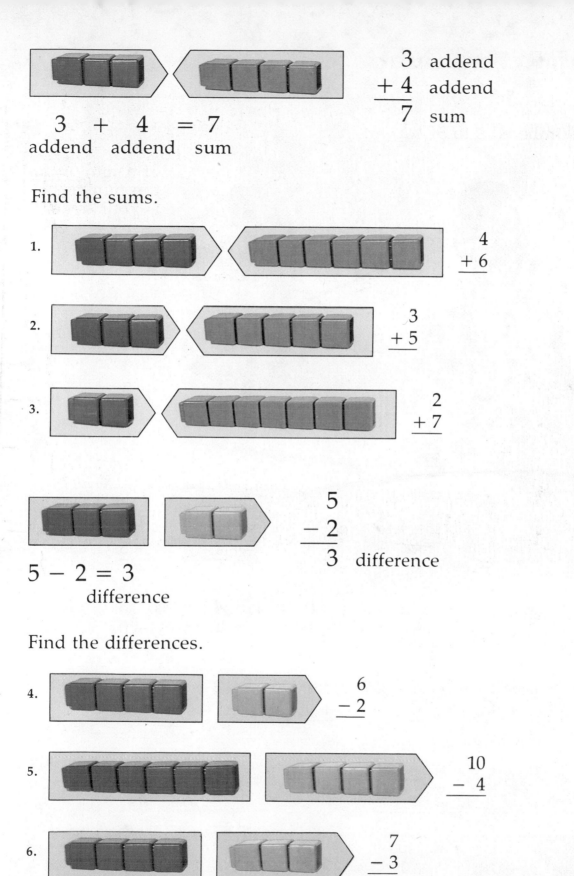

3 + 4 = 7
addend addend sum

$$\begin{array}{r} 3 \\ +4 \\ \hline 7 \end{array}$$ addend
addend
sum

Find the sums.

1. $$\begin{array}{r} 4 \\ +6 \\ \hline \end{array}$$

2. $$\begin{array}{r} 3 \\ +5 \\ \hline \end{array}$$

3. $$\begin{array}{r} 2 \\ +7 \\ \hline \end{array}$$

5 − 2 = 3
difference

$$\begin{array}{r} 5 \\ -2 \\ \hline 3 \end{array}$$ difference

Find the differences.

4. $$\begin{array}{r} 6 \\ -2 \\ \hline \end{array}$$

5. $$\begin{array}{r} 10 \\ -4 \\ \hline \end{array}$$

6. $$\begin{array}{r} 7 \\ -3 \\ \hline \end{array}$$

Addition facts

Cubes numbered 0 to 5

The sum of the
top numbers
is your score.

Score: ?

Add.

$$\begin{array}{r} 4 \\ +3 \\ \hline 7 \end{array}$$

Add.

1. $\begin{array}{r} 3 \\ +3 \\ \hline \end{array}$	2. $\begin{array}{r} 5 \\ +4 \\ \hline \end{array}$	3. $\begin{array}{r} 4 \\ +4 \\ \hline \end{array}$	4. $\begin{array}{r} 5 \\ +5 \\ \hline \end{array}$	5. $\begin{array}{r} 2 \\ +4 \\ \hline \end{array}$	6. $\begin{array}{r} 2 \\ +5 \\ \hline \end{array}$	7. $\begin{array}{r} 6 \\ +3 \\ \hline \end{array}$
8. $\begin{array}{r} 5 \\ +3 \\ \hline \end{array}$	9. $\begin{array}{r} 7 \\ +1 \\ \hline \end{array}$	10. $\begin{array}{r} 2 \\ +8 \\ \hline \end{array}$	11. $\begin{array}{r} 6 \\ +1 \\ \hline \end{array}$	12. $\begin{array}{r} 4 \\ +1 \\ \hline \end{array}$	13. $\begin{array}{r} 3 \\ +0 \\ \hline \end{array}$	14. $\begin{array}{r} 3 \\ +7 \\ \hline \end{array}$
15. $\begin{array}{r} 4 \\ +2 \\ \hline \end{array}$	16. $\begin{array}{r} 0 \\ +8 \\ \hline \end{array}$	17. $\begin{array}{r} 1 \\ +8 \\ \hline \end{array}$	18. $\begin{array}{r} 1 \\ +9 \\ \hline \end{array}$	19. $\begin{array}{r} 3 \\ +5 \\ \hline \end{array}$	20. $\begin{array}{r} 2 \\ +7 \\ \hline \end{array}$	21. $\begin{array}{r} 2 \\ +3 \\ \hline \end{array}$
22. $\begin{array}{r} 4 \\ +5 \\ \hline \end{array}$	23. $\begin{array}{r} 6 \\ +2 \\ \hline \end{array}$	24. $\begin{array}{r} 3 \\ +6 \\ \hline \end{array}$	25. $\begin{array}{r} 6 \\ +4 \\ \hline \end{array}$	26. $\begin{array}{r} 8 \\ +2 \\ \hline \end{array}$	27. $\begin{array}{r} 0 \\ +3 \\ \hline \end{array}$	28. $\begin{array}{r} 7 \\ +3 \\ \hline \end{array}$
29. $\begin{array}{r} 7 \\ +2 \\ \hline \end{array}$	30. $\begin{array}{r} 4 \\ +6 \\ \hline \end{array}$	31. $\begin{array}{r} 5 \\ +1 \\ \hline \end{array}$	32. $\begin{array}{r} 1 \\ +7 \\ \hline \end{array}$	33. $\begin{array}{r} 0 \\ +6 \\ \hline \end{array}$	34. $\begin{array}{r} 3 \\ +2 \\ \hline \end{array}$	35. $\begin{array}{r} 3 \\ +4 \\ \hline \end{array}$

Find the sums.

1. $7 + 3 = \square$
2. $2 + 2 = \square$
3. $8 + 1 = \square$
4. $6 + 2 = \square$

5. $9 + 1 = \square$
6. $2 + 8 = \square$
7. $0 + 5 = \square$
8. $5 + 2 = \square$

9. $7 + 2 = \square$
10. $0 + 0 = \square$
11. $5 + 5 = \square$
12. $5 + 3 = \square$

13. $3 + 2 = \square$
14. $3 + 1 = \square$
15. $3 + 6 = \square$
16. $5 + 1 = \square$

17. $6 + 4 = \square$
18. $2 + 1 = \square$
19. $4 + 4 = \square$
20. $3 + 3 = \square$

Give the missing numbers.

Add 2	
5	7
3	5
21. 6	▦
22. 4	▦
23. 7	▦
24. 2	▦

Add 4	
4	8
25. 5	▦
26. 3	▦
27. 6	▦
28. 2	▦
29. 0	▦

30. First number: 5
Second number: 3
Score: ?

Mark said, "3 years from now I'll be 10 years old." How old is Mark now?

☆ 31. Make two number cubes. Play a game with a friend.

More practice, page 324, Set A

Subtraction facts

First toss: 9
Second toss: 6
Difference: ?
Subtract.

The difference
is your score.

$$\begin{array}{r} 9 \\ -6 \\ \hline 3 \end{array}$$

JANE 3
BILL

Subtract.

1. $\begin{array}{r} 2 \\ -1 \\ \hline \end{array}$
2. $\begin{array}{r} 9 \\ -4 \\ \hline \end{array}$
3. $\begin{array}{r} 6 \\ -4 \\ \hline \end{array}$

4. $\begin{array}{r} 7 \\ -5 \\ \hline \end{array}$
5. $\begin{array}{r} 9 \\ -2 \\ \hline \end{array}$
6. $\begin{array}{r} 8 \\ -7 \\ \hline \end{array}$
7. $\begin{array}{r} 5 \\ -1 \\ \hline \end{array}$
8. $\begin{array}{r} 3 \\ -2 \\ \hline \end{array}$
9. $\begin{array}{r} 3 \\ -0 \\ \hline \end{array}$
10. $\begin{array}{r} 8 \\ -5 \\ \hline \end{array}$

11. $\begin{array}{r} 3 \\ -1 \\ \hline \end{array}$
12. $\begin{array}{r} 7 \\ -1 \\ \hline \end{array}$
13. $\begin{array}{r} 2 \\ -2 \\ \hline \end{array}$
14. $\begin{array}{r} 6 \\ -5 \\ \hline \end{array}$
15. $\begin{array}{r} 10 \\ -7 \\ \hline \end{array}$
16. $\begin{array}{r} 9 \\ -6 \\ \hline \end{array}$
17. $\begin{array}{r} 4 \\ -2 \\ \hline \end{array}$

18. $\begin{array}{r} 9 \\ -5 \\ \hline \end{array}$
19. $\begin{array}{r} 8 \\ -6 \\ \hline \end{array}$
20. $\begin{array}{r} 7 \\ -4 \\ \hline \end{array}$
21. $\begin{array}{r} 9 \\ -8 \\ \hline \end{array}$
22. $\begin{array}{r} 5 \\ -3 \\ \hline \end{array}$
23. $\begin{array}{r} 6 \\ -6 \\ \hline \end{array}$
24. $\begin{array}{r} 10 \\ -2 \\ \hline \end{array}$

25. $\begin{array}{r} 7 \\ -6 \\ \hline \end{array}$
26. $\begin{array}{r} 10 \\ -6 \\ \hline \end{array}$
27. $\begin{array}{r} 8 \\ -4 \\ \hline \end{array}$
28. $\begin{array}{r} 4 \\ -1 \\ \hline \end{array}$
29. $\begin{array}{r} 8 \\ -8 \\ \hline \end{array}$
30. $\begin{array}{r} 7 \\ -2 \\ \hline \end{array}$
31. $\begin{array}{r} 7 \\ -0 \\ \hline \end{array}$

Find the differences.

1. $7 - 2 = \square$ 2. $9 - 3 = \square$ 3. $8 - 4 = \square$

4. $6 - 2 = \square$ 5. $9 - 1 = \square$ 6. $6 - 3 = \square$

7. $5 - 2 = \square$ 8. $10 - 3 = \square$ 9. $8 - 7 = \square$

10. $10 - 5 = \square$ 11. $10 - 4 = \square$ 12. $10 - 6 = \square$

13. $10 - 7 = \square$ 14. $9 - 0 = \square$ 15. $8 - 6 = \square$

16. $7 - 4 = \square$ 17. $8 - 2 = \square$ 18. $6 - 1 = \square$ 19. $9 - 2 = \square$

20. $8 - 3 = \square$ 21. $9 - 7 = \square$ 22. $8 - 8 = \square$ 23. $10 - 1 = \square$

Give the missing numbers.

Subtract 3	
7	4
5	2
24. 8	▓
25. 6	▓
26. 4	▓
27. 9	▓

Subtract 4	
5	1
7	3
28. 6	▓
29. 10	▓
30. 4	▓
31. 9	▓

Find two numbers that have a sum of 9 and a difference of 9.

32. First toss: 10
    Second toss: 7
    Difference: ?

★ 33. Make a target.
    Play a game
    with a friend.

More practice, page 324, Set B

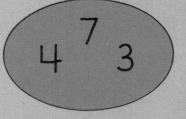

fact family numbers

$$4 + 3 = 7$$
$$3 + 4 = 7$$
$$7 - 3 = 4$$
$$7 - 4 = 3$$

Solve the equations.

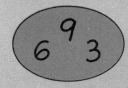

1. $6 + 3 = \square$

   $3 + 6 = \square$

   $9 - 3 = \square$

   $9 - 6 = \square$

2. $5 + 3 = \square$

   $3 + 5 = \square$

   $8 - 3 = \square$

   $8 - 5 = \square$

3. $4 + 6 = \square$

   $6 + 4 = \square$

   $10 - 6 = \square$

   $10 - 4 = \square$

4. $5 + 2 = \square$

   $2 + 5 = \square$

   $7 - 2 = \square$

   $7 - 5 = \square$

Solve the equations.

1. $2 + 3 = \square$ 2. $6 + 2 = \square$ 3. $4 + 5 = \square$

   $3 + 2 = \square$ $2 + 6 = \square$ $5 + 4 = \square$

   $5 - 3 = \square$ $8 - 2 = \square$ $9 - 5 = \square$

   $5 - 2 = \square$ $8 - 6 = \square$ $9 - 4 = \square$

4. $2 + 4 = \square$ 5. $7 + 2 = \square$ 6. $3 + 7 = \square$

   $4 + 2 = \square$ $2 + 7 = \square$ $7 + 3 = \square$

   $6 - 4 = \square$ $9 - 2 = \square$ $10 - 7 = \square$

   $6 - 2 = \square$ $9 - 7 = \square$ $10 - 3 = \square$

Find the differences.

7. $\begin{array}{r} 7 \\ -2 \\ \hline \end{array}$ 8. $\begin{array}{r} 9 \\ -5 \\ \hline \end{array}$ 9. $\begin{array}{r} 10 \\ -\ 5 \\ \hline \end{array}$ 10. $\begin{array}{r} 6 \\ -3 \\ \hline \end{array}$ 11. $\begin{array}{r} 8 \\ -3 \\ \hline \end{array}$ 12. $\begin{array}{r} 9 \\ -1 \\ \hline \end{array}$ 13. $\begin{array}{r} 7 \\ -1 \\ \hline \end{array}$

14. $\begin{array}{r} 9 \\ -3 \\ \hline \end{array}$ 15. $\begin{array}{r} 7 \\ -0 \\ \hline \end{array}$ 16. $\begin{array}{r} 10 \\ -\ 6 \\ \hline \end{array}$ 17. $\begin{array}{r} 8 \\ -1 \\ \hline \end{array}$ 18. $\begin{array}{r} 7 \\ -4 \\ \hline \end{array}$ 19. $\begin{array}{r} 8 \\ -7 \\ \hline \end{array}$ 20. $\begin{array}{r} 9 \\ -4 \\ \hline \end{array}$

21. $\begin{array}{r} 10 \\ -\ 8 \\ \hline \end{array}$ 22. $\begin{array}{r} 6 \\ -5 \\ \hline \end{array}$ 23. $\begin{array}{r} 9 \\ -2 \\ \hline \end{array}$ 24. $\begin{array}{r} 8 \\ -2 \\ \hline \end{array}$ 25. $\begin{array}{r} 10 \\ -\ 7 \\ \hline \end{array}$ 26. $\begin{array}{r} 9 \\ -6 \\ \hline \end{array}$ 27. $\begin{array}{r} 8 \\ -8 \\ \hline \end{array}$

Two numbers are we.
Nine is our sum.
Both greater than three,
Our difference is one.
Who are we?

Answers for Self-check   1. 10   2. 5   3. 9   4. 6   5. 9   6. 7   7. 3   8. 1   9. 3   10. 3   11. 4   12. 5
13. 10   14. 3   15. 8   16. 3   17. 5   18. 4   19. 5   20. 7   21. 7   22. 6   23. 10   24. 0

Self-check

Add or subtract.

1. $\begin{array}{r} 6 \\ + 4 \\ \hline \end{array}$ 2. $\begin{array}{r} 3 \\ + 2 \\ \hline \end{array}$ 3. $\begin{array}{r} 2 \\ + 7 \\ \hline \end{array}$ 4. $\begin{array}{r} 5 \\ + 1 \\ \hline \end{array}$ 5. $\begin{array}{r} 7 \\ + 2 \\ \hline \end{array}$ 6. $\begin{array}{r} 1 \\ + 6 \\ \hline \end{array}$

7. $\begin{array}{r} 9 \\ - 6 \\ \hline \end{array}$ 8. $\begin{array}{r} 8 \\ - 7 \\ \hline \end{array}$ 9. $\begin{array}{r} 8 \\ - 5 \\ \hline \end{array}$ 10. $\begin{array}{r} 6 \\ - 3 \\ \hline \end{array}$ 11. $\begin{array}{r} 8 \\ - 4 \\ \hline \end{array}$ 12. $\begin{array}{r} 10 \\ - 5 \\ \hline \end{array}$

13. $\begin{array}{r} 4 \\ + 6 \\ \hline \end{array}$ 14. $\begin{array}{r} 7 \\ - 4 \\ \hline \end{array}$ 15. $\begin{array}{r} 6 \\ + 2 \\ \hline \end{array}$ 16. $\begin{array}{r} 10 \\ - 7 \\ \hline \end{array}$ 17. $\begin{array}{r} 0 \\ + 5 \\ \hline \end{array}$ 18. $\begin{array}{r} 6 \\ - 2 \\ \hline \end{array}$

19. $\begin{array}{r} 2 \\ + 3 \\ \hline \end{array}$ 20. $\begin{array}{r} 10 \\ - 3 \\ \hline \end{array}$ 21. $\begin{array}{r} 5 \\ + 2 \\ \hline \end{array}$ 22. $\begin{array}{r} 9 \\ - 3 \\ \hline \end{array}$ 23. $\begin{array}{r} 3 \\ + 7 \\ \hline \end{array}$ 24. $\begin{array}{r} 5 \\ - 5 \\ \hline \end{array}$

Answers for Self-check—page 9

Test

Add or subtract.

1. $\begin{array}{r} 6 \\ + 3 \\ \hline \end{array}$ 2. $\begin{array}{r} 0 \\ + 7 \\ \hline \end{array}$ 3. $\begin{array}{r} 7 \\ + 3 \\ \hline \end{array}$ 4. $\begin{array}{r} 5 \\ + 3 \\ \hline \end{array}$ 5. $\begin{array}{r} 8 \\ + 2 \\ \hline \end{array}$ 6. $\begin{array}{r} 5 \\ + 4 \\ \hline \end{array}$

7. $\begin{array}{r} 8 \\ - 2 \\ \hline \end{array}$ 8. $\begin{array}{r} 5 \\ - 3 \\ \hline \end{array}$ 9. $\begin{array}{r} 10 \\ - 6 \\ \hline \end{array}$ 10. $\begin{array}{r} 7 \\ - 3 \\ \hline \end{array}$ 11. $\begin{array}{r} 9 \\ - 2 \\ \hline \end{array}$ 12. $\begin{array}{r} 6 \\ - 1 \\ \hline \end{array}$

13. $\begin{array}{r} 7 \\ + 1 \\ \hline \end{array}$ 14. $\begin{array}{r} 9 \\ - 7 \\ \hline \end{array}$ 15. $\begin{array}{r} 4 \\ + 5 \\ \hline \end{array}$ 16. $\begin{array}{r} 2 \\ + 5 \\ \hline \end{array}$ 17. $\begin{array}{r} 10 \\ - 4 \\ \hline \end{array}$ 18. $\begin{array}{r} 5 \\ - 2 \\ \hline \end{array}$

19. $\begin{array}{r} 3 \\ + 5 \\ \hline \end{array}$ 20. $\begin{array}{r} 7 \\ - 5 \\ \hline \end{array}$ 21. $\begin{array}{r} 3 \\ + 4 \\ \hline \end{array}$ 22. $\begin{array}{r} 9 \\ - 5 \\ \hline \end{array}$ 23. $\begin{array}{r} 8 \\ - 1 \\ \hline \end{array}$ 24. $\begin{array}{r} 3 \\ + 6 \\ \hline \end{array}$

A Nim Game

Try this game with a friend.

1. Start with 11 counters.

2. When it is your turn,
   pick up 1, 2, or 3
   counters.

3. To win, make your friend
   have to pick up the last
   counter.

Addition and Subtraction to 18

Getting started

Give each sum.

1.
9 + 5

10 + 4

2.
7 + 8

10 + 5

3.
8 + 6

10 + 4

4.
6 + 5

10 + 1

Solve the equations.
The papers above might help you.

1. $9 + 4 = \square$ 2. $7 + 6 = \square$

3. $8 + 3 = \square$ 4. $9 + 8 = \square$

5. $8 + 7 = \square$ 6. $9 + 7 = \square$

7. $8 + 6 = \square$ 8. $6 + 5 = \square$

9. $9 + 6 = \square$ 10. $8 + 5 = \square$

Addition

First toss: 7
Second toss: 9
Score: ?

Add.
$$\begin{array}{r} 7 \\ +\ 9 \\ \hline 16 \end{array}$$

The sum is your score.

Add.

1. $\begin{array}{r} 8 \\ +5 \\ \hline \end{array}$
2. $\begin{array}{r} 7 \\ +9 \\ \hline \end{array}$
3. $\begin{array}{r} 8 \\ +4 \\ \hline \end{array}$
4. $\begin{array}{r} 5 \\ +8 \\ \hline \end{array}$
5. $\begin{array}{r} 4 \\ +9 \\ \hline \end{array}$
6. $\begin{array}{r} 8 \\ +6 \\ \hline \end{array}$
7. $\begin{array}{r} 9 \\ +6 \\ \hline \end{array}$

8. $\begin{array}{r} 4 \\ +8 \\ \hline \end{array}$
9. $\begin{array}{r} 6 \\ +9 \\ \hline \end{array}$
10. $\begin{array}{r} 5 \\ +9 \\ \hline \end{array}$
11. $\begin{array}{r} 3 \\ +8 \\ \hline \end{array}$
12. $\begin{array}{r} 8 \\ +8 \\ \hline \end{array}$
13. $\begin{array}{r} 4 \\ +7 \\ \hline \end{array}$
14. $\begin{array}{r} 9 \\ +7 \\ \hline \end{array}$

15. $\begin{array}{r} 8 \\ +9 \\ \hline \end{array}$
16. $\begin{array}{r} 7 \\ +8 \\ \hline \end{array}$
17. $\begin{array}{r} 3 \\ +9 \\ \hline \end{array}$
18. $\begin{array}{r} 5 \\ +6 \\ \hline \end{array}$
19. $\begin{array}{r} 9 \\ +5 \\ \hline \end{array}$
20. $\begin{array}{r} 8 \\ +3 \\ \hline \end{array}$
21. $\begin{array}{r} 7 \\ +7 \\ \hline \end{array}$

22. $\begin{array}{r} 5 \\ +7 \\ \hline \end{array}$
23. $\begin{array}{r} 6 \\ +8 \\ \hline \end{array}$
24. $\begin{array}{r} 2 \\ +9 \\ \hline \end{array}$
25. $\begin{array}{r} 5 \\ +9 \\ \hline \end{array}$
26. $\begin{array}{r} 7 \\ +6 \\ \hline \end{array}$
27. $\begin{array}{r} 8 \\ +7 \\ \hline \end{array}$
28. $\begin{array}{r} 9 \\ +9 \\ \hline \end{array}$

Add.

29. $\begin{array}{r} 7 \\ +7 \\ \hline 14 \end{array}$ $\begin{array}{r} 8 \\ +7 \\ \hline ? \end{array}$
30. $\begin{array}{r} 6 \\ +6 \\ \hline 12 \end{array}$ $\begin{array}{r} 7 \\ +6 \\ \hline ? \end{array}$
31. $\begin{array}{r} 5 \\ +5 \\ \hline 10 \end{array}$ $\begin{array}{r} 5 \\ +6 \\ \hline ? \end{array}$

32. $\begin{array}{r} 9 \\ +9 \\ \hline 18 \end{array}$ $\begin{array}{r} 9 \\ +8 \\ \hline ? \end{array}$
33. $\begin{array}{r} 8 \\ +8 \\ \hline 16 \end{array}$ $\begin{array}{r} 7 \\ +8 \\ \hline ? \end{array}$
34. $\begin{array}{r} 7 \\ +7 \\ \hline 14 \end{array}$ $\begin{array}{r} 6 \\ +7 \\ \hline ? \end{array}$

Add.

1. $2 + 9$
2. $7 + 5$
3. $9 + 5$
4. $4 + 8$
5. $9 + 9$
6. $8 + 7$
7. $4 + 7$

8. $7 + 9$
9. $5 + 7$
10. $3 + 8$
11. $5 + 6$
12. $9 + 7$
13. $7 + 4$
14. $9 + 3$

15. $6 + 5$
16. $3 + 9$
17. $7 + 7$
18. $9 + 6$
19. $9 + 8$
20. $6 + 6$
21. $9 + 4$

22. $8 + 9$
23. $6 + 9$
24. $9 + 2$
25. $8 + 8$
26. $5 + 9$
27. $6 + 7$
28. $5 + 8$

Solve the equations.

29. $8 + 4 = \square$
30. $7 + 8 = \square$
31. $9 + 5 = \square$
32. $4 + 9 = \square$

33. $6 + 8 = \square$
34. $5 + 9 = \square$
35. $8 + 8 = \square$
36. $7 + 6 = \square$

37. $5 + 8 = \square$
38. $8 + 6 = \square$
39. $8 + 3 = \square$
40. $8 + 5 = \square$

41. First toss: 8
    Second toss: 4
    Score: ?

☆ 42. You try.
    Make a target.
    Play a game
    with a friend.

We have one digit each
And we're odd as odd can be.
Since our sum is just 16,
Our two names you'll surely see.
Who are we?

More practice, page 325, Set A

Fact families

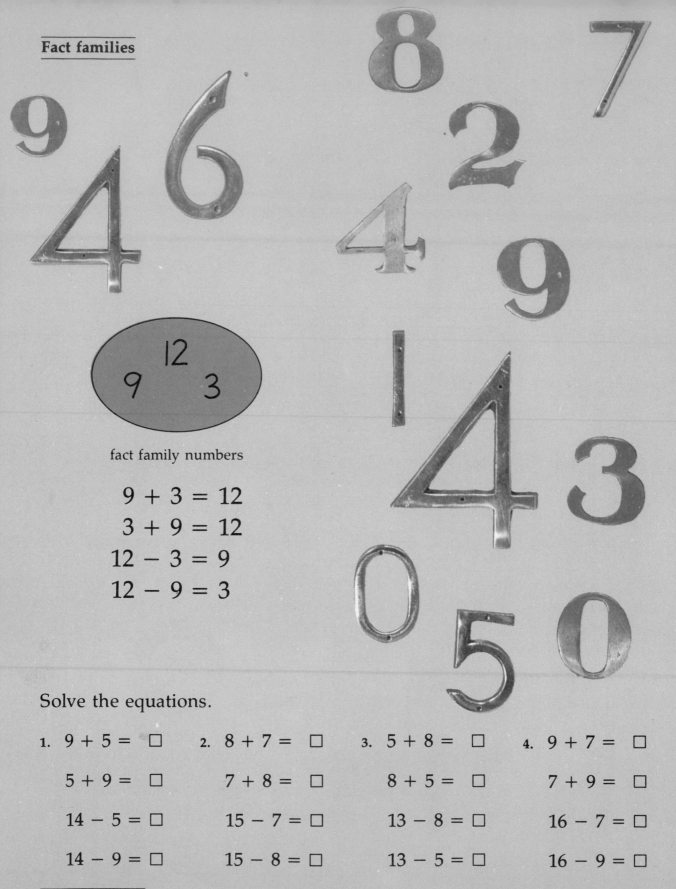

fact family numbers

$$9 + 3 = 12$$
$$3 + 9 = 12$$
$$12 - 3 = 9$$
$$12 - 9 = 3$$

Solve the equations.

1. $9 + 5 = \square$ 2. $8 + 7 = \square$ 3. $5 + 8 = \square$ 4. $9 + 7 = \square$

   $5 + 9 = \square$ $7 + 8 = \square$ $8 + 5 = \square$ $7 + 9 = \square$

   $14 - 5 = \square$ $15 - 7 = \square$ $13 - 8 = \square$ $16 - 7 = \square$

   $14 - 9 = \square$ $15 - 8 = \square$ $13 - 5 = \square$ $16 - 9 = \square$

Solve the equations.

1. $5 + 7 =$ ☐   2. $9 + 6 =$ ☐   3. $7 + 6 =$ ☐

    $7 + 5 =$ ☐ $6 + 9 =$ ☐ $6 + 7 =$ ☐

    $12 - 7 =$ ☐ $15 - 6 =$ ☐ $13 - 6 =$ ☐

    $12 - 5 =$ ☐ $15 - 9 =$ ☐ $13 - 7 =$ ☐

4. $8 + 9 =$ ☐   5. $6 + 5 =$ ☐   6. $8 + 6 =$ ☐

    $9 + 8 =$ ☐ $5 + 6 =$ ☐ $6 + 8 =$ ☐

    $17 - 9 =$ ☐ $11 - 5 =$ ☐ $14 - 6 =$ ☐

    $17 - 8 =$ ☐ $11 - 6 =$ ☐ $14 - 8 =$ ☐

Subtract.

7. $\begin{array}{r} 11 \\ -\ 3 \\ \hline \end{array}$ 8. $\begin{array}{r} 14 \\ -\ 7 \\ \hline \end{array}$ 9. $\begin{array}{r} 12 \\ -\ 8 \\ \hline \end{array}$ 10. $\begin{array}{r} 16 \\ -\ 8 \\ \hline \end{array}$ 11. $\begin{array}{r} 13 \\ -\ 9 \\ \hline \end{array}$ 12. $\begin{array}{r} 16 \\ -\ 7 \\ \hline \end{array}$

13. $\begin{array}{r} 12 \\ -\ 9 \\ \hline \end{array}$ 14. $\begin{array}{r} 13 \\ -\ 4 \\ \hline \end{array}$ 15. $\begin{array}{r} 14 \\ -\ 9 \\ \hline \end{array}$ 16. $\begin{array}{r} 11 \\ -\ 2 \\ \hline \end{array}$ 17. $\begin{array}{r} 17 \\ -\ 9 \\ \hline \end{array}$ 18. $\begin{array}{r} 12 \\ -\ 6 \\ \hline \end{array}$

19. $\begin{array}{r} 13 \\ -\ 8 \\ \hline \end{array}$ 20. $\begin{array}{r} 11 \\ -\ 5 \\ \hline \end{array}$ 21. $\begin{array}{r} 12 \\ -\ 7 \\ \hline \end{array}$ 22. $\begin{array}{r} 16 \\ -\ 9 \\ \hline \end{array}$ 23. $\begin{array}{r} 17 \\ -\ 8 \\ \hline \end{array}$ 24. $\begin{array}{r} 15 \\ -\ 9 \\ \hline \end{array}$

25. $\begin{array}{r} 18 \\ -\ 9 \\ \hline \end{array}$ 26. $\begin{array}{r} 14 \\ -\ 6 \\ \hline \end{array}$ 27. $\begin{array}{r} 12 \\ -\ 5 \\ \hline \end{array}$

28. $\begin{array}{r} 15 \\ -\ 8 \\ \hline \end{array}$ 29. $\begin{array}{r} 13 \\ -\ 7 \\ \hline \end{array}$ 30. $\begin{array}{r} 11 \\ -\ 4 \\ \hline \end{array}$

Think!

I'm the smallest number in my family. The other two are 11 and 8.
Who am I?

More practice, page 325, Set B

Practice for speed

Add.

1. 7
   + 8

2. 8
   + 4

3. 5
   + 8

4. 9
   + 2

5. 9
   + 6

6. 6
   + 6

7. 6
   + 8

8. 8
   + 3

9. 8
   + 5

10. 9
    + 8

11. 6
    + 7

12. 6
    + 9

13. 9
    + 9

14. 7
    + 7

15. 9
    + 3

16. 5
    + 9

17. 6
    + 5

18. 8
    + 6

19. 9
    + 4

20. 7
    + 9

21. 7
    + 4

22. 8
    + 9

23. 7
    + 5

24. 9
    + 5

25. 3
    + 9

26. 8
    + 8

27. 4
    + 9

28. 8
    + 7

Subtract.

29. 13
    − 8

30. 12
    − 3

31. 11
    − 8

32. 16
    − 7

33. 14
    − 9

34. 12
    − 4

35. 16
    − 9

36. 14
    − 5

37. 13
    − 7

38. 13
    − 4

39. 11
    − 4

40. 15
    − 9

41. 17
    − 8

42. 14
    − 6

43. 18
    − 9

44. 11
    − 5

45. 15
    − 7

46. 11
    − 2

47. 13
    − 5

48. 14
    − 8

49. 16
    − 8

50. 12
    − 5

51. 12
    − 7

52. 15
    − 8

Add or subtract.

1. $4 + 7$
2. $5 + 7$
3. $11 - 5$
4. $15 - 7$
5. $9 + 7$
6. $14 - 5$

7. $12 - 4$
8. $8 + 6$
9. $9 + 5$
10. $16 - 7$
11. $9 + 4$
12. $13 - 6$

13. $6 + 5$
14. $5 + 8$
15. $11 - 7$
16. $14 - 7$
17. $3 + 9$
18. $7 + 6$

19. $13 - 4$
20. $3 + 8$
21. $12 - 7$
22. $11 - 8$
23. $8 + 7$
24. $12 - 9$

Solve the equations.

25. $4 + 9 = \square$
26. $17 - 8 = \square$
27. $9 + 2 = \square$
28. $14 - 9 = \square$

29. $9 + 6 = \square$
30. $8 + 8 = \square$
31. $13 - 5 = \square$
32. $12 - 6 = \square$

33. $8 + 5 = \square$
34. $11 - 2 = \square$
35. $15 - 6 = \square$
36. $9 + 8 = \square$

Give the missing numbers.

Add 4	
7	11
37. 5	|||||
38. 8	|||||
39. 6	|||||
40. 9	|||||

Subtract 6	
12	6
41. 13	|||||
42. 11	|||||
43. 15	|||||
44. 14	|||||

Increase me by 5.
Then take away 7.
When you are done,
You should have 11.
Who am I?

Adding three numbers

What is the total score?   Cubes numbered 1 to 6

$4 + 2 + 3$
$6 + 3 = 9$

The score is 9.

Find the sums.

1. Add these first.
    $3 + 5 + 4 = \square$

2. Add these first.
    $3 + 5 + 4 = \square$

3. Add these first.
    $3 + 5 + 4 = \square$

Add any two numbers first.

4. $3 + 2 + 4 = \square$ 5. $5 + 2 + 6 = \square$ 6. $5 + 4 + 3 = \square$

7. $1 + 5 + 2 = \square$ 8. $7 + 1 + 8 = \square$ 9. $2 + 7 + 2 = \square$

10. $6 + 2 + 2 = \square$ 11. $3 + 6 + 2 = \square$ 12. $5 + 4 + 5 = \square$

13. $4 + 1 + 3 = \square$ 14. $7 + 2 + 6 = \square$ 15. $4 + 2 + 6 = \square$

Solve. Look for tens.

16. $7 + 3 + 2 = \square$ 17. $7 + 2 + 3 = \square$ 18. $6 + 3 + 1 = \square$

19. $5 + 6 + 5 = \square$ 20. $4 + 6 + 9 = \square$ 21. $7 + 8 + 2 = \square$

22. $9 + 8 + 1 = \square$ 23. $5 + 2 + 8 = \square$ 24. $8 + 5 + 2 = \square$

25. $6 + 2 + 4 = \square$ 26. $5 + 7 + 3 = \square$ 27. $9 + 5 + 5 = \square$

Adding down

$$\begin{array}{r} 3 \\ 4 \\ +\ 2 \\ \hline 9 \end{array}$$

Adding up

$$\begin{array}{r} 3 \\ 4 \\ +\ 2 \\ \hline 9 \end{array}$$

Add.

1. $\begin{array}{r} 2 \\ 3 \\ +\ 1 \\ \hline \end{array}$
2. $\begin{array}{r} 5 \\ 1 \\ +\ 6 \\ \hline \end{array}$
3. $\begin{array}{r} 1 \\ 4 \\ +\ 1 \\ \hline \end{array}$
4. $\begin{array}{r} 2 \\ 3 \\ +\ 2 \\ \hline \end{array}$
5. $\begin{array}{r} 4 \\ 2 \\ +\ 3 \\ \hline \end{array}$
6. $\begin{array}{r} 5 \\ 3 \\ +\ 2 \\ \hline \end{array}$
7. $\begin{array}{r} 2 \\ 5 \\ +\ 3 \\ \hline \end{array}$

8. $\begin{array}{r} 6 \\ 2 \\ +\ 1 \\ \hline \end{array}$
9. $\begin{array}{r} 7 \\ 1 \\ +\ 4 \\ \hline \end{array}$
10. $\begin{array}{r} 6 \\ 3 \\ +\ 5 \\ \hline \end{array}$
11. $\begin{array}{r} 2 \\ 8 \\ +\ 1 \\ \hline \end{array}$
12. $\begin{array}{r} 3 \\ 4 \\ +\ 3 \\ \hline \end{array}$
13. $\begin{array}{r} 4 \\ 5 \\ +\ 3 \\ \hline \end{array}$
14. $\begin{array}{r} 8 \\ 3 \\ +\ 1 \\ \hline \end{array}$

Add. Look for tens.

15. $\begin{array}{r} 2 \\ 4 \\ +\ 5 \\ \hline \end{array}$
16. $\begin{array}{r} 3 \\ 4 \\ +\ 3 \\ \hline \end{array}$
17. $\begin{array}{r} 6 \\ 2 \\ +\ 2 \\ \hline \end{array}$
18. $\begin{array}{r} 8 \\ 2 \\ +\ 4 \\ \hline \end{array}$
19. $\begin{array}{r} 7 \\ 5 \\ +\ 3 \\ \hline \end{array}$
20. $\begin{array}{r} 6 \\ 3 \\ +\ 5 \\ \hline \end{array}$
21. $\begin{array}{r} 3 \\ 6 \\ +\ 7 \\ \hline \end{array}$

22. $\begin{array}{r} 4 \\ 5 \\ +\ 5 \\ \hline \end{array}$
23. $\begin{array}{r} 6 \\ 3 \\ +\ 4 \\ \hline \end{array}$
24. $\begin{array}{r} 5 \\ 2 \\ +\ 5 \\ \hline \end{array}$
25. $\begin{array}{r} 3 \\ 7 \\ +\ 2 \\ \hline \end{array}$
26. $\begin{array}{r} 8 \\ 2 \\ +\ 8 \\ \hline \end{array}$
27. $\begin{array}{r} 9 \\ 6 \\ +\ 1 \\ \hline \end{array}$
28. $\begin{array}{r} 4 \\ 4 \\ +\ 6 \\ \hline \end{array}$

Give each score.

29.

30.

Think!

Three numbers are we.
Close as close can be.
Twelve's our sum you see.
Now who are we three?

Answers for Self-check   1. 15   2. 13   3. 14   4. 12   5. 12   6. 14   7. 7   8. 6   9. 5   10. 8   11. 7   12. 8   13. 15   14. 9   15. 17   16. 5   17. 16   18. 8   19. 8   20. 11   21. 11   22. 12   23. 14   24. 13

Self-check

1. 9
   + 6

2. 5
   + 8

3. 7
   + 7

4. 9
   + 3

5. 7
   + 5

6. 6
   + 8

7. 12
   − 5

8. 14
   − 8

9. 11
   − 6

10. 15
    − 7

11. 13
    − 6

12. 17
    − 9

13. $8 + 7 = \square$

14. $12 − 3 = \square$

15. $8 + 9 = \square$

16. $13 − 8 = \square$

17. $8 + 8 = \square$

18. $16 − 8 = \square$

19. 3
    3
    + 2

20. 4
    2
    + 5

21. 1
    7
    + 3

22. 4
    2
    + 6

23. 4
    3
    + 7

24. 5
    5
    + 3

Answers for Self-check—page 21

Test

1. 8
   + 7

2. 6
   + 5

3. 8
   + 4

4. 3
   + 9

5. 5
   + 8

6. 6
   + 9

7. 14
   − 6

8. 15
   − 7

9. 11
   − 4

10. 13
    − 8

11. 11
    − 8

12. 12
    − 9

13. $6 + 7 = \square$

14. $12 − 6 = \square$

15. $3 + 8 = \square$

16. $9 + 5 = \square$

17. $15 − 8 = \square$

18. $13 − 9 = \square$

19. 4
    1
    + 6

20. 7
    4
    + 3

21. 3
    8
    + 2

22. 5
    3
    + 6

23. 5
    6
    + 5

24. 4
    5
    + 3

Lucky Number Toss

Try this game with a friend.

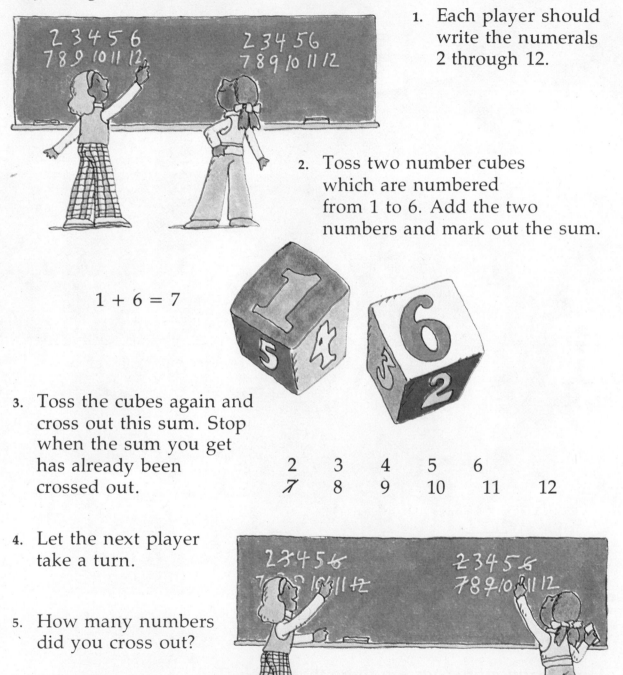

1. Each player should write the numerals 2 through 12.

2. Toss two number cubes which are numbered from 1 to 6. Add the two numbers and mark out the sum.

$$1 + 6 = 7$$

3. Toss the cubes again and cross out this sum. Stop when the sum you get has already been crossed out.

2	3	4	5	6
7̶	8	9	10	11	12

4. Let the next player take a turn.

5. How many numbers did you cross out?

The player with the most crossed out numbers wins.

8 cans

9 apples

4 cans

12 eggs

Getting started

1. How many cans are there in all?

2. How many more eggs are there than apples?

3. If 3 eggs are broken, how many good eggs are there?

4. What other problems can you solve?

Nora bought 7 sweet rolls and 9 dinner rolls. How many rolls did she buy?

7

9

How many rolls?

Add.

$$\begin{array}{r} 7 \\ + 9 \\ \hline 16 \end{array}$$

16 rolls seems right.

Solving Problems

1. Read carefully to find the facts.

2. Look for the question.

3. Decide what to do.

4. Find the answer.

5. Read again. Does your answer make sense?

Solve these short stories.

1. Laurie had 5 eggs. She broke 2 eggs. How many does she have now?

2. Alan has 6 bananas and 2 apples. How many pieces of fruit does he have?

A day at school

1. Singing:
   9 old songs
   8 new songs
   How many songs in all?

2. Playground:
   4 tables
   8 benches
   How many more benches
   than tables?

3. Pets:
   5 white mice
   7 fish
   How many pets in all?

4. Art:
   13 brushes
   9 paint jars
   How many more brushes
   than paint jars?

5. Math paper:
   12 problems
   Missed 3
   How many right?

6. Books:
   8 books on the shelf
   4 books on the table
   How many books in all?

7. Game:
7 players on one side
6 on the other
How many players in all?

8. Books:
Maria read 7.
Jim read 12.
How many more books
did Jim read?

9. Spelling:
First list—7 words
Second list—9 words
How many words in all?

10. Tables:
Lunchroom—16 tables
Library—7 tables
How many more tables
in the lunchroom?

11. Teams:
Stars won 16 games.
Miners won 8 games.
How many more games
did the Stars win?

12. Blocks from school:
Sandy—11 blocks
Randy—7 blocks
How many more blocks
for Sandy?

Frogs

All frogs were once tiny tadpoles. Tadpoles have tails and swim like fish. When they get older, their tails go away and they grow legs. Then they are frogs and can get out of the water.

You can learn more about frogs in these problems.

1. There were 5 tadpoles swimming in one pond. There were 8 in another. How many were in both?

2. One tadpole grew its back legs in 7 weeks. It grew its front legs in 5 weeks. How much longer did it take to grow its back legs?

3. The tail of a tadpole was 9 cm. The body was 4 cm. How long was the tadpole?

4. One tadpole was
   15 cm long.
   Another was only 6 cm.
   How much longer
   was the first?

5. Frogs catch bugs with
   their tongues. A frog
   ate 13 bugs one day.
   It ate 9 the next day.
   How many more did it
   eat the first day?

6. One day a frog was in the water 9 hours.
   Another day the frog was in the water 5 hours.
   How many hours for both days?

7. A small frog jumped 17 cm.
   Another jumped 8 cm.
   How much farther was the longer jump?

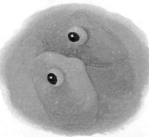

8. A large frog jumped 5 m.
   Then it jumped 4 m.
   How far did it jump in all?

Mike said,
"Guess my rule."

Gina said	Mike answered
3	5
8	10
5	7
2	4

Gina said,
"Your rule is
add 2."

1. Guess Sue's rule.
Give the missing
number.

Jim said	Sue answered
2	7
5	10
8	13
1	6
6	▥

Guess each rule. Then give the missing numbers.

	Bill said	Carol answered
	4	13
	6	15
	2	11
2.	7	▥
3.	9	▥
4.	▥	12
5.	▥	14

	Bill said	Carol answered
	8	1
	7	0
	10	3
6.	9	▥
7.	▥	6
8.	▥	8
9.	▥	7

	Bill said	Carol answered
	2	0
	4	0
	3	1
	5	1
	8	0
10.	6	▥
11.	11	▥

Guess my number

Scott and Brenda played "Guess My Number."

Try to find the numbers.

1. If you add 6 to my number, you get 10. What's my number?

2. If you add my number to 4, you get 8. What's my number?

☆ 3. Add 3 to my number. Then add 2. You should get 10. What's my number?

☆ 4. First subtract 6 from my number and then add 2. You should get 8. What's my number?

☆ 5. When you subtract 5 from my number, you get 9. What's my number?

☆ 6. Add my number to itself. Then add 4. You should get 10. What's my number?

Answers for Self-check   1. 8   2. 4   3. 15   4. 13   5. 13

Self-check

1. Had 12 eggs. Used 4.
   How many are left?

2. 11 balloons
   7 children
   How many more balloons
   than children?

3. 7 boys and 8 girls are
   playing a game.
   How many children?

4. Had 5 dollars.
   Earned 8 dollars more.
   Have how much now?

5. Give the missing number.

Bob said	Anna answered
7	15
3	11
6	14
5	▥

Answers for Self-check—page 31

Test

1. Had 15 cents.
   Spent 8 cents.
   How much is left?

2. 12 yellow pencils
   8 green pencils
   How many more yellow
   pencils?

3. Caught 7 butterflies.
   Then caught 6 more.
   How many in all?

4. 9 frogs
   6 tadpoles
   How many in all?

5. Give the missing number.

Nancy said	Jim answered
8	17
5	14
6	15
9	▥

Paper folding

Fold a paper once.

Open it. How many parts?

Fold a paper two times.

Open it. How many parts?

Fold a paper three times.

Open it. How many parts?

How many parts for each of these? Guess before you try.

Four folds   Five folds

Geometry 1

This pattern

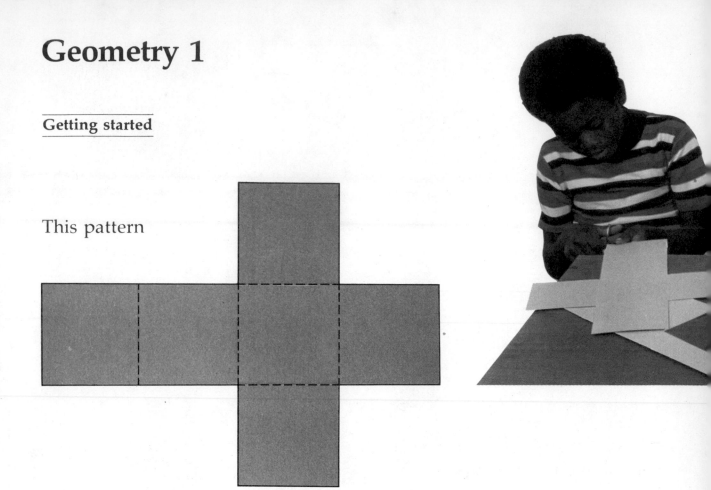

can be folded

and taped

to make a cube.

Trace the pattern and make a cube.

1. How many corners does your cube have? Each corner of your cube is a **point**.

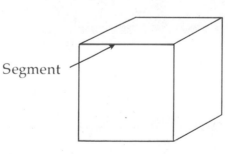

Point

2. How many edges does your cube have? Each edge of your cube is a **segment**.

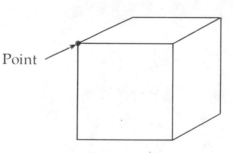

Segment

3. How many faces does your cube have? Each face of your cube has a **square** shape.

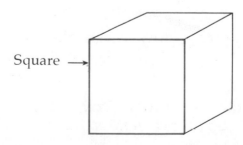

Square

There is geometry all around you.

A B

C D

E F

1. Which pictures show a square?

2. Which pictures show a triangle?

3. Which pictures show a rectangle?

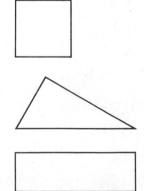

How many of each shape are in the figure?

1. squares

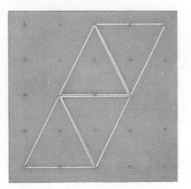

2. triangles

3. rectangles

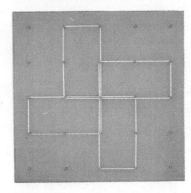

☆ **4. squares**

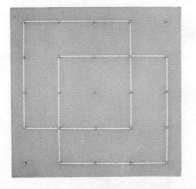

☆ **5. triangles**

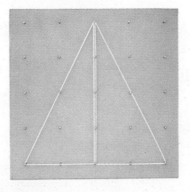

☆ **6. rectangles**

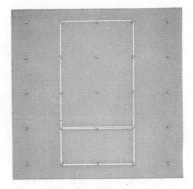

☆ **7. squares**

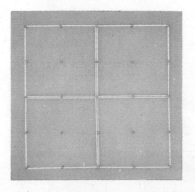

☆ **8. triangles**

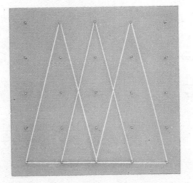

☆ **9. rectangles**

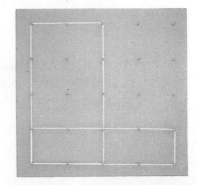

1. What shape has been made with the orange boards?

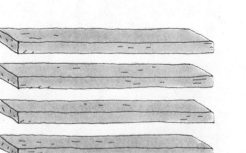

2. What shape could you make with the brown boards?

3. What shape could you make with the yellow boards?

Squares, triangles, and rectangles are made from segments.
Which figure can be made from which set of segments?

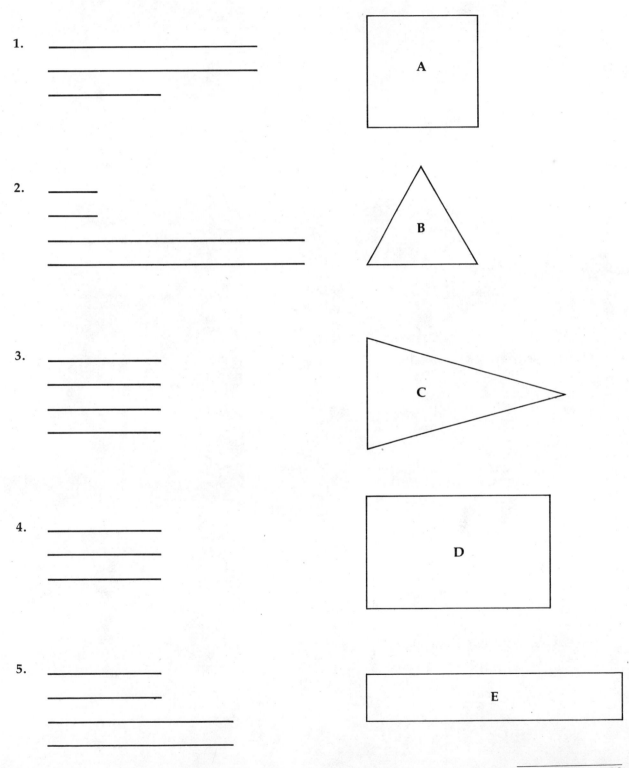

1.

2.

3.

4.

5.

A

B

C

D

E

1. How many circles
   can you find on the telephone?

2. How many other circles
   can you find in the picture?

1. **Circles** have a **center.**

   Which pencil is on the center of the circle?

2. Which pencil is on the circle?

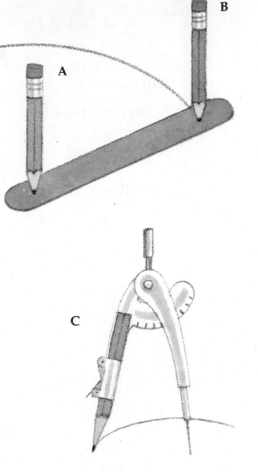

3. Here are some ways to draw circles.

A

With a round object

B

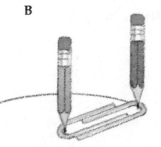

With two pencils and a paper clip

C

With a compass

Which of these ways uses the center point?

4. How many times would you need to fold a circle to find the center?

Edges even with each other

Answers for Self-check   1. C   2. A   3. A   4. B

Self-check

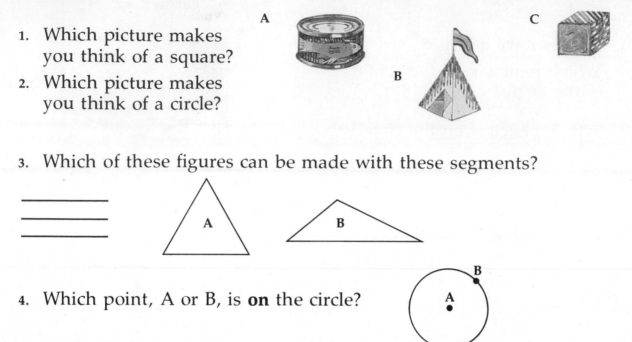

1. Which picture makes you think of a square?

2. Which picture makes you think of a circle?

3. Which of these figures can be made with these segments?

A B

4. Which point, A or B, is **on** the circle?

Answers for Self-check—page 41

Test

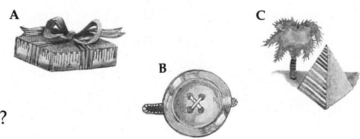

1. Which picture makes you think of a triangle?

2. Which picture makes you think of a rectangle?

3. Which of these figures can be made with these segments?

A B

4. Which point, A or B, is the **center** of the circle?

Inside or Outside?

This is a single loop of string.
Which things are inside the loop?

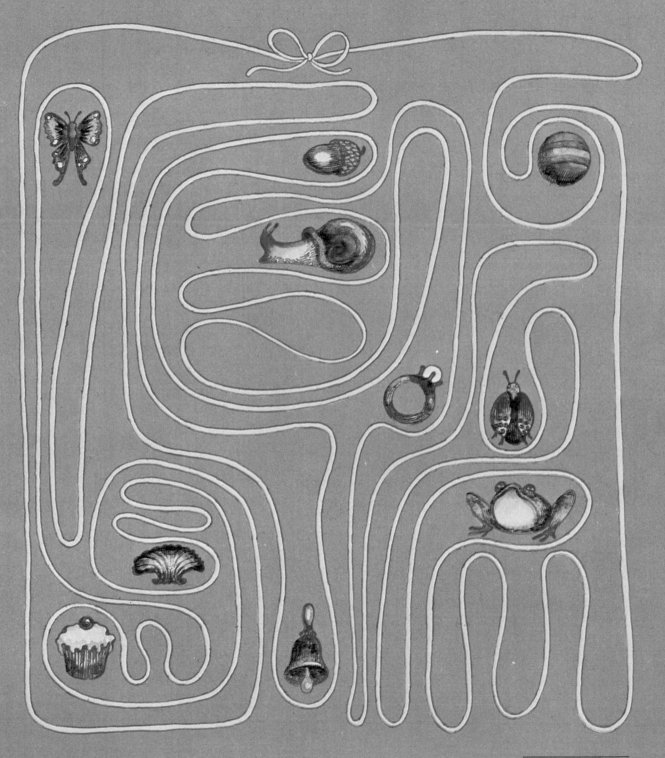

1. 3
    + 4

2. 2
    + 8

3. 5
    + 4

4. 7
    + 3

5. 3
    + 6

6. 2
    + 4

7. 8
    − 5

8. 10
    − 6

9. 9
    − 7

10. 7
    − 4

11. 10
    − 5

12. 8
    − 4

13. 5
    + 6

14. 7
    + 7

15. 9
    + 8

16. 6
    + 9

17. 8
    + 8

18. 7
    + 6

19. 12
    − 4

20. 17
    − 8

21. 18
    − 9

22. 13
    − 7

23. 15
    − 8

24. 14
    − 7

25. 6
    + 6

26. 11
    − 3

27. 7
    + 8

28. 16
    − 9

29. 9
    + 9

30. 14
    − 8

Solve.

31. 4 gray kittens
    3 black kittens
    How many in all?

32. First game: 9 points
    Second game: 14 points
    How many more points
    for the second game?

33. 12 turtles
    8 frogs
    How many more turtles?

34. 7 players on one team
    8 players on the other
    How many in all?

Level **12**

Place Value
Adding 2- and 3-digit Numbers
Subtracting 2- and 3-digit Numbers
Problem Solving—Using Your Skills
Measurement 1

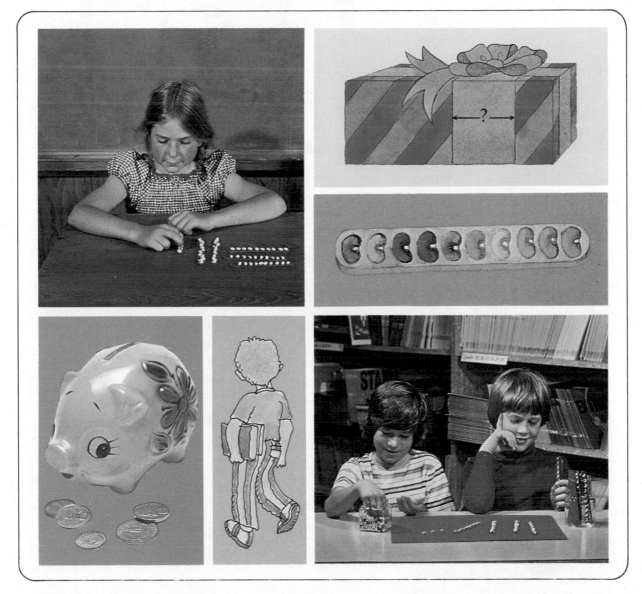

Place Value

Getting started

1 ten-stick has 10 beans

10 TENSTICKS

1 box has 10 ten-sticks

Suppose you made ten-sticks with these beans.

1. How many boxes could you fill?
2. How many extra ten-sticks would there be?
3. How many extra beans?

How many beans?

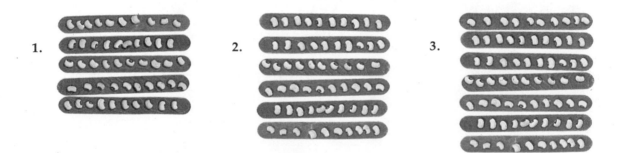

1.

2.

3.

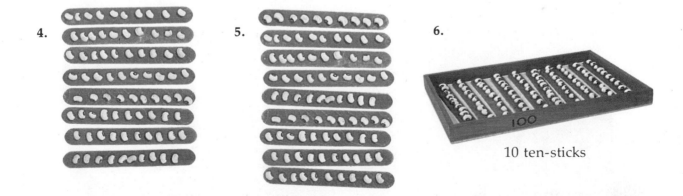

4.

5.

6.

10 ten-sticks

How many? Write the numeral.

1.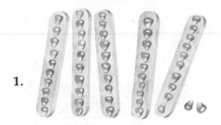

5 tens and 2 ones

2.

4 tens and 5 ones

3.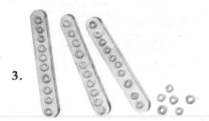

3 tens and 6 ones

4.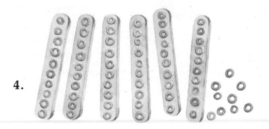

6 tens and 9 ones

5.

4 tens and 0 ones

6.

5 tens and 3 ones

Write the numeral.

1. 4 tens and 5 ones
   Answer: 45
2. 2 tens and 7 ones
3. 5 tens and 1 one

4. 3 tens and 2 ones
5. 6 tens and 0 ones
6. 4 tens and 8 ones

7. 7 tens and 4 ones
8. 5 tens and 9 ones
9. 8 tens and 2 ones

10. 6 tens and 5 ones
11. 8 tens and 3 ones
12. 7 tens and 0 ones

13. 4 tens and 2 ones
14. 1 ten and 0 ones
15. 3 tens and 9 ones

16. 9 tens and 2 ones
17. 7 tens and 7 ones
18. 9 tens and 9 ones

Complete the counting.

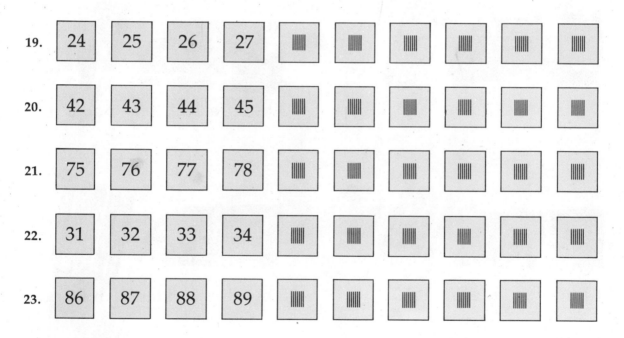

19. 24 25 26 27

20. 42 43 44 45

21. 75 76 77 78

22. 31 32 33 34

23. 86 87 88 89

 Think!

1. My digits are 6 and 2.
   I come before 30.
   Who am I?

2. One of my digits is 0.
   I'm between 60 and 80.
   Who am I?

We write: 245

How many? Write the numeral.

1.

2 hundreds, 3 tens, and 4 ones

2.

3 hundreds, 2 tens, and 5 ones

3.
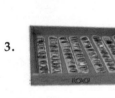

1 hundred, 4 tens, and 2 ones

4.

2 hundreds, 5 tens, and 0 ones

5.

3 hundreds, 0 tens, and 2 ones

6.

1 hundred, 3 tens, and 4 ones

Write the numeral.

1. 3 hundreds, 2 tens, and 6 ones
2. 5 hundreds, 0 tens, and 0 ones
3. 4 hundreds, 7 tens, and 2 ones
4. 6 hundreds, 2 tens, and 7 ones
5. 6 hundreds, 5 tens, and 0 ones
6. 1 hundred, 0 tens, and 0 ones
7. 2 hundreds, 0 tens, and 1 one
8. 7 hundreds, 8 tens, and 5 ones
9. 3 hundreds, 8 tens, and 0 ones
10. 9 hundreds, 2 tens, and 4 ones

11. two hundred eighty-three
12. six hundred fifty-four
13. five hundred sixty-seven
14. three hundred thirty-nine
15. nine hundred forty-one
16. seven hundred twenty-eight
17. seven hundred twenty
18. seven hundred eight
19. seven hundred
20. seven hundred eighty

Give the missing numbers.

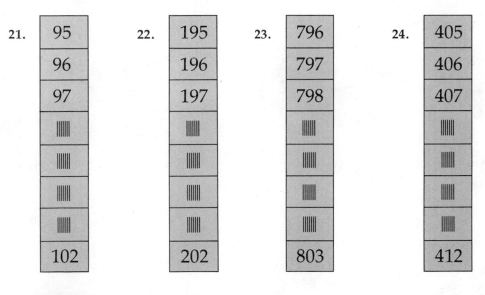

21.
| 95 |
| 96 |
| 97 |
102

22.
| 195 |
| 196 |
| 197 |
202

23.
| 796 |
| 797 |
| 798 |
803

24.
| 405 |
| 406 |
| 407 |
412

1. Find the smallest 3-digit number that uses 3 different digits.
2. Find the largest 3-digit number that uses 3 different digits.

Thousands

One thousand is 10 hundreds.

| 1 thousand | 2 hundreds | 3 tens | 2 ones |

We write: 1232

How many? Write the numeral.

1.

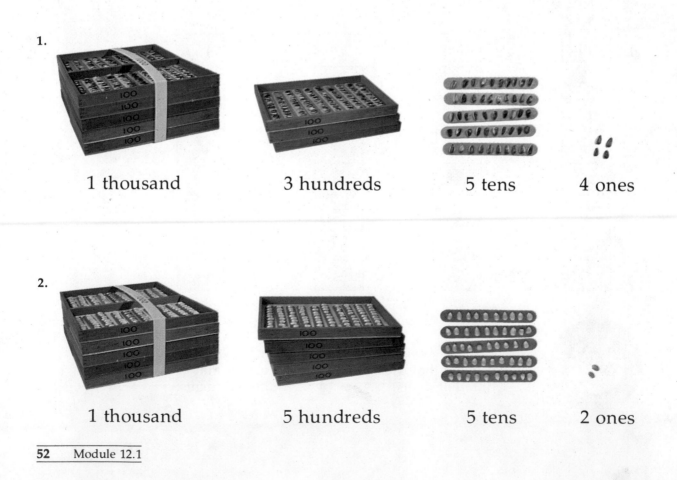

| 1 thousand | 3 hundreds | 5 tens | 4 ones |

2.

| 1 thousand | 5 hundreds | 5 tens | 2 ones |

Give the number for each row.

	thousands	hundreds	tens	ones
3.	1	2	9	4
4.	2	8	6	1
5.	7	0	5	4
6.	9	2	0	6
7.	3	4	3	0
8.	8	7	6	5

Read each numeral aloud.

Example: For 4751 we say, "four thousand, seven hundred, fifty-one."

9. 4751   10. 2029   11. 5846   12. 1975

13. 8010   14. 1002   15. 3678   16. 6027

17. 8942   18. 2341   19. 1391   20. 5300

21. 7924   22. 8516   23. 9406   24. 2345

25. 1058   26. 7643   27. 9999   28. 4251

29. 3031   30. 5249   31. 8317   32. 8808

33. 6152   34. 7843   35. 3012   36. 6532

1. Find the smallest 4-digit number that uses just 3 different digits.

2. Find the largest 4-digit number that uses just 3 different digits.

Answers for Self-check   1. 36   2. 26   3. 50   4. 475   5. 261   6. 2570   7. 4605
8. 209, 210, 211, 212, 213, 214   9. 799, 800, 801, 802, 803, 804

Self-check

Write the numeral.

1. 3 tens and 6 ones

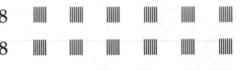

2. 2 tens and 6 ones

3. 5 tens and 0 ones

4. 4 hundreds, 7 tens, and 5 ones

5. 2 hundreds, 6 tens, and 1 one

6. 2 thousands, 5 hundreds, 7 tens, and 0 ones

7. 4 thousands, 6 hundreds, 0 tens, and 5 ones

Complete the counting.

8. 205   206   207   208 ||||| ||||| ||||| ||||| ||||| |||||

9. 795   796   797   798 ||||| ||||| ||||| ||||| ||||| |||||

Answers for Self-check—page 53

Test

Write the numeral.

1. 2 tens and 4 ones

2. 6 tens and 4 ones

3. 5 tens and 0 ones

4. 2 hundreds, 9 tens, and 7 ones

5. 6 hundreds, 2 tens, and 5 ones

6. 4 thousands, 5 hundreds, 0 tens, and 3 ones

7. 6 thousands, 2 hundreds, 5 tens, and 0 ones

Complete the counting.

8. 124   125   126   127 ||||| ||||| ||||| ||||| ||||| |||||

9. 814   815   816   817 ||||| ||||| ||||| ||||| ||||| |||||

One-Ten-Hundred Game

On a cube print:
100 on one face
10 on two faces
1 on three faces

Try this game with a classmate.

1. Each player gets 10 tosses of the cube.

2. Keep a tally of each other's score.

3. The player with the highest total score for the 10 tosses wins.

WAYLAND		DIANE	
100	I	100	II
10	III	10	II
1	ЖHI	1	ЖHI
TOTAL	136		226

Adding 2- and 3-Digit Numbers

Getting started

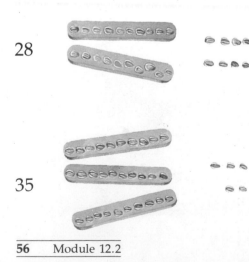

28

35

Put them all together.

1. How many ten-sticks in all?
2. How many extra beans?

Trade: 10 beans for
      1 ten-stick

3. How many ten-sticks now?
4. How many extra beans?

When you can, think of trading:

10 beans for 1 ten-stick

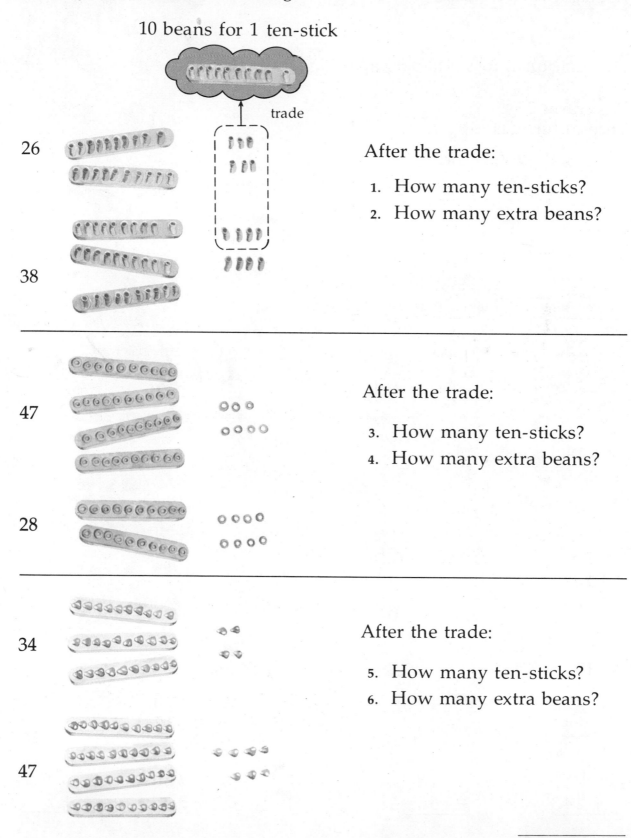

trade

26

38

After the trade:

1. How many ten-sticks?
2. How many extra beans?

47

28

After the trade:

3. How many ten-sticks?
4. How many extra beans?

34

47

After the trade:

5. How many ten-sticks?
6. How many extra beans?

Adding without regrouping

For each turn, toss 5 paper clips.

First turn: 23
Second turn: 41

What is the total score?

Finding the answer

First add the ones	→	Then add the tens

```
  23          23
+ 41        + 41
----        ----
   4          64
```

The total score is 64.

Other examples

```
  13          75         256
+ 24        + 60       + 431
----        ----       -----
  37         135         687
```

Add.

1.
```
  23
+ 42
```

2.
```
  42
+ 26
```

3.
```
  52
+ 17
```

4.
```
  96
+ 32
```

5.
```
  24
+ 50
```

6.
```
  740
+ 243
```

7.
```
  518
+ 160
```

8.
```
  655
+ 431
```

9.
```
  820
+ 340
```

10.
```
  127
+ 740
```

Find the sums.

1.	231	2.	231	3.	412	4.	511	5.	323
	+356		+432		+ 31		+100		+704

6.	416	7.	502	8.	370	9.	40	10.	300
	+103		+830		+400		+952		+400

Find the sums.

Example:

	32	11.	21	12.	32	13.	41	14.	75	15.	32
	14		13		40		12		21		42
	+43		+41		+23		+13		+42		+63
	89										

16.	20	17.	31	18.	42	19.	14	20.	22	21.	15
	30		40		60		50		30		31
	+40		+10		+27		+42		+46		+43

Solve.

22. First turn: 44

   Second turn: 25

   What is the total score?

23. Nina's score: 32

   Liza's score: 51

   How many points for both?

Tom had 10 marbles.

Bill said, "If you give me 2 of your marbles, then we'll both have the same number."

How many marbles did Bill have?

More practice, page 326

Adding with regrouping

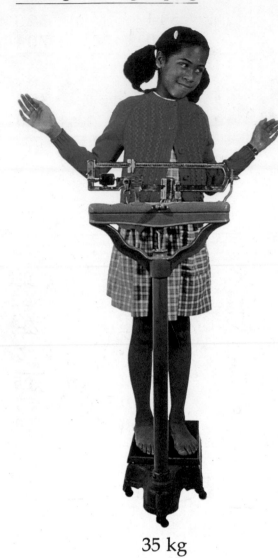

35 kg

What is the total number
of kilograms?

Finding the answer

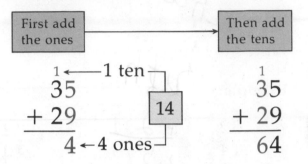

There are 64 kg in all.

Other examples

$$\begin{array}{r}\overset{1}{16}\\ +48\\ \hline 64\end{array} \qquad \begin{array}{r}\overset{1}{28}\\ +67\\ \hline 95\end{array} \qquad \begin{array}{r}\overset{1}{65}\\ +78\\ \hline 143\end{array}$$

Add.

1. $\begin{array}{r}24\\ +17\end{array}$ 2. $\begin{array}{r}36\\ +47\end{array}$ 3. $\begin{array}{r}54\\ +29\end{array}$ 4. $\begin{array}{r}18\\ +68\end{array}$ 5. $\begin{array}{r}25\\ +28\end{array}$ 6. $\begin{array}{r}36\\ +26\end{array}$

7. $\begin{array}{r}73\\ +19\end{array}$ 8. $\begin{array}{r}46\\ +45\end{array}$ 9. $\begin{array}{r}27\\ +45\end{array}$ 10. $\begin{array}{r}48\\ +36\end{array}$ 11. $\begin{array}{r}37\\ +24\end{array}$ 12. $\begin{array}{r}14\\ +68\end{array}$

13. $\begin{array}{r}26\\ +69\end{array}$ 14. $\begin{array}{r}52\\ +29\end{array}$ 15. $\begin{array}{r}46\\ +17\end{array}$ 16. $\begin{array}{r}54\\ +28\end{array}$ 17. $\begin{array}{r}25\\ +48\end{array}$ 18. $\begin{array}{r}39\\ +82\end{array}$

Find the sums.

1. 86
    + 29

2. 52
    + 79

3. 27
    + 97

4. 58
    + 67

5. 95
    + 85

6. 75
    + 48

7. 67
    + 66

8. 56
    + 56

9. 83
    + 39

10. 56
    + 78

11. 88
    + 33

12. 95
    + 48

13. 76
    + 72

14. 66
    + 84

15. 97
    + 14

16. 59
    + 79

17. 88
    + 76

18. 28
    + 46

19. 52
    + 77

20. 67
    + 76

21. 52
    + 43

22. 79
    + 46

23. 85
    + 67

24. 62
    + 40

29 kg

25. Paula: 36 kg
    Maria: 39 kg
    How many kilograms in all?

☆ 26. You: ▥ kg
    A friend: ▥ kg
    How many kilograms in all?

Find the missing digits.

     4 6   7 ▥
   + 3 ▥   + ▥ 6
   ▥ 3   ▥ 3 4

More practice, page 327

Finding larger sums

How many kilometers is
it from Kent to Clay?

Finding the answer

First add the ones	Then add the tens	Then add the hundreds

$$
\begin{array}{r}
\overset{1}{185} \\
+\,267 \\
\hline
2
\end{array}
\qquad
\begin{array}{r}
\overset{1\,1}{185} \\
+\,267 \\
\hline
52
\end{array}
\qquad
\begin{array}{r}
\overset{1\,1}{185} \\
+\,267 \\
\hline
452
\end{array}
$$

It is 452 km from Kent to Clay.

Other examples

$$
\begin{array}{r}
\overset{1}{237} \\
+\,146 \\
\hline
383
\end{array}
\qquad
\begin{array}{r}
\overset{1\,1}{384} \\
+\,127 \\
\hline
511
\end{array}
\qquad
\begin{array}{r}
\overset{1\,1}{659} \\
+\,873 \\
\hline
1532
\end{array}
$$

Add.

1. $\begin{array}{r} 136 \\ +\,217 \\ \hline \end{array}$
2. $\begin{array}{r} 325 \\ +\,129 \\ \hline \end{array}$
3. $\begin{array}{r} 248 \\ +\,278 \\ \hline \end{array}$
4. $\begin{array}{r} 462 \\ +\,189 \\ \hline \end{array}$
5. $\begin{array}{r} 658 \\ +\,247 \\ \hline \end{array}$

6. $\begin{array}{r} 589 \\ +\,736 \\ \hline \end{array}$
7. $\begin{array}{r} 655 \\ +\,408 \\ \hline \end{array}$
8. $\begin{array}{r} 493 \\ +\,537 \\ \hline \end{array}$
9. $\begin{array}{r} 576 \\ +\,986 \\ \hline \end{array}$
10. $\begin{array}{r} 843 \\ +\,567 \\ \hline \end{array}$

11. $\begin{array}{r} 235 \\ +\,345 \\ \hline \end{array}$
12. $\begin{array}{r} 507 \\ +\,167 \\ \hline \end{array}$
13. $\begin{array}{r} 156 \\ +\,669 \\ \hline \end{array}$
14. $\begin{array}{r} 708 \\ +\,287 \\ \hline \end{array}$
15. $\begin{array}{r} 297 \\ +\,465 \\ \hline \end{array}$

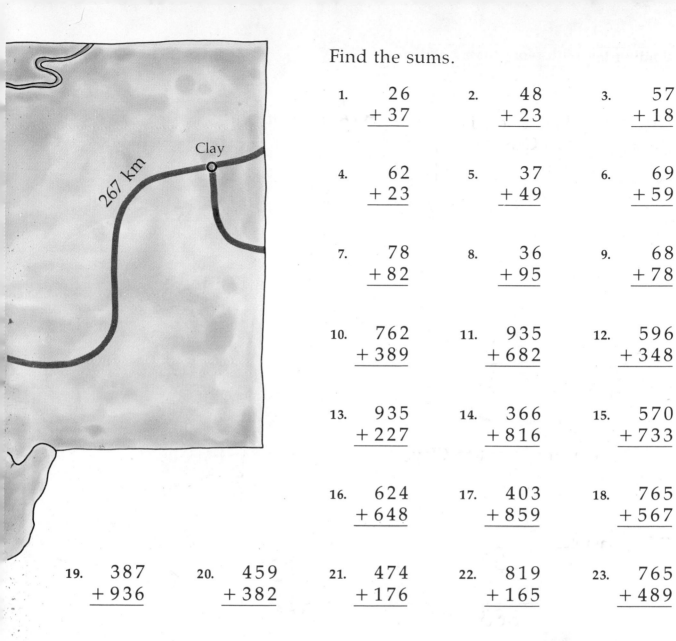

Find the sums.

1.	26 + 37	2.	48 + 23	3.	57 + 18
4.	62 + 23	5.	37 + 49	6.	69 + 59
7.	78 + 82	8.	36 + 95	9.	68 + 78
10.	762 + 389	11.	935 + 682	12.	596 + 348
13.	935 + 227	14.	366 + 816	15.	570 + 733
16.	624 + 648	17.	403 + 859	18.	765 + 567

19.	387 + 936	20.	459 + 382	21.	474 + 176	22.	819 + 165

23. 765 + 489

24. Driving:
Before noon: 265 km
After noon: 195 km
How far in all?

☆ 25. How far is it from your
city to another?
How far there and back?

I can be found
Halfway between
Twenty-seven
And seventeen.
Who am I?

17 •••••••••• 27

More practice, page 328

Regrouping with more than 2 addends

Favorite sport

How many voted?

Baseball	卌 卌 卌					19
Soccer	卌				8
Hockey	卌 卌 卌		16

Finding the answer

| First add the ones | → | Then add the tens |

$$
\begin{array}{r}
2 \leftarrow \text{2 tens} \\
19 \\
8 \\
+ 16 \\
\hline
3 \leftarrow \text{3 ones}
\end{array}
\quad \boxed{23}
$$

$$
\begin{array}{r}
2 \\
19 \\
8 \\
+ 16 \\
\hline
43
\end{array}
$$

43 voted.

Other examples

$$
\begin{array}{r}
1 \\
25 \\
32 \\
+ 17 \\
\hline
74
\end{array}
\qquad
\begin{array}{r}
2 \\
38 \\
27 \\
+ 19 \\
\hline
84
\end{array}
\qquad
\begin{array}{r}
2 \\
75 \\
28 \\
+ 39 \\
\hline
142
\end{array}
$$

Add.

1. $\begin{array}{r} 16 \\ 22 \\ +18 \\ \hline \end{array}$
2. $\begin{array}{r} 35 \\ 14 \\ +23 \\ \hline \end{array}$
3. $\begin{array}{r} 48 \\ 8 \\ +27 \\ \hline \end{array}$
4. $\begin{array}{r} 17 \\ 39 \\ +28 \\ \hline \end{array}$
5. $\begin{array}{r} 26 \\ 15 \\ +49 \\ \hline \end{array}$
6. $\begin{array}{r} 37 \\ 47 \\ +37 \\ \hline \end{array}$

7. $\begin{array}{r} 28 \\ 67 \\ +59 \\ \hline \end{array}$
8. $\begin{array}{r} 72 \\ 9 \\ +64 \\ \hline \end{array}$
9. $\begin{array}{r} 56 \\ 27 \\ +49 \\ \hline \end{array}$
10. $\begin{array}{r} 62 \\ 53 \\ +72 \\ \hline \end{array}$
11. $\begin{array}{r} 19 \\ 24 \\ +46 \\ \hline \end{array}$
12. $\begin{array}{r} 35 \\ 67 \\ +15 \\ \hline \end{array}$

Examples:

$$\begin{array}{r} {\scriptstyle 1\ 1} \\ 324 \\ 756 \\ +\ 248 \\ \hline 1328 \end{array} \qquad \begin{array}{r} {\scriptstyle 2} \\ 32 \\ 46 \\ 27 \\ +\ 15 \\ \hline 120 \end{array} \qquad \begin{array}{r} {\scriptstyle 1\ 2} \\ 287 \\ 309 \\ 458 \\ +\ 121 \\ \hline 1175 \end{array}$$

Find the sums.

1.
$$\begin{array}{r} 12 \\ 15 \\ 13 \\ +\ 14 \end{array}$$

2.
$$\begin{array}{r} 16 \\ 3 \\ 11 \\ +\ 14 \end{array}$$

3.
$$\begin{array}{r} 12 \\ 10 \\ 17 \\ +\ 14 \end{array}$$

4.
$$\begin{array}{r} 23 \\ 42 \\ 16 \\ +\ 5 \end{array}$$

5.
$$\begin{array}{r} 17 \\ 48 \\ 15 \\ +\ 32 \end{array}$$

6.
$$\begin{array}{r} 216 \\ 344 \\ +\ 122 \end{array}$$

7.
$$\begin{array}{r} 367 \\ 105 \\ +\ 214 \end{array}$$

8.
$$\begin{array}{r} 335 \\ 125 \\ +\ 114 \end{array}$$

9.
$$\begin{array}{r} 263 \\ 752 \\ +\ 237 \end{array}$$

10.
$$\begin{array}{r} 136 \\ 465 \\ +\ 674 \end{array}$$

☆ 11.
$$\begin{array}{r} 326 \\ 415 \\ 203 \\ +\ 141 \end{array}$$

☆ 12.
$$\begin{array}{r} 346 \\ 110 \\ 218 \\ +\ 314 \end{array}$$

☆ 13.
$$\begin{array}{r} 263 \\ 141 \\ 100 \\ +\ 320 \end{array}$$

☆ 14.
$$\begin{array}{r} 418 \\ 175 \\ 216 \\ +\ 342 \end{array}$$

☆ 15.
$$\begin{array}{r} 131 \\ 204 \\ 432 \\ +\ 205 \end{array}$$

16. Naming favorite desserts:

Pie: 18
Cake: 9
Ice cream: 18

How many voted?

☆ 17. Ask your friends to name their favorite color.

Red: ||||| Green: |||||
Blue: ||||| Orange: |||||

How many voted?

Think!

1. My digits are 7, 2, and 5. I'm between 500 and 550. **Who am I?**

2. My digits are 6, 0, and 3. I'm smaller than 350. **Who am I?**

Answers for Self-check   1. 56   2. 77   3. 62   4. 131   5. 143   6. 361   7. 375   8. 513   9. 89   10. 79
11. 434   12. 1239   13. 1164   14. 1324   15. 1157

Self-check

Add.

1. 22
    + 34

2. 31
    + 46

3. 34
    + 28

4. 56
    + 75

5. 87
    + 56

6. 236
    + 125

7. 248
    + 127

8. 385
    + 128

9. 42
    13
    + 34

10. 46
    25
    + 8

11. 256
    + 178

12. 845
    + 394

13. 735
    + 429

14. 548
    127
    + 649

15. 324
    497
    + 336

Answers for Self-check—page 65

Test

Add.

1. 24
    + 52

2. 35
    + 12

3. 46
    + 17

4. 28
    + 74

5. 75
    + 59

6. 324
    + 152

7. 416
    + 128

8. 475
    + 865

9. 23
    42
    + 14

10. 16
    35
    + 62

11. 549
    + 835

12. 718
    + 296

13. 635
    + 192

14. 665
    443
    + 276

15. 181
    819
    + 454

Magic squares

Find the sum along each arrow.

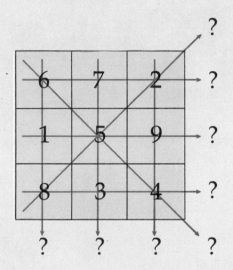

6	7	2
1	5	9
8	3	4

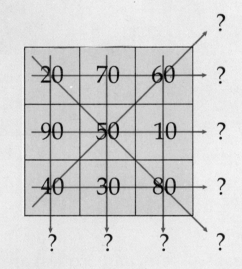

20	70	60
90	50	10
40	30	80

Copy the squares and find the missing numbers.

A 15 square

6	1	8
7		3

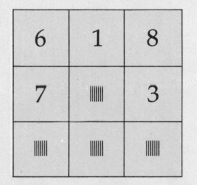
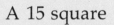

An 18 square

3		
10		2
5	4	

Subtracting 2- and 3-Digit Numbers

Getting started

43 beans (4 tens and 3 ones) are on the table.

Which of these numbers of beans could you pick up **without a trade**?

1. 23	2. 31	3. 32	4. 39
5. 25	6. 21	7. 17	8. 12
9. 42	10. 14	11. 4	12. 8

Now trade one ten (a ten-stick) for ten ones (beans).

13. 25 beans?   14. 14 beans?   15. 39 beans?   16. 8 beans?

Trade a ten-stick.

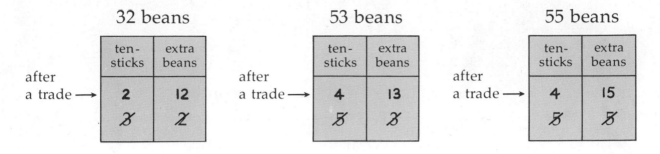

32 beans				53 beans				55 beans		
after a trade →	ten-sticks	extra beans		after a trade →	ten-sticks	extra beans		after a trade →	ten-sticks	extra beans
	2 ~~3~~	**12** ~~2~~			**4** ~~5~~	**13** ~~3~~			**4** ~~5~~	**15** ~~5~~

Give the numbers after the trade.

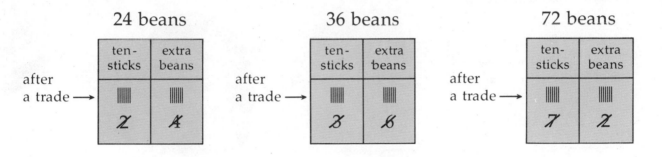

24 beans				36 beans				72 beans		
after a trade →	ten-sticks	extra beans		after a trade →	ten-sticks	extra beans		after a trade →	ten-sticks	extra beans
	||||| ~~2~~	|||| ~~4~~			||||| ~~3~~	|||||| ~~6~~			||||| ~~7~~	|| ~~2~~

Trade a ten.

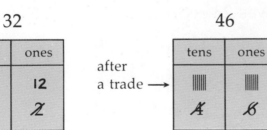

32				46				83		
after a trade →	tens	ones		after a trade →	tens	ones		after a trade →	tens	ones
	2 ~~3~~	**12** ~~2~~			||||| ~~4~~	|||||| ~~6~~			||||| ~~8~~	||||| ~~3~~

Copy the number. Trade a ten.

Example for 34:   ~~34~~ (2 14)

1. 32   2. 46   3. 83   4. 53   5. 86   6. 42

7. 65   8. 71   9. 26   10. 33   11. 82   12. 44

Subtracting (no regrouping)

Guessing a minute

Jan's guess: 75 seconds
Ted's guess: 52 seconds
What was the difference?

Finding the answer

First subtract the ones	Then subtract the tens

$$\begin{array}{r} 75 \\ -52 \\ \hline 3 \end{array} \qquad \begin{array}{r} 75 \\ -52 \\ \hline 23 \end{array}$$

The difference in guesses was 23 seconds.

Other examples

$$\begin{array}{r} 36 \\ -12 \\ \hline 24 \end{array} \qquad \begin{array}{r} 59 \\ -52 \\ \hline 7 \end{array} \qquad \begin{array}{r} 95 \\ -65 \\ \hline 30 \end{array}$$

Subtract.

1. $\begin{array}{r} 45 \\ -21 \\ \hline \end{array}$
2. $\begin{array}{r} 56 \\ -34 \\ \hline \end{array}$
3. $\begin{array}{r} 73 \\ -2 \\ \hline \end{array}$
4. $\begin{array}{r} 84 \\ -50 \\ \hline \end{array}$
5. $\begin{array}{r} 59 \\ -36 \\ \hline \end{array}$
6. $\begin{array}{r} 37 \\ -24 \\ \hline \end{array}$

7. $\begin{array}{r} 65 \\ -25 \\ \hline \end{array}$
8. $\begin{array}{r} 92 \\ -10 \\ \hline \end{array}$
9. $\begin{array}{r} 39 \\ -21 \\ \hline \end{array}$
10. $\begin{array}{r} 89 \\ -6 \\ \hline \end{array}$
11. $\begin{array}{r} 67 \\ -62 \\ \hline \end{array}$
12. $\begin{array}{r} 58 \\ -4 \\ \hline \end{array}$

Find the differences.

Example:

```
  654
- 123
-----
  531
```

1.  ```
      754
    - 122
    ```

2.  ```
      483
    -  51
    ```

3.  ```
      269
    - 133
    ```

4.  ```
      538
    - 217
    ```

5.  ```
      796
    - 546
    ```

6.  ```
      587
    -  75
    ```

7.  ```
      643
    - 441
    ```

8.  ```
      726
    -   5
    ```

9.  ```
      834
    - 812
    ```

10. ```
      927
    - 723
    ```

11. ```
      865
    -  43
    ```

12. ```
      746
    -   6
    ```

13. ```
      872
    - 501
    ```

14. ```
      934
    - 710
    ```

15. ```
      764
    -  23
    ```

16. ```
      642
    - 321
    ```

17. ```
      758
    -  37
    ```

18. ```
      457
    - 235
    ```

19. ```
      455
    -  11
    ```

20. ```
      784
    - 680
    ```

21. Donna's guess: 41 seconds
    Bill's guess: 56 seconds
    What is the difference?

☆ 22. Close your eyes and try
    to guess a minute. How
    close to 60 seconds were
    you?

The sum of two numbers is 20. Their difference is 4. What are the numbers?

More practice, page 330, Set A

Subtracting with regrouping

Jim takes 24 breaths a minute when sitting down.
He takes 53 breaths a minute after running.

How many more breaths does he take after running?

Finding the answer

You need more ones	→	Trade a ten	→	Subtract the ones	→	Subtract the tens

$$
\begin{array}{r} 53 \\ -24 \\ \hline \end{array}
\qquad
\begin{array}{r} \overset{4\ 13}{\cancel{53}} \\ -24 \\ \hline \end{array}
\qquad
\begin{array}{r} \overset{4\ 13}{\cancel{53}} \\ -24 \\ \hline 9 \end{array}
\qquad
\begin{array}{r} \overset{4\ 13}{\cancel{53}} \\ -24 \\ \hline 29 \end{array}
$$

Jim takes 29 more breaths after running.

Other examples

$$
\begin{array}{r} \overset{6\ 14}{\cancel{74}} \\ -26 \\ \hline 48 \end{array}
\qquad
\begin{array}{r} \overset{5\ 10}{\cancel{60}} \\ -23 \\ \hline 37 \end{array}
\qquad
\begin{array}{r} \overset{3\ 13}{\cancel{43}} \\ -38 \\ \hline 5 \end{array}
$$

Subtract.

1. $\begin{array}{r} 52 \\ -37 \\ \hline \end{array}$
2. $\begin{array}{r} 34 \\ -15 \\ \hline \end{array}$
3. $\begin{array}{r} 40 \\ -17 \\ \hline \end{array}$
4. $\begin{array}{r} 76 \\ -18 \\ \hline \end{array}$
5. $\begin{array}{r} 64 \\ -58 \\ \hline \end{array}$
6. $\begin{array}{r} 81 \\ -19 \\ \hline \end{array}$

7. $\begin{array}{r} 65 \\ -23 \\ \hline \end{array}$
8. $\begin{array}{r} 37 \\ -28 \\ \hline \end{array}$
9. $\begin{array}{r} 67 \\ -49 \\ \hline \end{array}$
10. $\begin{array}{r} 60 \\ -24 \\ \hline \end{array}$
11. $\begin{array}{r} 50 \\ -31 \\ \hline \end{array}$
12. $\begin{array}{r} 72 \\ -15 \\ \hline \end{array}$

$$\begin{array}{r} {}^{1\ 15}\\ 12\!\!\!\diagup\!\!5 \\ -\ 57 \\ \hline 68 \end{array} \qquad \begin{array}{r} {}^{3\ 12}\\ 1\!\!\!\diagup\!\!4\!\!\!\diagup\!\!2 \\ -\ 64 \\ \hline 78 \end{array} \qquad \begin{array}{r} {}^{7\ 15}\\ 8\!\!\!\diagup\!\!5 \\ -\ 9 \\ \hline 76 \end{array}$$

Find the differences.

1. $\begin{array}{r} 122 \\ -\ 43 \\ \hline \end{array}$
2. $\begin{array}{r} 46 \\ -\ 9 \\ \hline \end{array}$
3. $\begin{array}{r} 131 \\ -\ 76 \\ \hline \end{array}$
4. $\begin{array}{r} 75 \\ -26 \\ \hline \end{array}$
5. $\begin{array}{r} 82 \\ -\ 4 \\ \hline \end{array}$

6. $\begin{array}{r} 143 \\ -\ 77 \\ \hline \end{array}$
7. $\begin{array}{r} 95 \\ -48 \\ \hline \end{array}$
8. $\begin{array}{r} 182 \\ -\ 92 \\ \hline \end{array}$
9. $\begin{array}{r} 62 \\ -\ 8 \\ \hline \end{array}$
10. $\begin{array}{r} 147 \\ -\ 85 \\ \hline \end{array}$

11. $\begin{array}{r} 123 \\ -\ 34 \\ \hline \end{array}$
12. $\begin{array}{r} 60 \\ -57 \\ \hline \end{array}$
13. $\begin{array}{r} 153 \\ -\ 67 \\ \hline \end{array}$
14. $\begin{array}{r} 71 \\ -12 \\ \hline \end{array}$
15. $\begin{array}{r} 134 \\ -\ 46 \\ \hline \end{array}$

16. $\begin{array}{r} 150 \\ -\ 72 \\ \hline \end{array}$
17. $\begin{array}{r} 126 \\ -\ 56 \\ \hline \end{array}$
18. $\begin{array}{r} 135 \\ -\ 89 \\ \hline \end{array}$
19. $\begin{array}{r} 72 \\ -15 \\ \hline \end{array}$
20. $\begin{array}{r} 123 \\ -\ 95 \\ \hline \end{array}$

21. Rose's breathing rate:
Sitting down—
   26 breaths a minute
After running—
   51 breaths a minute
How many more breaths
does she take after running?

☆ 22. Your breathing rate:
Sitting down— ▥
After running— ▥
How many more breaths
do you take after running?

It's true our sum is 60,
And we differ by just 2.
If you want to find our names,
Some thinking you must do.
Who are we?

More practice, page 330, Set B; page 330A; page 330B; page 331, Set A

Subtracting 3-digit numbers

365 days in a year
180 days in school

How many days are not spent in school?

Finding the answer

Subtract the ones	→	You need more tens	→	Trade a hundred	→	Subtract the tens	→	Subtract the hundreds

$$\begin{array}{r} 365 \\ -180 \\ \hline 5 \end{array} \qquad \begin{array}{r} 365 \\ -180 \\ \hline ?5 \end{array} \qquad \begin{array}{r} {\small 2\ 16} \\ 3\cancel{6}5 \\ -180 \\ \hline 5 \end{array} \qquad \begin{array}{r} {\small 2\ 16} \\ \cancel{3}\cancel{6}5 \\ -180 \\ \hline 85 \end{array} \qquad \begin{array}{r} {\small 2\ 16} \\ \cancel{3}\cancel{6}5 \\ -180 \\ \hline 185 \end{array}$$

185 days are not spent in school.

Other examples

$$\begin{array}{r} {\small 4\ 13} \\ \cancel{5}\cancel{3}7 \\ -162 \\ \hline 375 \end{array} \qquad \begin{array}{r} {\small 4\ 12} \\ 6\cancel{5}\cancel{2} \\ -215 \\ \hline 437 \end{array} \qquad \begin{array}{r} {\small 2\ 15} \\ \cancel{3}\cancel{5}6 \\ -\ 82 \\ \hline 274 \end{array}$$

Subtract.

1. $\begin{array}{r} 725 \\ -142 \\ \hline \end{array}$
2. $\begin{array}{r} 627 \\ -161 \\ \hline \end{array}$
3. $\begin{array}{r} 853 \\ -215 \\ \hline \end{array}$
4. $\begin{array}{r} 532 \\ -217 \\ \hline \end{array}$
5. $\begin{array}{r} 643 \\ -\ 80 \\ \hline \end{array}$

6. $\begin{array}{r} 426 \\ -\ 52 \\ \hline \end{array}$
7. $\begin{array}{r} 653 \\ -\ 24 \\ \hline \end{array}$
8. $\begin{array}{r} 714 \\ -132 \\ \hline \end{array}$
9. $\begin{array}{r} 943 \\ -618 \\ \hline \end{array}$
10. $\begin{array}{r} 726 \\ -682 \\ \hline \end{array}$

Find the differences.

1. 647
  − 385

2. 712
  − 605

3. 546
  − 293

4. 425
  − 272

5. 318
  − 222

6. 674
  − 435

7. 963
  − 758

8. 291
  − 87

9. 172
  − 68

10. 862
  − 527

11. 718
  − 543

12. 459
  − 382

13. 672
  − 458

14. 526
  − 318

15. 863
  − 546

16. 942
  − 381

17. 725
  − 625

18. 541
  − 328

19. 678
  − 492

20. 375
  − 148

21. Days in a year: 365
Sunny days: 190
How many days were not sunny?

☆ 22. Find how many days are in this year. How many Saturdays and Sundays are in this year? Subtract to find how many weekdays are in this year.

Think!

I'm less than thirty-one
And more than twenty-three.
Just half way in between
Is where I'm sure to be.
Who am I?

More practice, page 331, Set B; page 331A; page 331B; page 332, Set A

More about subtracting

How many more students in Grant School?

Grant School	545 students
Fremont School	356 students

Finding the answer

You need more ones	→	Trade a ten and subtract	→	You need more tens	→	Trade a hundred and subtract

$$\begin{array}{r} 545 \\ -356 \\ \hline \end{array}$$

$$\begin{array}{r} {\scriptstyle 3\ 15} \\ 5\cancel{4}\cancel{5} \\ -356 \\ \hline 9 \end{array}$$

$$\begin{array}{r} {\scriptstyle 3\ 15} \\ 5\cancel{4}\cancel{5} \\ -356 \\ \hline ?9 \end{array}$$

$$\begin{array}{r} {\scriptstyle 4\ 13\ 15} \\ \cancel{5}\cancel{4}\cancel{5} \\ -356 \\ \hline 189 \end{array}$$

There are 189 more students in Grant School.

Other examples

$$\begin{array}{r} {\scriptstyle 6\ 12\ 14} \\ \cancel{7}\cancel{3}\cancel{4} \\ -259 \\ \hline 475 \end{array}$$

$$\begin{array}{r} {\scriptstyle 8\ 11\ 16} \\ \cancel{9}\cancel{2}\cancel{6} \\ -\ 37 \\ \hline 889 \end{array}$$

$$\begin{array}{r} {\scriptstyle 5\ 13\ 12} \\ \cancel{6}\cancel{4}\cancel{2} \\ -585 \\ \hline 57 \end{array}$$

Find the differences.

1. $\begin{array}{r} 758 \\ -489 \\ \hline \end{array}$ 2. $\begin{array}{r} 312 \\ -276 \\ \hline \end{array}$ 3. $\begin{array}{r} 695 \\ -468 \\ \hline \end{array}$ 4. $\begin{array}{r} 734 \\ -675 \\ \hline \end{array}$

5. $\begin{array}{r} 831 \\ -647 \\ \hline \end{array}$ 6. $\begin{array}{r} 424 \\ -385 \\ \hline \end{array}$ 7. $\begin{array}{r} 627 \\ -409 \\ \hline \end{array}$ 8. $\begin{array}{r} 574 \\ -389 \\ \hline \end{array}$

More practice, page 332, Set B; page 332A

Find the differences.

1. 626
  − 258

2. 843
  − 467

3. 531
  − 282

4. 922
  − 246

5. 354
  − 89

6. 430
  − 156

7. 635
  − 342

8. 462
  − 175

9. 945
  − 618

10. 746
  − 77

11. 865
  − 576

12. 574
  − 199

13. 640
  − 475

14. 812
  − 434

15. 553
  − 68

16. 723
  − 698

17. Marshall School: 724 students
Wilson School: 586 students
How many more students are
in Marshall School?

☆ 18. Your school: ‖‖‖ students
A nearby school: ‖‖‖ students
Which school has more?
How many more?

Find the missing
digits.

  6 2 ‖‖‖
− 2 ‖‖‖ 6
  3 4 7

More about subtracting

302 pages in all
Read 149 pages.
How many pages must
be read to finish
the book?

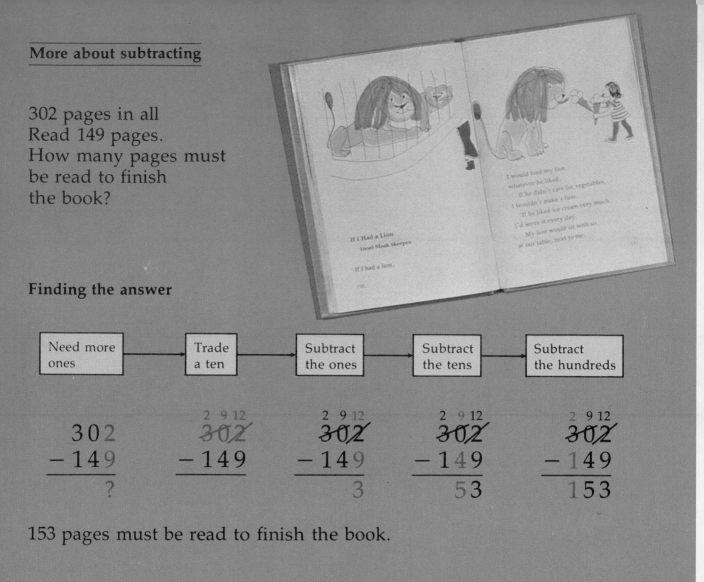

Finding the answer

| Need more ones | → | Trade a ten | → | Subtract the ones | → | Subtract the tens | → | Subtract the hundreds |

$$
\begin{array}{r} 302 \\ -149 \\ \hline ? \end{array}
\qquad
\begin{array}{r} {\scriptstyle 2\ \ 9\ 12} \\ \cancel{302} \\ -149 \\ \hline \end{array}
\qquad
\begin{array}{r} {\scriptstyle 2\ \ 9\ 12} \\ \cancel{302} \\ -149 \\ \hline 3 \end{array}
\qquad
\begin{array}{r} {\scriptstyle 2\ \ 9\ 12} \\ \cancel{302} \\ -149 \\ \hline 53 \end{array}
\qquad
\begin{array}{r} {\scriptstyle 2\ \ 9\ 12} \\ \cancel{302} \\ -149 \\ \hline 153 \end{array}
$$

153 pages must be read to finish the book.

Other examples

$$
\begin{array}{r} {\scriptstyle 5\ 9\ 14} \\ \cancel{604} \\ -278 \\ \hline 326 \end{array}
\qquad
\begin{array}{r} {\scriptstyle 6\ 9\ 15} \\ \cancel{705} \\ -658 \\ \hline 47 \end{array}
\qquad
\begin{array}{r} {\scriptstyle 4\ 9\ 10} \\ \cancel{500} \\ -149 \\ \hline 351 \end{array}
$$

Subtract.

1. $\begin{array}{r} 502 \\ -314 \\ \hline \end{array}$
2. $\begin{array}{r} 704 \\ -157 \\ \hline \end{array}$
3. $\begin{array}{r} 500 \\ -296 \\ \hline \end{array}$
4. $\begin{array}{r} 706 \\ -228 \\ \hline \end{array}$
5. $\begin{array}{r} 900 \\ -658 \\ \hline \end{array}$

6. $\begin{array}{r} 803 \\ -354 \\ \hline \end{array}$
7. $\begin{array}{r} 600 \\ -495 \\ \hline \end{array}$
8. $\begin{array}{r} 904 \\ -657 \\ \hline \end{array}$
9. $\begin{array}{r} 500 \\ -398 \\ \hline \end{array}$
10. $\begin{array}{r} 806 \\ -159 \\ \hline \end{array}$

More examples

$$
\begin{array}{r}
\overset{5\ 11\ 13}{\cancel{623}} \\
-248 \\
\hline
375
\end{array}
\qquad
\begin{array}{r}
\overset{7\ 9\ 12}{\cancel{802}} \\
-\ \ 56 \\
\hline
746
\end{array}
\qquad
\begin{array}{r}
\overset{8\ 9\ 10}{\cancel{900}} \\
-\ \ \ \ 7 \\
\hline
893
\end{array}
$$

Find the differences.

1. 812
    −156

2. 703
    −278

3. 524
    −132

4. 936
    −346

5. 604
    −176

6. 472
    −231

7. 729
    −532

8. 804
    − 56

9. 321
    −247

10. 500
    −185

11. 630
    −266

12. 902
    − 37

13. 234
    − 68

14. 416
    −354

15. 975
    −468

16. 800
    − 9

17. 706
    −164

18. 614
    − 52

19. 832
    −267

20. 501
    −139

21. Bird book: 304 pages
    Fish book: 156 pages
    How many more pages are
    in the bird book?

☆ 22. Choose 2 books.
    First book: ▥ pages
    Second book: ▥ pages
    Difference: ?

Find each sum quickly without
pencil and paper.

1. $1 + 5 + 9$

2. $1 + 50 + 99$

3. $1 + 2 + 50 + 98 + 99$

Answers for Self-check   1. 35   2. 25   3. 35   4. 54   5. 47   6. 552   7. 66   8. 45   9. 327   10. 588
11. 52   12. 568   13. 484   14. 242   15. 276

Subtract.

1. 58
    -23

2. 42
    -17

3. 64
    -29

4. 70
    -16

5. 82
    -35

6. 675
    -123

7. 124
    -58

8. 135
    -90

9. 483
    -156

10. 817
    -229

11. 523
    -471

12. 706
    -138

13. 526
    -42

14. 500
    -258

15. 711
    -435

Answers for Self-check—page 79

Test

Subtract.

1. 65
    -42

2. 71
    -54

3. 95
    -29

4. 132
    -78

5. 83
    -67

6. 465
    -139

7. 628
    -352

8. 723
    -189

9. 604
    -347

10. 572
    -86

11. 804
    -659

12. 386
    -109

13. 700
    -487

14. 611
    -324

15. 743
    -268

Smallest Difference Game

1. Make this set of cards.

2. Mix the cards facedown.

3. Give 4 cards to each player.

4. Make a subtraction problem.

$$\begin{array}{r} 7\ 4 \\ -\ 6\ 5 \\ \hline 9 \end{array}$$
$$\begin{array}{r} 3\ 6 \\ -\ 2\ 9 \\ \hline 7 \end{array}$$

winner

5. The problem with the smallest difference wins a point.

6. The first player with 10 points wins the game.

Problem Solving
Using Your Skills

8 books

42 books

38 books

139 cm

165 cm

Getting started

1. How many books are on the 2 bottom shelves?

2. How much taller is the bookcase than the child?

3. What other problems can you solve?

Solving Problems

1. Read carefully to find the facts.

2. Look for the question.

3. Decide what to do.

4. Find the answer.

5. Read again. Does your answer make sense?

Add +
or
Subtract −

1. Lunch:
   Hot dog: 45¢
   Milk shake: 40¢
   How much for both?

?	45¢
+ or −	40¢

2. Tuna sandwich: 60¢
   Cheese sandwich: 45¢
   How much more for tuna?

?	60¢
+ or −	45¢

3. Had 25¢.
   Bought milk for 17¢.
   How much is left?

?	25¢
+ or −	17¢

4. Drank a 25¢ orange.
   Then drank a 25¢ root beer.
   Spent how much?

?	25¢
+ or −	25¢

1. Going to the beach:
   38 km
   Coming home: 38 km
   How far in all?

2. 45 minutes to get there
   35 minutes to get home
   How many minutes for both?

3. Counted 52 cars going.
   Counted 38 coming home.
   How many more going?

4. Paula took 50 cents
   to the beach.
   She spent 35 cents.
   How much was left?

5. Ted had 138 shells.
   He found 76 more.
   How many does
   he have now?

6. Jane has 123 rocks
   from the beach.
   Tom has 75.
   How many more has Jane?

7. Lisa found 206 shells.
   She gave away 78 shells.
   How many did she keep?

8. Pam found 37 small shells.
   She found 18 large shells.
   How many shells did she find?

9. Bill found 72 rocks.
   He took 35 of them home.
   How many did he
   leave behind?

10. Lena has 213 rocks
    and 157 shells.
    How many more rocks?

11. 27 white shells
    35 pink shells
    18 brown shells
    How many in all?

12. Car game:
    205 points for Tina
    137 points for Ted
    How many more for Tina?

Dolphins

Dolphins are very smart animals.
They even have a way of talking
to each other. Dolphins like to play
and can be taught to do many tricks.

1. In one day a dolphin
   ate 36 small fish
   and 19 large ones.
   How many fish did
   the dolphin eat?

2. One dolphin was 210 cm
   long. Another was
   193 cm long. How
   much longer was
   the first dolphin?

3. One dolphin had 88 teeth.
   Another had only 85.
   How many teeth for both?

6. A large dolphin had a mass of 78 kg. A small dolphin had a mass of 47 kg. How many kilograms for both?

4. Dolphins often swim in schools. One school had 15 dolphins. Another had 27. How many dolphins in all?

7. A baby dolphin swam for 12 minutes. Then it jumped for 15 minutes. Then it rested for 45 minutes. How many minutes in all?

5. Dolphins can jump high in the air. One dolphin jumped 523 cm high. Then it jumped 478 cm. How much higher was the first jump?

8. Dolphins are fast swimmers. One swam a kilometer in 87 seconds. Another swam a kilometer in 102 seconds. How much longer did the second dolphin take?

Adding and subtracting amounts of money

What is the total cost
for both games?

$1.00 is 100 cents.

Finding the answer

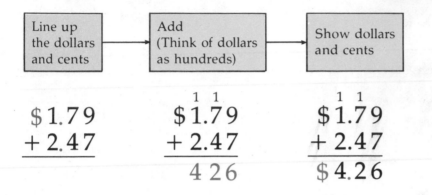

| Line up the dollars and cents | → | Add (Think of dollars as hundreds) | → | Show dollars and cents |

$$\begin{array}{r} \$1.79 \\ +2.47 \end{array}$$

$$\begin{array}{r} {}^{1\ 1} \\ \$1.79 \\ +2.47 \\ \hline 4\ 2\ 6 \end{array}$$

$$\begin{array}{r} {}^{1\ 1} \\ \$1.79 \\ +2.47 \\ \hline \$4.26 \end{array}$$

The total cost for both games is $4.26.

Other examples

$$\begin{array}{r} {}^{1\ 1} \\ \$5.98 \\ +1.49 \\ \hline \$7.47 \end{array} \qquad \begin{array}{r} {}^{1} \\ \$12.50 \\ +\ \ 5.95 \\ \hline \$18.45 \end{array} \qquad \begin{array}{r} {}^{2\ 2} \\ \$11.49 \\ 0.57 \\ +\ \ 2.98 \\ \hline \$15.04 \end{array}$$

Find the total amounts.

1. $$\begin{array}{r} \$2.39 \\ +3.48 \end{array}$$

2. $$\begin{array}{r} \$1.98 \\ +2.49 \end{array}$$

3. $$\begin{array}{r} \$10.88 \\ +\ \ 1.48 \end{array}$$

4. $$\begin{array}{r} \$2.56 \\ +0.49 \end{array}$$

5. $$\begin{array}{r} \$1.39 \\ 0.56 \\ +2.33 \end{array}$$

6. $$\begin{array}{r} \$0.47 \\ 0.56 \\ +0.38 \end{array}$$

7. $$\begin{array}{r} \$2.35 \\ 1.88 \\ +3.57 \end{array}$$

8. $$\begin{array}{r} \$12.43 \\ 5.98 \\ +10.56 \end{array}$$

Subtraction examples

$$
\begin{array}{r}
{\scriptstyle 2\ 14\ 10} \\
\$\cancel{3.50} \\
-\ 1.98 \\
\hline
\$1.52
\end{array}
\qquad
\begin{array}{r}
{\scriptstyle 4\ 9\ 10} \\
\$\cancel{5.00} \\
-\ 1.49 \\
\hline
\$3.51
\end{array}
\qquad
\begin{array}{r}
{\scriptstyle 6\ 10} \\
\$\cancel{7.00} \\
-\ 2.50 \\
\hline
\$4.50
\end{array}
$$

Find the differences.

1. $\begin{array}{r}\$2.45 \\ -\ 1.25 \\ \hline\end{array}$	2. $\begin{array}{r}\$3.49 \\ -\ 1.50 \\ \hline\end{array}$	3. $\begin{array}{r}\$4.56 \\ -\ 1.39 \\ \hline\end{array}$	4. $\begin{array}{r}\$3.50 \\ -\ 1.35 \\ \hline\end{array}$
5. $\begin{array}{r}\$5.50 \\ -\ 1.75 \\ \hline\end{array}$	6. $\begin{array}{r}\$6.75 \\ -\ 1.98 \\ \hline\end{array}$	7. $\begin{array}{r}\$5.00 \\ -\ 2.35 \\ \hline\end{array}$	8. $\begin{array}{r}\$9.45 \\ -\ 5.50 \\ \hline\end{array}$

Solve.

9. Chess: $11.98
   Dominos: $2.49
   How much for both?

10. Table tennis balls: $2.25
    Net: $1.95
    Paddles: $2.55
    How much in all?

11. Had a 5 dollar bill.
    Spent $1.98.
    How much change?

12. Had $3.50.
    Spent $1.25.
    How much is left?

13. Checkers: $2.98
    Cards: $1.35
    How much for both?

Comparing numbers

Magic book:
436 pages

Dog book:
452 pages

Which book
has more pages?

Finding the answer

Look at the hundreds' digits	Look at the tens' digits	Look at the ones' digits

4**3**6
4**5**2
Same

4**3**6
4**5**2
5 is greater
than 3.

The tens are
different. You
need not look at
the ones.

452 is greater than 436.

452 > 436   The dog book has more pages.

Which of the two numbers is greater?

1. 427
    441

2. 652
    658

3. 791
    698

4. 526
    523

5. 964
    864

6. 6247
    6238

7. 5436
    3478

8. 2651
    2653

9. 4724
    4720

10. 8642
    8579

472 is greater than 459.   673 is less than 678.

We write: 472 > 459   We write: 673 < 678

Write > or < for each ⬤ .

1. 256 ⬤ 259   2. 314 ⬤ 312   3. 768 ⬤ 758

4. 435 ⬤ 485   5. 350 ⬤ 349   6. 678 ⬤ 680

7. 901 ⬤ 899   8. 702 ⬤ 698   9. 435 ⬤ 427

10. 768 ⬤ 771   11. 497 ⬤ 654   12. 684 ⬤ 721

13. 4321 ⬤ 4326   14. 5786 ⬤ 5784   15. 6437 ⬤ 6476

16. 5300 ⬤ 5280   17. 7000 ⬤ 6999   18. 3898 ⬤ 4010

19. Which book has more pages?   20. Which book has more pages?

787 pages   804 pages

288 pages   302 pages

☆ 21.   Choose 2 books.
First book: ▌▌▌ pages
Second book: ▌▌▌ pages
Which book has more pages?

Answers for Self-check   1. 83   2. 158   3. $1.25   4. $5.29   5. $5.41   6. $6.04   7. $1.55   8. 682
9. 789 < 793

Self-check

1. Found 38 shells before lunch.
   Found 45 after lunch.
   How many in all?

2. There were 214 fish
   in a school. 56 swam away.
   How many were left
   in the school?

3. Ken had $4.00.
   He spent $2.75.
   How much does he have left?

4. $3.79
   +1.50

5. $8.00
   −2.59

6. $2.15
   +3.89

7. $7.44
   −5.89

8. Which is greater,
   678 or 682?

9. Write > or < for ⬤ .
   789 ⬤ 793

Answers for Self-check—page 91

Test

1. 83 rocks
   49 shells
   How many more rocks?

2. One dolphin was 198 cm long.
   Another was 175 cm long.
   How much longer was the
   first dolphin?

3. Anna had $2.76.
   She earned $1.45 more.
   How much does
   she have now?

4. $1.39
   +2.56

5. $5.00
   −1.25

6. $6.25
   +1.99

7. $5.18
   −3.59

8. Which is greater,
   461 or 457?

9. Write > or < for ⬤ .
   612 ⬤ 620

The Magic Answer

1. Choose a 3-digit number.   **3 6 7**

2. Reverse the digits.   **7 6 3**

3. Find the difference.

$$\begin{array}{r} 763 \\ -\ 367 \\ \hline 396 \end{array}$$

   3 9 6

4. Reverse the digits.   **6 9 3**

5. Find the sum.

$$\begin{array}{r} 396 \\ +\ 693 \\ \hline 1089 \end{array}$$

1089

The Magic Answer

Now you try the 5 steps with some of these numbers:
624, 259, 348, or 926. Try a number of your own.
Do you think the trick will always work?

Measurement 1

A paper clip

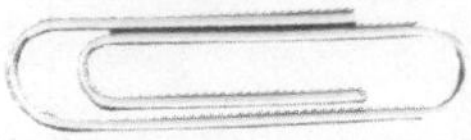

can be used as a **unit** to make a ruler.

Paper clip units

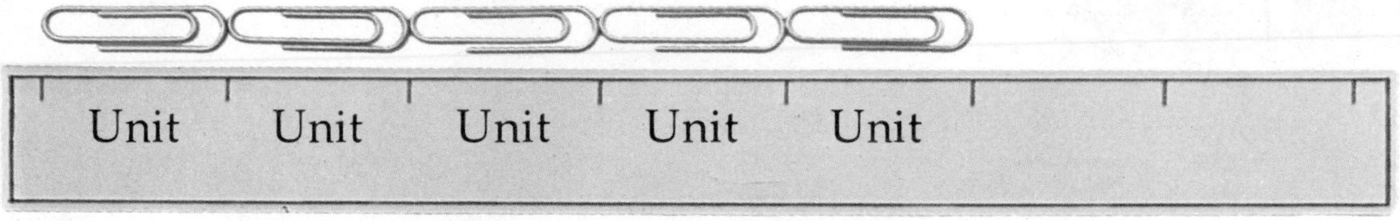

How many paper clips long is each of these?

1.

2.

3.

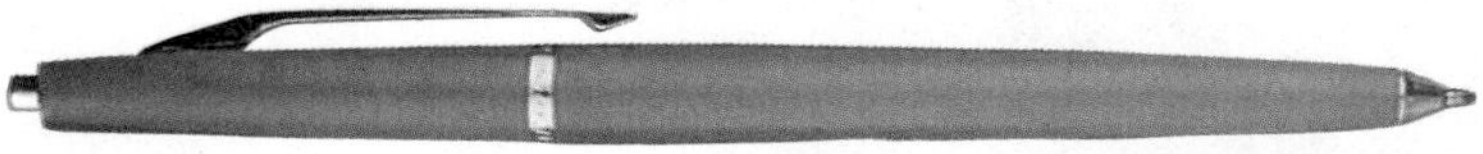

4.

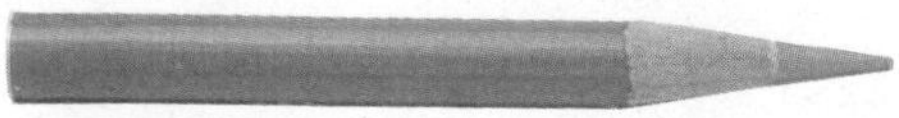

Think of each object as a unit.
Guess about how many of each unit
will fit between the red lines.

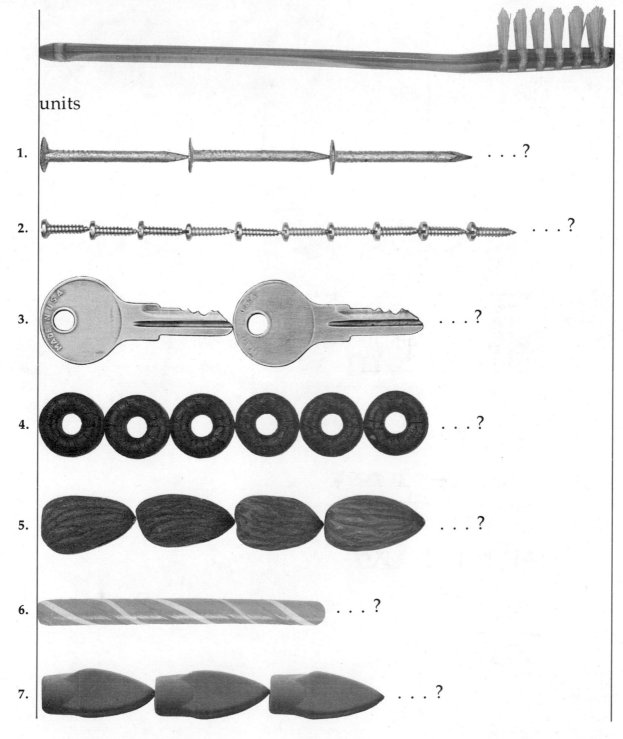

units

1. . . . ?

2. . . . ?

3. . . . ?

4. . . . ?

5. . . . ?

6. . . . ?

7. . . . ?

Can you find a way to check your guesses?

Measuring with centimeter units

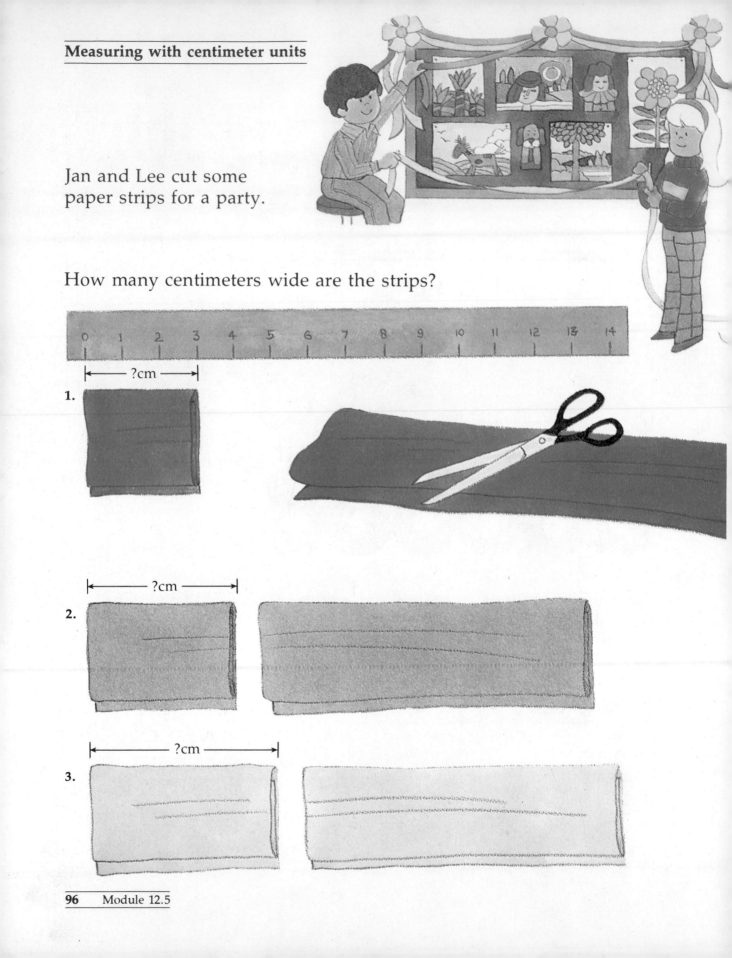

Jan and Lee cut some paper strips for a party.

How many centimeters wide are the strips?

|← ?cm →|

1.

|←   ?cm   →|

2.

|←   ?cm   →|

3.

Jan and Lee helped wrap some game prizes.
Answer the questions
using centimeters.

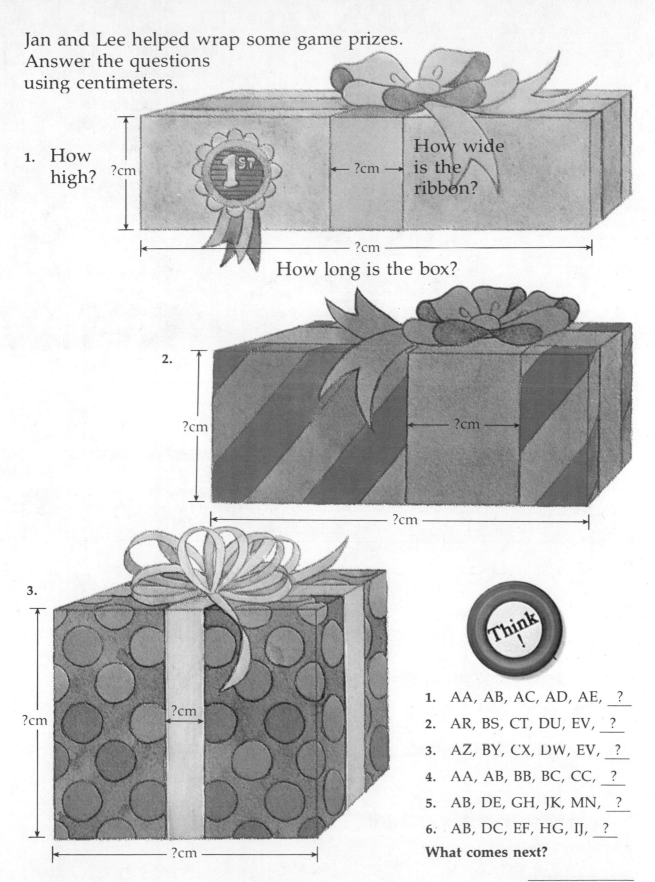

1. How
    high?

?cm

1ˢᵀ

?cm

How wide
is the
ribbon?

?cm

How long is the box?

2.

?cm

?cm

?cm

3.

?cm

?cm

?cm

Think
!

1. AA, AB, AC, AD, AE, _?_
2. AR, BS, CT, DU, EV, _?_
3. AZ, BY, CX, DW, EV, _?_
4. AA, AB, BB, BC, CC, _?_
5. AB, DE, GH, JK, MN, _?_
6. AB, DC, EF, HG, IJ, _?_

What comes next?

Each piece of yarn just fits around the child's wrist.

| 0 | 1 | 2 | 3 | 4 | 5 | 6 | 7 | 8 | 9 | 10 | 11 | 12 | 13 | 14 | 15 |

cm

Paul's wrist is 14 cm (to the nearest centimeter).

Give each of these wrist measures to the nearest centimeter.

1.

Rita's wrist

2.

Larry's wrist

3.

Molly's wrist

Some of the children
measured their spans.

Find each span to
the nearest centimeter.

Rita's span
1.

Larry's span
2.

Paul's span
3.

Molly's span
4.

5. Can you find your own wrist measure and span?

Larger units for length

A **meter** (m) is 100 centimeters.

A **kilometer** (km) is 1000 meters.

You might walk 1 kilometer
in 10 minutes.

Estimate each of these lengths in meters.

1. How wide is your classroom?

2. How long is your chalkboard?

3. Find the height of a door.

4. What is the difference in the
   distances shown on the sign?

Chimney Rock 7km

Sea Lion Cove 2km

Answer **more** or **less** than 1 meter.

1. Your height

2. Your shoe

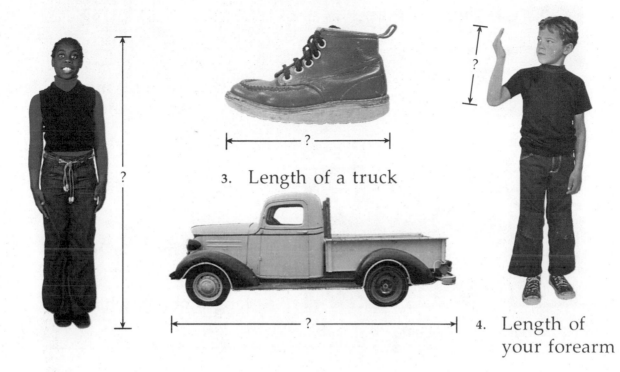

3. Length of a truck

4. Length of your forearm

Answer **more** or **less** than 1 kilometer.

5. Distance from your classroom to the school office

6. Distance a bicycle rider can go in 30 minutes

Answers for Self-check   1. 6 cm   2. 8 cm   3. 5 cm   4. more   5. less

Self-check

Find each length to the nearest centimeter.

1.

2.

3.

4. Answer **more** or **less** than a meter.

    height of a door

5. Answer **more** or **less** than a kilometer.

    length of a city block

Answers for Self-check—page 101

Test

Find the length. Use your ruler.

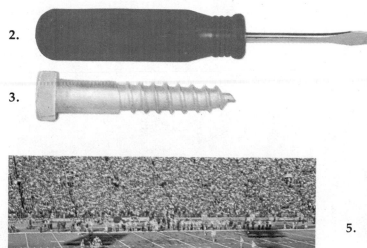

1.

2.

3.

4. Answer **more** or **less** than a meter.

    length of your forearm

5. Answer **more** or **less** than a kilometer.

    length of a football field

Dots and Segments

The three segments have different lengths.

How many more segments can you find
with lengths different from these?

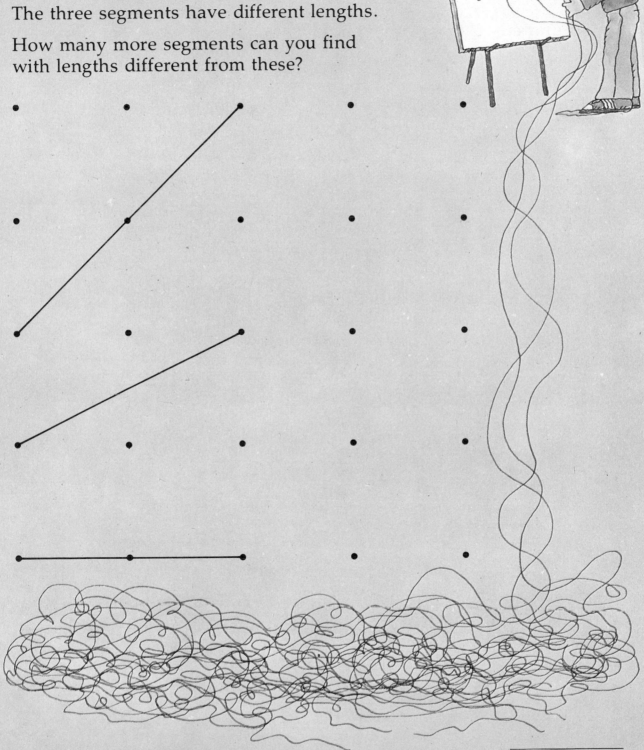

Level 12 review

Write the numeral.

1. 3 tens and 1 one

2. 8 tens and 0 ones

3. 4 hundreds, 2 tens, and 5 ones

4. 7 hundreds, 1 ten, and 9 ones

5. 2 thousands, 7 hundreds, 6 tens, and 8 ones

6. 9 thousands, 0 hundreds, 3 tens, and 6 ones

Complete the counting.

7. 84   85   86   87

8. 715   716   717   718

Add.

9. $\begin{array}{r} 32 \\ +65 \\ \hline \end{array}$

10. $\begin{array}{r} 73 \\ +88 \\ \hline \end{array}$

11. $\begin{array}{r} 65 \\ +37 \\ \hline \end{array}$

12. $\begin{array}{r} 26 \\ +49 \\ \hline \end{array}$

13. $\begin{array}{r} 48 \\ +94 \\ \hline \end{array}$

14. $\begin{array}{r} 418 \\ +259 \\ \hline \end{array}$

15. $\begin{array}{r} 782 \\ +597 \\ \hline \end{array}$

16. $\begin{array}{r} 506 \\ +385 \\ \hline \end{array}$

17. $\begin{array}{r} 695 \\ +786 \\ \hline \end{array}$

18. $\begin{array}{r} 387 \\ +461 \\ \hline \end{array}$

Subtract.

19. $\begin{array}{r} 25 \\ -12 \\ \hline \end{array}$

20. $\begin{array}{r} 32 \\ -28 \\ \hline \end{array}$

21. $\begin{array}{r} 71 \\ -46 \\ \hline \end{array}$

22. $\begin{array}{r} 50 \\ -37 \\ \hline \end{array}$

23. $\begin{array}{r} 93 \\ -66 \\ \hline \end{array}$

24. $\begin{array}{r} 538 \\ -274 \\ \hline \end{array}$

25. $\begin{array}{r} 342 \\ -165 \\ \hline \end{array}$

26. $\begin{array}{r} 602 \\ -345 \\ \hline \end{array}$

27. $\begin{array}{r} 811 \\ -634 \\ \hline \end{array}$

28. $\begin{array}{r} 735 \\ -489 \\ \hline \end{array}$

Level  **13**

Multiplication
Smaller Multiplication Facts
Multiplication Facts
Problem Solving—Using Your Skills
Geometry 2

Multiplication

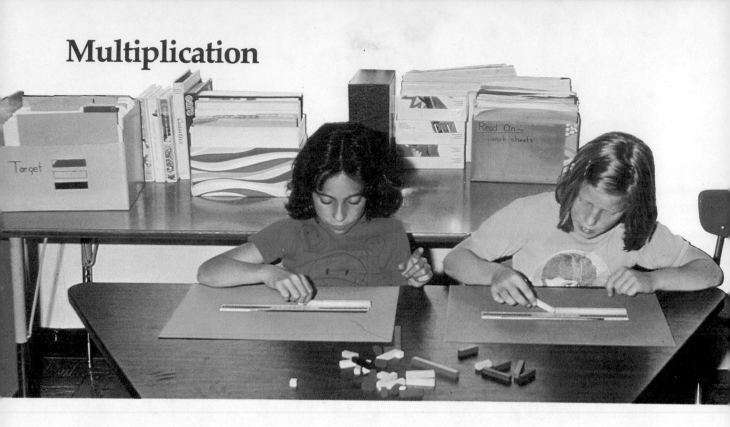

Getting started

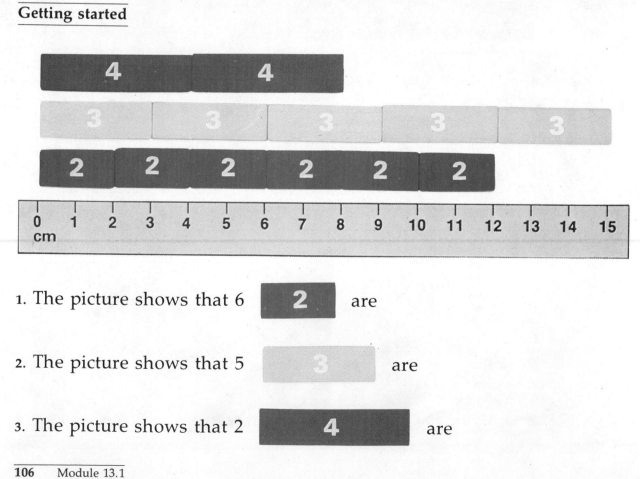

1. The picture shows that 6 $\boxed{2}$ are

2. The picture shows that 5 $\boxed{3}$ are

3. The picture shows that 2 $\boxed{4}$ are

We see:

We think: 3 twos are 6

We write: $3 \times 2 = 6$

We say: "Three times two equals six."

Solve.

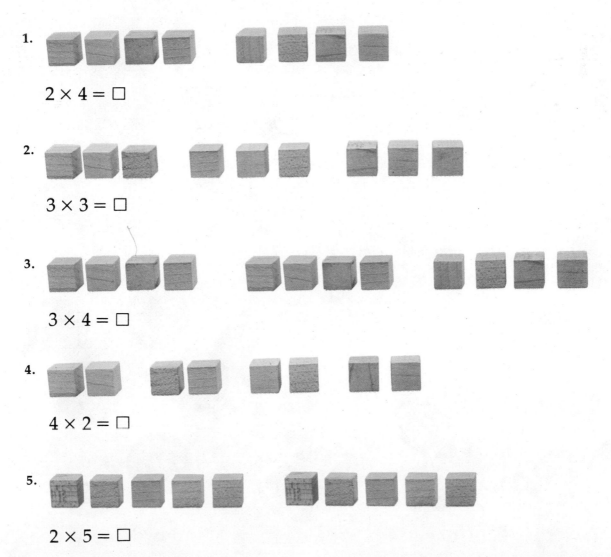

1. $2 \times 4 = \square$

2. $3 \times 3 = \square$

3. $3 \times 4 = \square$

4. $4 \times 2 = \square$

5. $2 \times 5 = \square$

Multiplication and sets

Give the missing numbers.

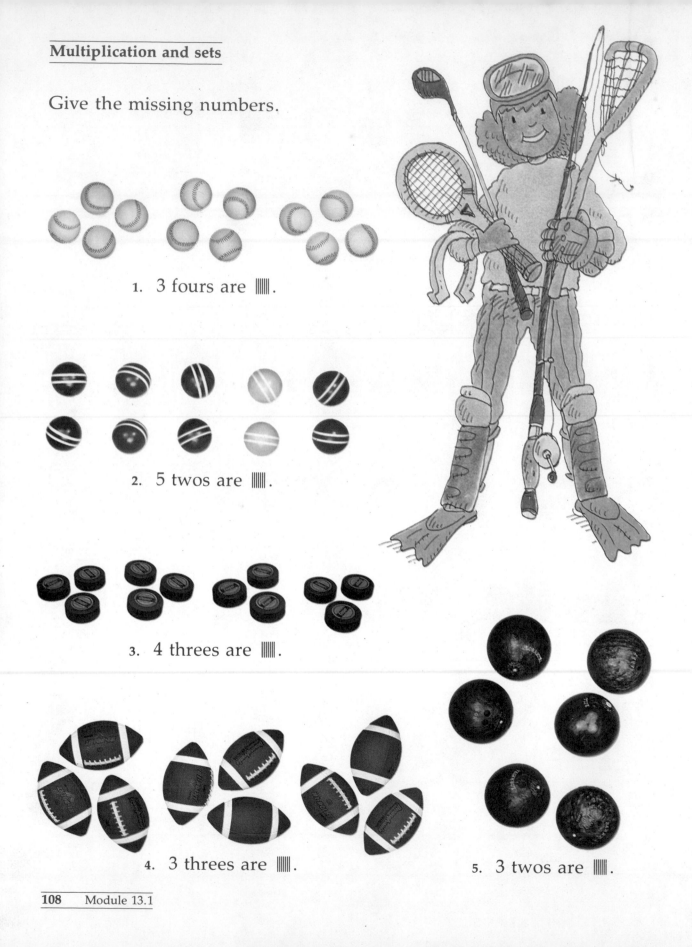

1. 3 fours are ▥.

2. 5 twos are ▥.

3. 4 threes are ▥.

4. 3 threes are ▥.

5. 3 twos are ▥.

Solve the equations.

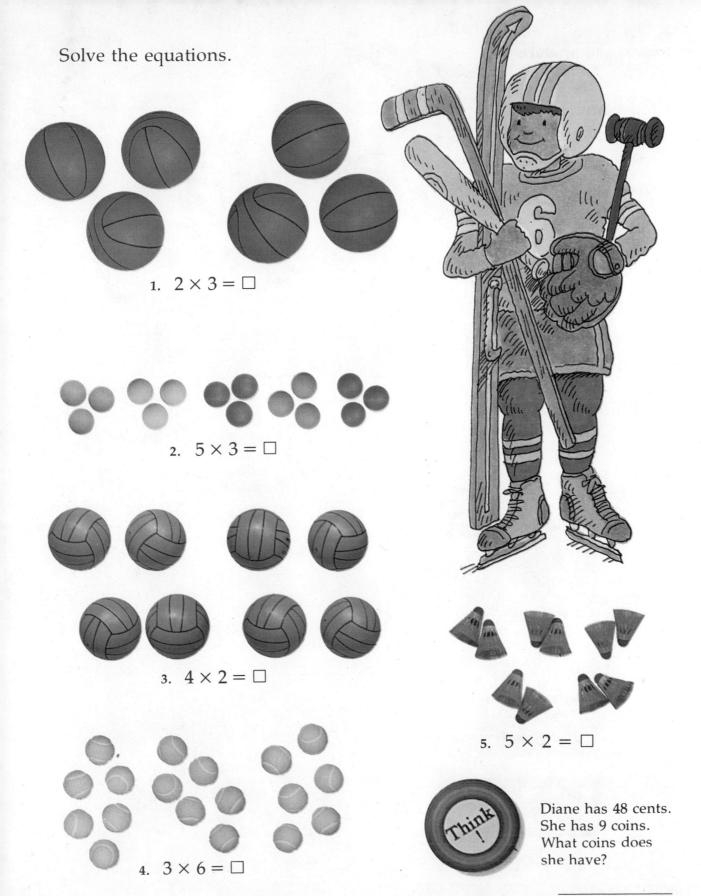

1. $2 \times 3 = \square$

2. $5 \times 3 = \square$

3. $4 \times 2 = \square$

4. $3 \times 6 = \square$

5. $5 \times 2 = \square$

Think!

Diane has 48 cents.
She has 9 coins.
What coins does
she have?

Factors and products

Card game:

4 players

3 cards each

How many cards?

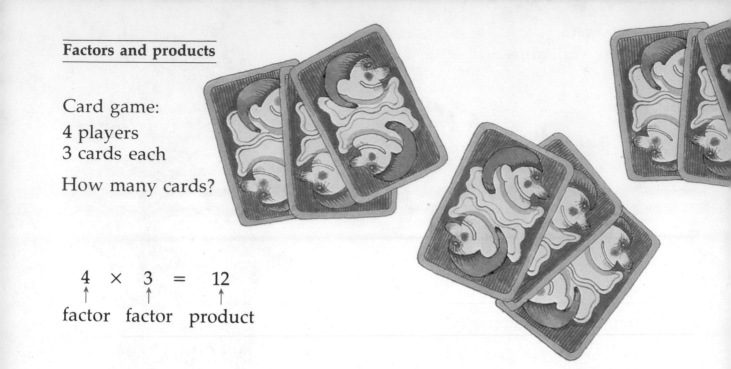

$$4 \times 3 = 12$$

factor   factor   product

Find the products.

1.

$3 \times 4 = \square$

2.

$2 \times 3 = \square$

3.

$4 \times 4 = \square$

4.

$3 \times 3 = \square$

Find the products.

1.

$3 \times 5 = \square$

2.

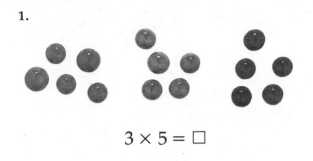

$5 \times 2 = \square$

3.

$2 \times 6 = \square$

4.

$4 \times 2 = \square$

5.

$2 \times 4 = \square$

Larry has 73 cents. What is the smallest number of coins he could have?

Multiplication and addition

You can think of adding when you find products.

How many nails?

$3 + 3 + 3 + 3 = 12$

$4 \times 3 = 12$

Find the sums and products.

1.

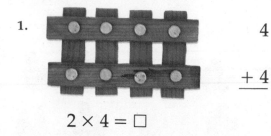

$$\begin{array}{r} 4 \\ + 4 \\ \hline \end{array}$$

$2 \times 4 = \square$

2.

$2 + 2 + 2 + 2 = \square$

$4 \times 2 = \square$

3.

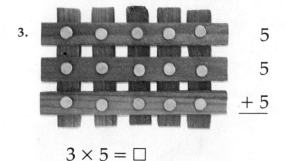

$$\begin{array}{r} 5 \\ 5 \\ + 5 \\ \hline \end{array}$$

$3 \times 5 = \square$

4.

$3 + 3 + 3 + 3 + 3 = \square$

$5 \times 3 = \square$

5.

$$\begin{array}{r} 5 \\ 5 \\ 5 \\ + 5 \\ \hline \end{array}$$

$4 \times 5 = \square$

6.

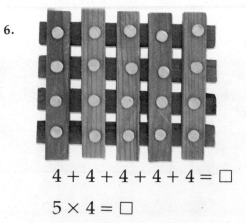

$4 + 4 + 4 + 4 + 4 = \square$

$5 \times 4 = \square$

Find the products.

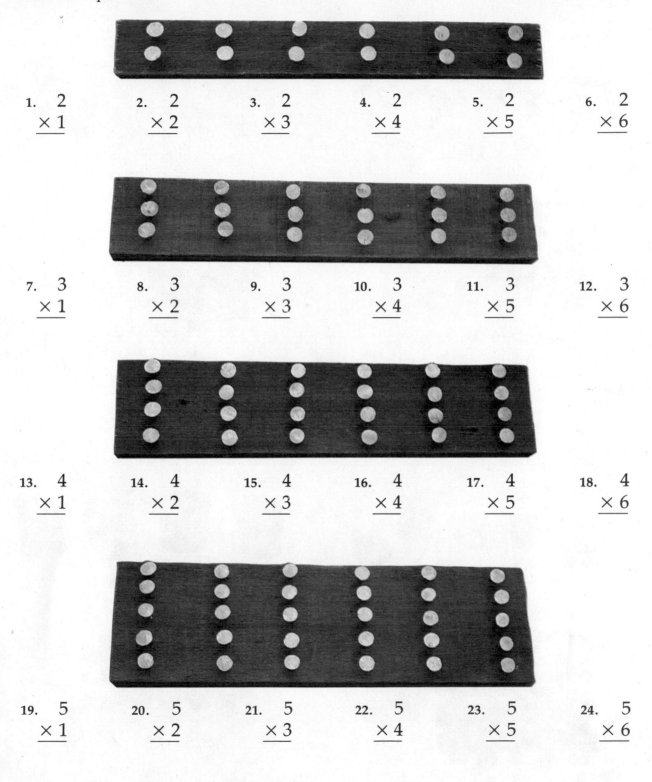

1. 2
    × 1

2. 2
    × 2

3. 2
    × 3

4. 2
    × 4

5. 2
    × 5

6. 2
    × 6

7. 3
    × 1

8. 3
    × 2

9. 3
    × 3

10. 3
    × 4

11. 3
    × 5

12. 3
    × 6

13. 4
    × 1

14. 4
    × 2

15. 4
    × 3

16. 4
    × 4

17. 4
    × 5

18. 4
    × 6

19. 5
    × 1

20. 5
    × 2

21. 5
    × 3

22. 5
    × 4

23. 5
    × 5

24. 5
    × 6

Answers for Self-check   1. 12   2. 10   3. 9   4. 12

Self-check

Solve.

1.

$$4 \times 3 = \square$$

2.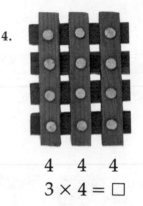

$$2 \times 5 = \square$$

3. 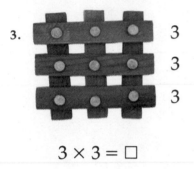 3
    3
    3

$$3 \times 3 = \square$$

4.

4 4 4
$$3 \times 4 = \square$$

Answers for Self-check—page 113

Test

Solve.

1.

$$5 \times 3 = \square$$

2.

$$4 \times 4 = \square$$

3.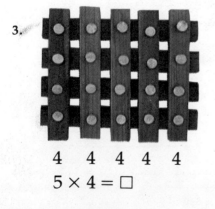

4 4 4 4 4
$$5 \times 4 = \square$$

4. 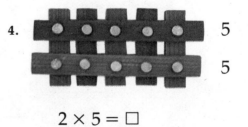 5
    5

$$2 \times 5 = \square$$

Finding the Letter

Find the answer to the riddle.

What do birds say at Halloween?

T_ ?_ ?_ ?_ ?_ ?_ ?_ ?_ ?_ ?_ ?_ ?_

2,9 5,4 8,7 3,6 4,2   7,1 5,4   2,9 6,8 9,3 9,3 2,9

To answer the riddle follow the first number over and the second number up.

Smaller Multiplication Facts

Make one of these sets of cards.
Put the products on the back.

Multiplying by 3

$$\frac{0}{\times 3} \quad \frac{1}{\times 3} \quad \frac{2}{\times 3} \quad \frac{3}{\times 3} \quad \frac{4}{\times 3} \quad \frac{5}{\times 3} \quad \frac{6}{\times 3} \quad \frac{7}{\times 3} \quad \frac{8}{\times 3} \quad \frac{9}{\times 3}$$

Multiplying by 4

$$\frac{0}{\times 4} \quad \frac{1}{\times 4} \quad \frac{2}{\times 4} \quad \frac{3}{\times 4} \quad \frac{4}{\times 4} \quad \frac{5}{\times 4} \quad \frac{6}{\times 4} \quad \frac{7}{\times 4} \quad \frac{8}{\times 4} \quad \frac{9}{\times 4}$$

Multiplying by 5

$$\frac{0}{\times 5} \quad \frac{1}{\times 5} \quad \frac{2}{\times 5} \quad \frac{3}{\times 5} \quad \frac{4}{\times 5} \quad \frac{5}{\times 5} \quad \frac{6}{\times 5} \quad \frac{7}{\times 5} \quad \frac{8}{\times 5} \quad \frac{9}{\times 5}$$

Mix up your cards.
Ask a friend to show you the front of some cards.
Try to give the products.

X	0	1	2	3	4	5	6	7	8	9
3	0	3	6	9	12	15	18	21	24	27
4	0	4	8	12	16	20	24	28	32	36
5	0	5	10	15	20	25	30	35	40	45

Try to remember the facts.
If you forget a fact, try to
figure it out.

Give these products.

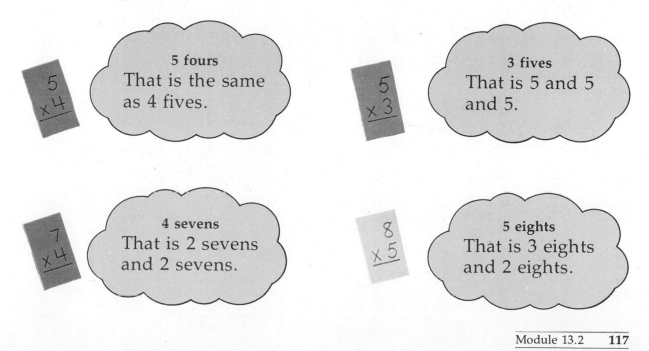

5
× 4

5 fours
That is the same
as 4 fives.

5
× 3

3 fives
That is 5 and 5
and 5.

7
× 4

4 sevens
That is 2 sevens
and 2 sevens.

8
× 5

5 eights
That is 3 eights
and 2 eights.

The easy facts

Zero times any number is zero.	$\begin{array}{r}0\\ \times 0\\ \hline 0\end{array}$	$\begin{array}{r}1\\ \times 0\\ \hline 0\end{array}$	$\begin{array}{r}2\\ \times 0\\ \hline 0\end{array}$	$\begin{array}{r}3\\ \times 0\\ \hline 0\end{array}$	$\begin{array}{r}4\\ \times 0\\ \hline 0\end{array}$	. . .
One times any number is that number.	$\begin{array}{r}0\\ \times 1\\ \hline 0\end{array}$	$\begin{array}{r}1\\ \times 1\\ \hline 1\end{array}$	$\begin{array}{r}2\\ \times 1\\ \hline 2\end{array}$	$\begin{array}{r}3\\ \times 1\\ \hline 3\end{array}$	$\begin{array}{r}4\\ \times 1\\ \hline 4\end{array}$	. . .
For two times a number, you can think of adding.	$\begin{array}{r}(0+0)\\ 0\\ \times 2\\ \hline 0\end{array}$	$\begin{array}{r}(1+1)\\ 1\\ \times 2\\ \hline 2\end{array}$	$\begin{array}{r}(2+2)\\ 2\\ \times 2\\ \hline 4\end{array}$	$\begin{array}{r}(3+3)\\ 3\\ \times 2\\ \hline 6\end{array}$	$\begin{array}{r}(4+4)\\ 4\\ \times 2\\ \hline 8\end{array}$	. . . .

Multiply.

1. $\begin{array}{r}5\\ \times 2\\ \hline\end{array}$
2. $\begin{array}{r}4\\ \times 1\\ \hline\end{array}$
3. $\begin{array}{r}4\\ \times 0\\ \hline\end{array}$
4. $\begin{array}{r}6\\ \times 2\\ \hline\end{array}$
5. $\begin{array}{r}5\\ \times 0\\ \hline\end{array}$
6. $\begin{array}{r}6\\ \times 1\\ \hline\end{array}$
7. $\begin{array}{r}2\\ \times 0\\ \hline\end{array}$

8. $\begin{array}{r}4\\ \times 2\\ \hline\end{array}$
9. $\begin{array}{r}8\\ \times 1\\ \hline\end{array}$
10. $\begin{array}{r}1\\ \times 2\\ \hline\end{array}$
11. $\begin{array}{r}0\\ \times 0\\ \hline\end{array}$
12. $\begin{array}{r}2\\ \times 2\\ \hline\end{array}$
13. $\begin{array}{r}7\\ \times 1\\ \hline\end{array}$
14. $\begin{array}{r}3\\ \times 0\\ \hline\end{array}$

15. $\begin{array}{r}1\\ \times 1\\ \hline\end{array}$
16. $\begin{array}{r}3\\ \times 2\\ \hline\end{array}$
17. $\begin{array}{r}1\\ \times 0\\ \hline\end{array}$
18. $\begin{array}{r}9\\ \times 1\\ \hline\end{array}$
19. $\begin{array}{r}0\\ \times 2\\ \hline\end{array}$
20. $\begin{array}{r}7\\ \times 0\\ \hline\end{array}$
21. $\begin{array}{r}2\\ \times 1\\ \hline\end{array}$

22. $\begin{array}{r}5\\ \times 1\\ \hline\end{array}$
23. $\begin{array}{r}7\\ \times 2\\ \hline\end{array}$
24. $\begin{array}{r}8\\ \times 0\\ \hline\end{array}$
25. $\begin{array}{r}0\\ \times 1\\ \hline\end{array}$
26. $\begin{array}{r}8\\ \times 2\\ \hline\end{array}$
27. $\begin{array}{r}3\\ \times 1\\ \hline\end{array}$
28. $\begin{array}{r}9\\ \times 2\\ \hline\end{array}$

Solve the equations.

1. $2 \times 1 = \square$ 2. $1 \times 4 = \square$ 3. $0 \times 4 = \square$ 4. $1 \times 2 = \square$

5. $2 \times 5 = \square$ 6. $0 \times 7 = \square$ 7. $1 \times 9 = \square$ 8. $0 \times 6 = \square$

9. $2 \times 3 = \square$ 10. $1 \times 7 = \square$ 11. $2 \times 6 = \square$ 12. $0 \times 3 = \square$

13. $1 \times 6 = \square$ 14. $0 \times 9 = \square$ 15. $2 \times 7 = \square$ 16. $1 \times 0 = \square$

17. $0 \times 1 = \square$ 18. $2 \times 2 = \square$ 19. $1 \times 5 = \square$ 20. $0 \times 8 = \square$

21. $1 \times 3 = \square$ 22. $0 \times 2 = \square$ 23. $2 \times 0 = \square$ 24. $2 \times 8 = \square$

Multiply.

25. $\begin{array}{r} 3 \\ \times 2 \\ \hline \end{array}$ 26. $\begin{array}{r} 5 \\ \times 2 \\ \hline \end{array}$ 27. $\begin{array}{r} 4 \\ \times 2 \\ \hline \end{array}$ 28. $\begin{array}{r} 2 \\ \times 2 \\ \hline \end{array}$ 29. $\begin{array}{r} 6 \\ \times 2 \\ \hline \end{array}$ 30. $\begin{array}{r} 8 \\ \times 2 \\ \hline \end{array}$ 31. $\begin{array}{r} 3 \\ \times 2 \\ \hline \end{array}$

32. $\begin{array}{r} 5 \\ \times 2 \\ \hline \end{array}$ 33. $\begin{array}{r} 9 \\ \times 2 \\ \hline \end{array}$ 34. $\begin{array}{r} 8 \\ \times 2 \\ \hline \end{array}$ 35. $\begin{array}{r} 7 \\ \times 2 \\ \hline \end{array}$ 36. $\begin{array}{r} 2 \\ \times 2 \\ \hline \end{array}$ 37. $\begin{array}{r} 4 \\ \times 2 \\ \hline \end{array}$ 38. $\begin{array}{r} 9 \\ \times 2 \\ \hline \end{array}$

39. $\begin{array}{r} 9 \\ \times 2 \\ \hline \end{array}$ 40. $\begin{array}{r} 6 \\ \times 2 \\ \hline \end{array}$ 41. $\begin{array}{r} 5 \\ \times 2 \\ \hline \end{array}$ 42. $\begin{array}{r} 8 \\ \times 2 \\ \hline \end{array}$ 43. $\begin{array}{r} 7 \\ \times 2 \\ \hline \end{array}$ 44. $\begin{array}{r} 6 \\ \times 2 \\ \hline \end{array}$ 45. $\begin{array}{r} 7 \\ \times 2 \\ \hline \end{array}$

Multiply by 1	
3	3
8	8
46. 2	|||||
47. 6	|||||
48. 0	|||||
49. 1	|||||

Multiply by 2	
4	8
50. 6	|||||
51. 3	|||||
52. 9	|||||
53. 0	|||||
54. 1	|||||

2 children.
Each child has 4 dogs.
Each dog has 3 fleas.
How many fleas?

Multiplying by 3

Find the products.

0	1	2	3	4	5	6	7	8	9
×3	×3	×3	×3	×3	×3	×3	×3	×3	×3

Multiply.

1. 4
×3

2. 6
×3

3. 7
×3

4. 9
×3

5. 8
×3

6. 3
×3

7. 5
×3

8. 6
×3

9. 2
×3

10. 0
×3

11. 8
×3

12. 4
×3

13. 9
×3

14. 7
×3

15. 2
×3

16. 9
×3

17. 7
×3

18. 5
×3

19. 1
×3

20. 8
×3

21. 3
×3

Multiply.

22. 6
×2

23. 4
×3

24. 9
×1

25. 2
×3

26. 4
×2

27. 6
×0

28. 6
×3

29. 3
×2

30. 8
×0

31. 3
×3

32. 9
×2

33. 5
×3

34. 6
×1

35. 7
×3

36. 1
×2

37. 8
×3

I'm more than 8 and 8,
and less than 5 times 4,
3 times some other number.
You need to know no more.

Who am I?

The downhill race

Put a marker on start.
To get down the hill,
follow these rules.

1. Roll the cube.
2. Multiply the top
   number by 3.
3. Say your product.
4. If you are right, move
   the number of spaces of
   the tens' digit (1 or 2).

The cube has
4, 5, 6, 7, 8, 9
on its faces.

5. Take turns. The player
   who gets down the
   hill first wins.

Multiplying by 4

If the clip
lands on 7,
what's the score?

Multiply by 4.

$$\begin{array}{r} 7 \\ \times\ 4 \\ \hline 28 \end{array}$$

The score is 28.

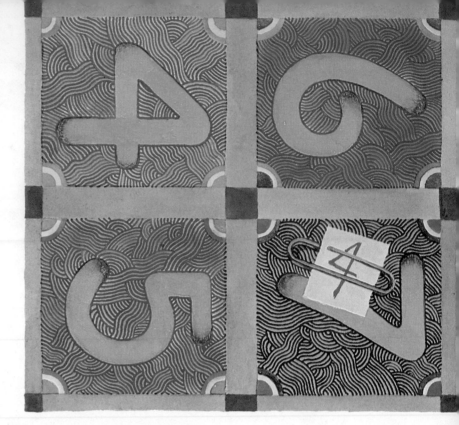

Multiply.

0	1	2	3	4	5	6	7	8	9
×4	×4	×4	×4	×4	×4	×4	×4	×4	×4

1. 4
  × 4

2. 6
  × 4

3. 7
  × 4

4. 9
  × 4

5. 8
  × 4

6. 3
  × 4

7. 5
  × 4

8. 6
  × 4

9. 5
  × 4

10. 0
  × 4

11. 8
  × 4

12. 2
  × 4

13. 9
  × 4

14. 7
  × 4

15. 2
  × 4

16. 9
  × 4

17. 7
  × 4

18. 5
  × 4

19. 6
  × 4

20. 8
  × 4

21. 4
  × 4

22. 9
  × 4

23. 6
  × 4

24. 3
  × 4

25. 8
  × 4

26. 1
  × 4

27. 5
  × 4

28. 7
  × 4

Solve the equations.

1. $4 \times 7 = \square$ 2. $4 \times 4 = \square$ 3. $4 \times 8 = \square$

4. $4 \times 1 = \square$ 5. $4 \times 5 = \square$ 6. $4 \times 9 = \square$

7. $4 \times 0 = \square$ 8. $4 \times 7 = \square$ 9. $4 \times 8 = \square$

10. $4 \times 6 = \square$ 11. $4 \times 3 = \square$ 12. $4 \times 2 = \square$

Multiply.

13. $\begin{array}{r} 5 \\ \times 2 \\ \hline \end{array}$ 14. $\begin{array}{r} 5 \\ \times 4 \\ \hline \end{array}$ 15. $\begin{array}{r} 4 \\ \times 3 \\ \hline \end{array}$ 16. $\begin{array}{r} 8 \\ \times 2 \\ \hline \end{array}$

17. $\begin{array}{r} 1 \\ \times 4 \\ \hline \end{array}$ 18. $\begin{array}{r} 8 \\ \times 3 \\ \hline \end{array}$ 19. $\begin{array}{r} 9 \\ \times 3 \\ \hline \end{array}$

20. $\begin{array}{r} 5 \\ \times 0 \\ \hline \end{array}$ 21. $\begin{array}{r} 9 \\ \times 4 \\ \hline \end{array}$ 22. $\begin{array}{r} 4 \\ \times 2 \\ \hline \end{array}$ 23. $\begin{array}{r} 9 \\ \times 2 \\ \hline \end{array}$ 24. $\begin{array}{r} 7 \\ \times 3 \\ \hline \end{array}$ 25. $\begin{array}{r} 6 \\ \times 4 \\ \hline \end{array}$ 26. $\begin{array}{r} 7 \\ \times 2 \\ \hline \end{array}$

27. $\begin{array}{r} 8 \\ \times 4 \\ \hline \end{array}$ 28. $\begin{array}{r} 4 \\ \times 4 \\ \hline \end{array}$ 29. $\begin{array}{r} 0 \\ \times 4 \\ \hline \end{array}$ 30. $\begin{array}{r} 2 \\ \times 3 \\ \hline \end{array}$ 31. $\begin{array}{r} 3 \\ \times 4 \\ \hline \end{array}$ 32. $\begin{array}{r} 5 \\ \times 3 \\ \hline \end{array}$ 33. $\begin{array}{r} 7 \\ \times 4 \\ \hline \end{array}$

Multiply by 4	
7	28
34. 5	|||||
35. 2	|||||
36. 8	|||||
37. 0	|||||
38. 4	|||||

39. What is the score?

☆ 40. Try the clip game with a friend. The player with the higher total after 5 tosses wins.

If you add me to myself
Then multiply by two,
It's 12 plus 4 you're
sure to get.
You need no other clue.
Who am I?

Multiplying by 5

Find the products.

0	1	2	3	4	5	6	7	8	9
×5	×5	×5	×5	×5	×5	×5	×5	×5	×5

Multiply.

1. 4 ×5	2. 6 ×5	3. 7 ×5	4. 9 ×5	5. 8 ×5	6. 3 ×5	7. 5 ×5
8. 6 ×5	9. 5 ×5	10. 0 ×5	11. 8 ×5	12. 4 ×5	13. 9 ×5	14. 7 ×5
15. 2 ×5	16. 9 ×5	17. 7 ×5	18. 5 ×5	19. 6 ×5	20. 8 ×5	21. 4 ×5

Multiply.

22. 3 ×5	23. 6 ×3	24. 6 ×5	25. 5 ×4	26. 6 ×2	27. 7 ×5	28. 7 ×4
29. 7 ×3	30. 9 ×5	31. 9 ×4	32. 8 ×5	33. 1 ×5	34. 3 ×3	35. 4 ×2

Think!

What number should
be on the tag?

20 ? 40

Score lines

Use a spinner like this.

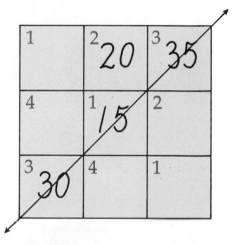

Each player should make a
score board like this.

1	2	3
4	1	2
3	4	1

Rules
1. Spin the spinner.

2. Multiply your number by 5.

3. Put your product in a square so that
   the tens' digit matches the red digit.

4. First player to line up three products
   ($\updownarrow$ $\leftrightarrow$ $\nearrow$ $\searrow$) wins.

Note: Sometimes you may not be able
to put your score in any square.
If not, you lose a turn.

A winner's board.

1	2 20	3 35
4	1 15	2
3 30	4	1

Answers for Self-check   1. 8   2. 5   3. 14   4. 30   5. 24   6. 9   7. 7   8. 18   9. 45   10. 12   11. 0   12. 24
13. 20   14. 18   15. 12   16. 21   17. 3   18. 28   19. 27   20. 12   21. 35   22. 0   23. 40   24. 32

More practice, page 334

Multiply.

1. $\begin{array}{r} 2 \\ \times 4 \\ \hline \end{array}$
2. $\begin{array}{r} 5 \\ \times 1 \\ \hline \end{array}$
3. $\begin{array}{r} 7 \\ \times 2 \\ \hline \end{array}$
4. $\begin{array}{r} 6 \\ \times 5 \\ \hline \end{array}$
5. $\begin{array}{r} 6 \\ \times 4 \\ \hline \end{array}$
6. $\begin{array}{r} 3 \\ \times 3 \\ \hline \end{array}$

7. $\begin{array}{r} 7 \\ \times 1 \\ \hline \end{array}$
8. $\begin{array}{r} 6 \\ \times 3 \\ \hline \end{array}$
9. $\begin{array}{r} 9 \\ \times 5 \\ \hline \end{array}$
10. $\begin{array}{r} 3 \\ \times 4 \\ \hline \end{array}$
11. $\begin{array}{r} 6 \\ \times 0 \\ \hline \end{array}$
12. $\begin{array}{r} 8 \\ \times 3 \\ \hline \end{array}$

13. $4 \times 5 = \square$
14. $2 \times 9 = \square$
15. $3 \times 4 = \square$
16. $3 \times 7 = \square$

17. $1 \times 3 = \square$
18. $4 \times 7 = \square$
19. $3 \times 9 = \square$
20. $2 \times 6 = \square$

21. $5 \times 7 = \square$
22. $0 \times 2 = \square$
23. $5 \times 8 = \square$
24. $4 \times 8 = \square$

Answers for Self-check—page 125

Multiply.

1. $\begin{array}{r} 5 \\ \times 2 \\ \hline \end{array}$
2. $\begin{array}{r} 8 \\ \times 3 \\ \hline \end{array}$
3. $\begin{array}{r} 7 \\ \times 2 \\ \hline \end{array}$
4. $\begin{array}{r} 4 \\ \times 5 \\ \hline \end{array}$
5. $\begin{array}{r} 9 \\ \times 4 \\ \hline \end{array}$
6. $\begin{array}{r} 3 \\ \times 0 \\ \hline \end{array}$

7. $\begin{array}{r} 5 \\ \times 5 \\ \hline \end{array}$
8. $\begin{array}{r} 7 \\ \times 4 \\ \hline \end{array}$
9. $\begin{array}{r} 9 \\ \times 3 \\ \hline \end{array}$
10. $\begin{array}{r} 7 \\ \times 5 \\ \hline \end{array}$
11. $\begin{array}{r} 1 \\ \times 1 \\ \hline \end{array}$
12. $\begin{array}{r} 4 \\ \times 4 \\ \hline \end{array}$

13. $5 \times 6 = \square$
14. $4 \times 5 = \square$
15. $3 \times 6 = \square$
16. $2 \times 4 = \square$

17. $2 \times 6 = \square$
18. $1 \times 8 = \square$
19. $2 \times 8 = \square$
20. $3 \times 5 = \square$

21. $4 \times 8 = \square$
22. $5 \times 8 = \square$
23. $4 \times 6 = \square$
24. $5 \times 9 = \square$

Number Name Game

Can you find the number for each set of letters?

Example:

WOT   TWO

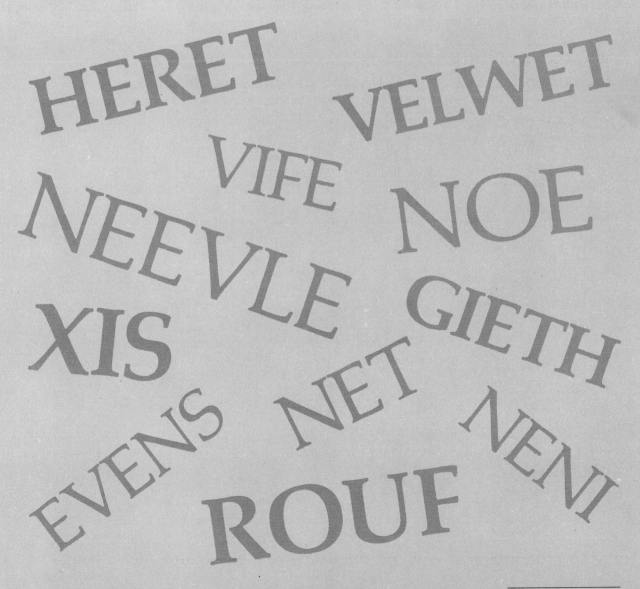

HERET

VELWET

VIFE

NEEVLE

NOE

XIS

GIETH

EVENS

NET

NENI

ROUF

Multiplication Facts

x	0	1	2	3	4	5	6	7	8	9
6	0	6	12	18	24	30	36	42	48	54
7	0	7	14	21	28	35	42	49	56	63
8	0	8	16	24	32	40	48	56	64	72
9	0	9	18	27	36	45	54	63	72	81

Getting started

Choose one of these sets of cards.
Make the ones with a star. Put the products on the back.

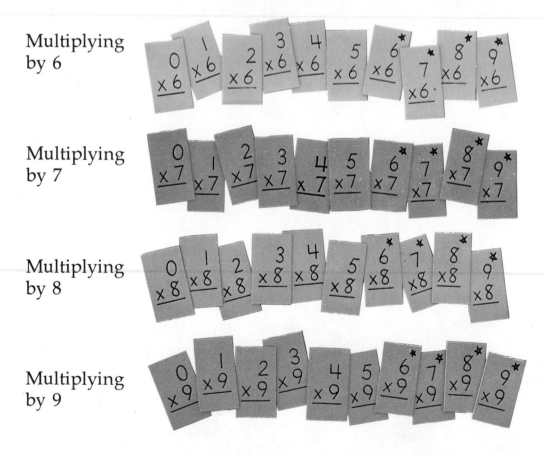

Multiplying by 6

Multiplying by 7

Multiplying by 8

Multiplying by 9

Try to remember all your products. Have a classmate check you.

These two cards have the same product.

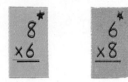

1. How many other cards with stars have the same product?

2. Do you remember this card?

What is the product for this card?

3. Give the product for each pair of cards.

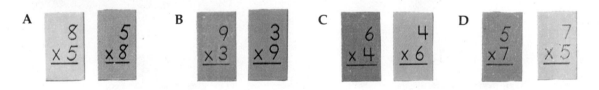

A 8 ×5   5 ×8

B 9 ×3   3 ×9

C 6 ×4   4 ×6

D 5 ×7   7 ×5

4. Give the missing products.

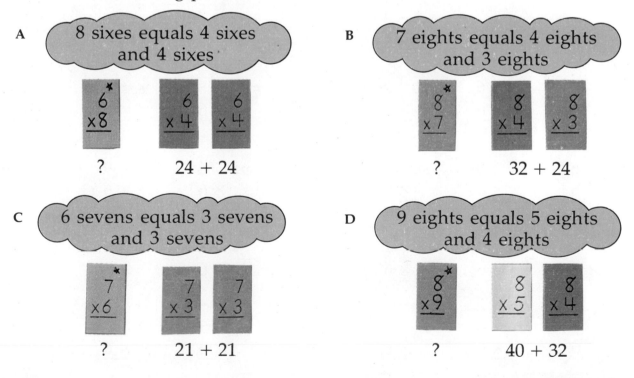

A 8 sixes equals 4 sixes and 4 sixes

6 ×8   6 ×4   6 ×4

?   24 + 24

B 7 eights equals 4 eights and 3 eights

8 ×7   8 ×4   8 ×3

?   32 + 24

C 6 sevens equals 3 sevens and 3 sevens

7 ×6   7 ×3   7 ×3

?   21 + 21

D 9 eights equals 5 eights and 4 eights

8 ×9   8 ×5   8 ×4

?   40 + 32

Multiplying by 6

Open a book with your eyes closed.
Find the last digit of the page number. 5
Multiply by 6.

What is the product?

$6 \times 5 = 30$

Find these products.

0	1	2	3	4	5
×6	×6	×6	×6	×6	×6

Now find these products.

Use the table on page 128 to check your answers.

6	7	8	9
×6	×6	×6	×6

Find the products.

1. 4	2. 6	3. 7	4. 9	5. 8	6. 3	7. 5
×6	×6	×6	×6	×6	×6	×6

8. 6	9. 5	10. 0	11. 8	12. 4	13. 9	14. 7
×6	×6	×6	×6	×6	×6	×6

15. 2	16. 9	17. 7	18. 5	19. 6	20. 8	21. 4
×6	×6	×6	×6	×6	×6	×6

22. 9	23. 6	24. 2	25. 8	26. 1	27. 5	28. 7
×6	×6	×6	×6	×6	×6	×6

Solve the equations.

1. $6 \times 5 = \square$ 2. $6 \times 8 = \square$ 3. $6 \times 3 = \square$ 4. $6 \times 7 = \square$

5. $6 \times 0 = \square$ 6. $6 \times 6 = \square$ 7. $6 \times 4 = \square$ 8. $6 \times 9 = \square$

9. $6 \times 7 = \square$ 10. $6 \times 6 = \square$ 11. $6 \times 8 = \square$ 12. $6 \times 4 = \square$

13. $6 \times 5 = \square$ 14. $6 \times 2 = \square$ 15. $6 \times 3 = \square$ 16. $6 \times 9 = \square$

Multiply as quickly as you can.

17. $\begin{array}{r} 5 \\ \times 6 \\ \hline \end{array}$	18. $\begin{array}{r} 5 \\ \times 3 \\ \hline \end{array}$	19. $\begin{array}{r} 7 \\ \times 6 \\ \hline \end{array}$	20. $\begin{array}{r} 5 \\ \times 5 \\ \hline \end{array}$	21. $\begin{array}{r} 9 \\ \times 4 \\ \hline \end{array}$	22. $\begin{array}{r} 6 \\ \times 3 \\ \hline \end{array}$	23. $\begin{array}{r} 4 \\ \times 5 \\ \hline \end{array}$
24. $\begin{array}{r} 4 \\ \times 4 \\ \hline \end{array}$	25. $\begin{array}{r} 9 \\ \times 6 \\ \hline \end{array}$	26. $\begin{array}{r} 6 \\ \times 2 \\ \hline \end{array}$	27. $\begin{array}{r} 8 \\ \times 6 \\ \hline \end{array}$	28. $\begin{array}{r} 6 \\ \times 5 \\ \hline \end{array}$	29. $\begin{array}{r} 5 \\ \times 4 \\ \hline \end{array}$	30. $\begin{array}{r} 9 \\ \times 5 \\ \hline \end{array}$
31. $\begin{array}{r} 7 \\ \times 3 \\ \hline \end{array}$	32. $\begin{array}{r} 0 \\ \times 6 \\ \hline \end{array}$	33. $\begin{array}{r} 2 \\ \times 5 \\ \hline \end{array}$	34. $\begin{array}{r} 4 \\ \times 6 \\ \hline \end{array}$	35. $\begin{array}{r} 8 \\ \times 2 \\ \hline \end{array}$	36. $\begin{array}{r} 2 \\ \times 6 \\ \hline \end{array}$	37. $\begin{array}{r} 7 \\ \times 4 \\ \hline \end{array}$
38. $\begin{array}{r} 3 \\ \times 5 \\ \hline \end{array}$	39. $\begin{array}{r} 6 \\ \times 6 \\ \hline \end{array}$	40. $\begin{array}{r} 8 \\ \times 3 \\ \hline \end{array}$	41. $\begin{array}{r} 7 \\ \times 5 \\ \hline \end{array}$	42. $\begin{array}{r} 1 \\ \times 6 \\ \hline \end{array}$	43. $\begin{array}{r} 8 \\ \times 5 \\ \hline \end{array}$	44. $\begin{array}{r} 3 \\ \times 6 \\ \hline \end{array}$

45. Multiply the last digit by 6.

What is the product?

☆ 46. Try the page game with a friend.
Each player takes 5 turns.
Add your answers.
High score wins.

Which amounts can
you pay with 3 coins?

1. 7¢   2. 14¢
3. 15¢   4. 16¢
5. 30¢   6. 31¢

Multiplying by 7

The cube is numbered from 4 to 9.

Multiply the top number by 7.

$7 \times 8 = 56$

The score is 56.

Find these products.

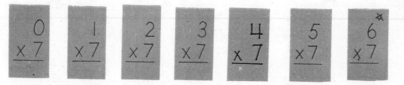

Now find these products.

Use the table on page 128 to check your answers.

| 7
×7 | 8
×7 | 9
×7 |

Find the products.

1. 4
   ×7
2. 6
   ×7
3. 7
   ×7
4. 9
   ×7
5. 8
   ×7
6. 3
   ×7
7. 5
   ×7

8. 6
   ×7
9. 5
   ×7
10. 0
    ×7
11. 8
    ×7
12. 4
    ×7
13. 9
    ×7
14. 7
    ×7

15. 2
    ×7
16. 9
    ×7
17. 7
    ×7
18. 5
    ×7
19. 6
    ×7
20. 8
    ×7
21. 4
    ×7

22. 9
    ×7
23. 6
    ×7
24. 3
    ×7
25. 8
    ×7
26. 1
    ×7
27. 5
    ×7
28. 7
    ×7

Solve the equations.

1. $7 \times 5 = \square$ 2. $7 \times 8 = \square$ 3. $7 \times 3 = \square$

4. $7 \times 7 = \square$ 5. $7 \times 0 = \square$ 6. $7 \times 6 = \square$

7. $7 \times 2 = \square$ 8. $7 \times 9 = \square$ 9. $7 \times 7 = \square$

10. $7 \times 6 = \square$ 11. $7 \times 8 = \square$ 12. $7 \times 4 = \square$

Multiply as quickly as you can.

13. $\begin{array}{r} 8 \\ \times 4 \\ \hline \end{array}$ 14. $\begin{array}{r} 6 \\ \times 7 \\ \hline \end{array}$ 15. $\begin{array}{r} 6 \\ \times 6 \\ \hline \end{array}$ 16. $\begin{array}{r} 4 \\ \times 7 \\ \hline \end{array}$ 17. $\begin{array}{r} 7 \\ \times 5 \\ \hline \end{array}$

18. $\begin{array}{r} 3 \\ \times 6 \\ \hline \end{array}$ 19. $\begin{array}{r} 5 \\ \times 7 \\ \hline \end{array}$ 20. $\begin{array}{r} 9 \\ \times 2 \\ \hline \end{array}$ 21. $\begin{array}{r} 8 \\ \times 6 \\ \hline \end{array}$ 22. $\begin{array}{r} 7 \\ \times 6 \\ \hline \end{array}$ 23. $\begin{array}{r} 5 \\ \times 5 \\ \hline \end{array}$ 24. $\begin{array}{r} 8 \\ \times 7 \\ \hline \end{array}$

25. $\begin{array}{r} 7 \\ \times 4 \\ \hline \end{array}$ 26. $\begin{array}{r} 2 \\ \times 7 \\ \hline \end{array}$ 27. $\begin{array}{r} 9 \\ \times 7 \\ \hline \end{array}$ 28. $\begin{array}{r} 8 \\ \times 5 \\ \hline \end{array}$ 29. $\begin{array}{r} 0 \\ \times 7 \\ \hline \end{array}$ 30. $\begin{array}{r} 6 \\ \times 3 \\ \hline \end{array}$ 31. $\begin{array}{r} 2 \\ \times 6 \\ \hline \end{array}$

32. $\begin{array}{r} 7 \\ \times 7 \\ \hline \end{array}$ 33. $\begin{array}{r} 6 \\ \times 5 \\ \hline \end{array}$ 34. $\begin{array}{r} 9 \\ \times 4 \\ \hline \end{array}$ 35. $\begin{array}{r} 5 \\ \times 6 \\ \hline \end{array}$ 36. $\begin{array}{r} 3 \\ \times 7 \\ \hline \end{array}$ 37. $\begin{array}{r} 4 \\ \times 6 \\ \hline \end{array}$ 38. $\begin{array}{r} 5 \\ \times 4 \\ \hline \end{array}$

39.

Multiply
by 7.
What is the
score?

Whenever I'm a factor,
I think I'm quite a hero.
You'll always get a product
That ends in five or zero.
Who am I?

☆ 40. Try the cube game with
a friend. Number a cube
from 4 to 9. Toss the cube.
Multiply by 7. Copy the table.
Record your answers.

×	4	5	6	7	8	9
7						

First player to complete their
table wins.

Multiplying by 8

A number from 0 to 9 is on each card.
Multiply the card number by 8.

$$8 \times 6 = 48$$

The score for the first turn is 48.

Find these products.

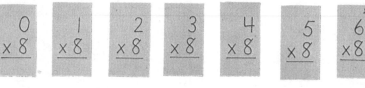

Now find these products.

Use the table on page 128
to check your answers.

Find the products.

1. $\begin{array}{r} 4 \\ \times 8 \end{array}$	2. $\begin{array}{r} 6 \\ \times 8 \end{array}$	3. $\begin{array}{r} 7 \\ \times 8 \end{array}$	4. $\begin{array}{r} 9 \\ \times 8 \end{array}$	5. $\begin{array}{r} 8 \\ \times 8 \end{array}$	6. $\begin{array}{r} 3 \\ \times 8 \end{array}$	7. $\begin{array}{r} 5 \\ \times 8 \end{array}$
8. $\begin{array}{r} 6 \\ \times 8 \end{array}$	9. $\begin{array}{r} 5 \\ \times 8 \end{array}$	10. $\begin{array}{r} 0 \\ \times 8 \end{array}$	11. $\begin{array}{r} 8 \\ \times 8 \end{array}$	12. $\begin{array}{r} 2 \\ \times 8 \end{array}$	13. $\begin{array}{r} 9 \\ \times 8 \end{array}$	14. $\begin{array}{r} 7 \\ \times 8 \end{array}$
15. $\begin{array}{r} 2 \\ \times 8 \end{array}$	16. $\begin{array}{r} 9 \\ \times 8 \end{array}$	17. $\begin{array}{r} 7 \\ \times 8 \end{array}$	18. $\begin{array}{r} 5 \\ \times 8 \end{array}$	19. $\begin{array}{r} 6 \\ \times 8 \end{array}$	20. $\begin{array}{r} 8 \\ \times 8 \end{array}$	21. $\begin{array}{r} 4 \\ \times 8 \end{array}$
22. $\begin{array}{r} 9 \\ \times 8 \end{array}$	23. $\begin{array}{r} 6 \\ \times 8 \end{array}$	24. $\begin{array}{r} 4 \\ \times 8 \end{array}$	25. $\begin{array}{r} 8 \\ \times 8 \end{array}$	26. $\begin{array}{r} 1 \\ \times 8 \end{array}$	27. $\begin{array}{r} 5 \\ \times 8 \end{array}$	28. $\begin{array}{r} 7 \\ \times 8 \end{array}$

Solve the equations.

1. $8 \times 5 = \square$ 2. $8 \times 8 = \square$ 3. $8 \times 3 = \square$

4. $8 \times 7 = \square$ 5. $8 \times 0 = \square$ 6. $8 \times 6 = \square$

7. $8 \times 4 = \square$ 8. $8 \times 9 = \square$ 9. $8 \times 5 = \square$

10. $8 \times 7 = \square$ 11. $8 \times 8 = \square$ 12. $8 \times 4 = \square$

13. $8 \times 1 = \square$ 14. $8 \times 6 = \square$ 15. $8 \times 2 = \square$

Multiply as quickly as you can.

| 16. $\begin{array}{r} 5 \\ \times 6 \\ \hline \end{array}$ | 17. $\begin{array}{r} 4 \\ \times 8 \\ \hline \end{array}$ | 18. $\begin{array}{r} 9 \\ \times 7 \\ \hline \end{array}$ | 19. $\begin{array}{r} 8 \\ \times 8 \\ \hline \end{array}$ | 20. $\begin{array}{r} 7 \\ \times 4 \\ \hline \end{array}$ | 21. $\begin{array}{r} 6 \\ \times 7 \\ \hline \end{array}$ | 22. $\begin{array}{r} 6 \\ \times 8 \\ \hline \end{array}$ |

| 23. $\begin{array}{r} 9 \\ \times 8 \\ \hline \end{array}$ | 24. $\begin{array}{r} 7 \\ \times 7 \\ \hline \end{array}$ | 25. $\begin{array}{r} 7 \\ \times 3 \\ \hline \end{array}$ | 26. $\begin{array}{r} 3 \\ \times 6 \\ \hline \end{array}$ | 27. $\begin{array}{r} 1 \\ \times 8 \\ \hline \end{array}$ | 28. $\begin{array}{r} 9 \\ \times 3 \\ \hline \end{array}$ | 29. $\begin{array}{r} 3 \\ \times 8 \\ \hline \end{array}$ |

| 30. $\begin{array}{r} 5 \\ \times 8 \\ \hline \end{array}$ | 31. $\begin{array}{r} 7 \\ \times 2 \\ \hline \end{array}$ | 32. $\begin{array}{r} 7 \\ \times 8 \\ \hline \end{array}$ | 33. $\begin{array}{r} 9 \\ \times 6 \\ \hline \end{array}$ | 34. $\begin{array}{r} 6 \\ \times 5 \\ \hline \end{array}$ | 35. $\begin{array}{r} 8 \\ \times 7 \\ \hline \end{array}$ | 36. $\begin{array}{r} 7 \\ \times 6 \\ \hline \end{array}$ |

| 37. $\begin{array}{r} 8 \\ \times 4 \\ \hline \end{array}$ | 38. $\begin{array}{r} 0 \\ \times 8 \\ \hline \end{array}$ | 39. $\begin{array}{r} 7 \\ \times 5 \\ \hline \end{array}$ | 40. $\begin{array}{r} 9 \\ \times 8 \\ \hline \end{array}$ | 41. $\begin{array}{r} 5 \\ \times 7 \\ \hline \end{array}$ | 42. $\begin{array}{r} 2 \\ \times 8 \\ \hline \end{array}$ | 43. $\begin{array}{r} 8 \\ \times 8 \\ \hline \end{array}$ |

☆ 44. Try the card game with a friend.
Take turns picking up a card.
Find your score.
Player with highest total
after 4 turns wins.

Multiply me by myself.
You're almost up to fifty.
Though I am a little odd,
I think I'm pretty nifty.
Who am I?

Multiplying by 9

The spinner landed on 9.
Multiply 9 by 9.

$$9 \times 9 = 81$$

The score is 81.

Find these products.

Use the table on page 128
to check your answers.

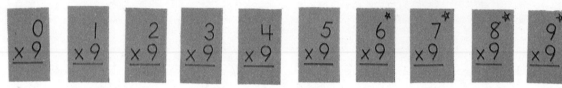

Find the products.

1. 4
   × 9

2. 6
   × 9

3. 7
   × 9

4. 9
   × 9

5. 8
   × 9

6. 3
   × 9

7. 5
   × 9

8. 6
   × 9

9. 5
   × 9

10. 0
   × 9

11. 8
   × 9

12. 2
   × 9

13. 9
   × 9

14. 7
   × 9

15. 2
   × 9

16. 9
   × 9

17. 7
   × 9

18. 5
   × 9

19. 6
   × 9

20. 8
   × 9

21. 4
   × 9

22. 9
   × 9

23. 6
   × 9

24. 4
   × 9

25. 8
   × 9

26. 1
   × 9

27. 5
   × 9

28. 7
   × 9

29. 4
   × 9

30. 7
   × 9

31. 8
   × 9

32. 5
   × 9

33. 3
   × 9

34. 6
   × 9

35. 9
   × 9

Solve the equations.

1. $9 \times 5 = \square$ 2. $9 \times 8 = \square$ 3. $9 \times 3 = \square$ 4. $9 \times 7 = \square$

5. $9 \times 0 = \square$ 6. $9 \times 6 = \square$ 7. $9 \times 4 = \square$ 8. $9 \times 9 = \square$

9. $9 \times 6 = \square$ 10. $9 \times 7 = \square$ 11. $9 \times 8 = \square$ 12. $9 \times 4 = \square$

13. $9 \times 1 = \square$ 14. $9 \times 5 = \square$ 15. $9 \times 2 = \square$ 16. $9 \times 9 = \square$

Multiply as quickly as you can.

17. $\begin{array}{r} 4 \\ \times 8 \\ \hline \end{array}$
18. $\begin{array}{r} 5 \\ \times 9 \\ \hline \end{array}$
19. $\begin{array}{r} 6 \\ \times 8 \\ \hline \end{array}$
20. $\begin{array}{r} 4 \\ \times 7 \\ \hline \end{array}$
21. $\begin{array}{r} 6 \\ \times 9 \\ \hline \end{array}$
22. $\begin{array}{r} 7 \\ \times 7 \\ \hline \end{array}$
23. $\begin{array}{r} 9 \\ \times 3 \\ \hline \end{array}$

24. $\begin{array}{r} 0 \\ \times 9 \\ \hline \end{array}$
25. $\begin{array}{r} 8 \\ \times 7 \\ \hline \end{array}$
26. $\begin{array}{r} 4 \\ \times 9 \\ \hline \end{array}$
27. $\begin{array}{r} 8 \\ \times 8 \\ \hline \end{array}$
28. $\begin{array}{r} 6 \\ \times 4 \\ \hline \end{array}$
29. $\begin{array}{r} 8 \\ \times 9 \\ \hline \end{array}$
30. $\begin{array}{r} 9 \\ \times 5 \\ \hline \end{array}$

31. $\begin{array}{r} 9 \\ \times 6 \\ \hline \end{array}$
32. $\begin{array}{r} 8 \\ \times 5 \\ \hline \end{array}$
33. $\begin{array}{r} 7 \\ \times 9 \\ \hline \end{array}$
34. $\begin{array}{r} 5 \\ \times 8 \\ \hline \end{array}$
35. $\begin{array}{r} 3 \\ \times 8 \\ \hline \end{array}$
36. $\begin{array}{r} 2 \\ \times 9 \\ \hline \end{array}$
37. $\begin{array}{r} 6 \\ \times 6 \\ \hline \end{array}$

38. $\begin{array}{r} 9 \\ \times 7 \\ \hline \end{array}$
39. $\begin{array}{r} 3 \\ \times 9 \\ \hline \end{array}$
40. $\begin{array}{r} 9 \\ \times 8 \\ \hline \end{array}$
41. $\begin{array}{r} 1 \\ \times 9 \\ \hline \end{array}$
42. $\begin{array}{r} 9 \\ \times 4 \\ \hline \end{array}$
43. $\begin{array}{r} 9 \\ \times 9 \\ \hline \end{array}$
44. $\begin{array}{r} 7 \\ \times 8 \\ \hline \end{array}$

45.

Multiply by 9.
What is the score?

☆ 46. Try the spinner game with a friend.
Make a spinner. Take turns.
Player with highest total
after 4 spins wins.

What patterns do you notice
in the "9" facts?

$2 \times 9 = 18$ $1 + 8 = ?$
$3 \times 9 = 27$ $2 + 7 = ?$
$4 \times 9 = 36$ $3 + 6 = ?$

Is the pattern true for all
the "9" facts? Try it.

More practice, page 335

Practice for speed

Multiplying by 0, 1, 2, 3, 4, or 5

1. 5
    × 4

2. 6
    × 5

3. 3
    × 1

4. 8
    × 5

5. 6
    × 3

6. 7
    × 4

7. 7
    × 2

8. 5
    × 3

9. 3
    × 4

10. 9
    × 2

11. 0
    × 5

12. 4
    × 4

13. 8
    × 0

14. 8
    × 3

15. 9
    × 4

16. 2
    × 5

17. 4
    × 3

18. 6
    × 2

19. 7
    × 5

20. 6
    × 4

21. 3
    × 5

22. 7
    × 3

23. 5
    × 0

24. 8
    × 2

25. 8
    × 4

26. 7
    × 1

27. 9
    × 3

28. 1
    × 5

Multiplying by 6, 7, 8, or 9

29. 6
    × 8

30. 4
    × 6

31. 5
    × 9

32. 6
    × 7

33. 8
    × 8

34. 7
    × 9

35. 2
    × 7

36. 8
    × 9

37. 7
    × 6

38. 4
    × 7

39. 3
    × 8

40. 2
    × 6

41. 8
    × 7

42. 4
    × 8

43. 8
    × 6

44. 1
    × 9

45. 5
    × 7

46. 9
    × 8

47. 5
    × 6

48. 9
    × 9

49. 5
    × 8

50. 4
    × 9

51. 3
    × 6

52. 7
    × 7

53. 6
    × 6

54. 6
    × 9

55. 0
    × 7

56. 7
    × 8

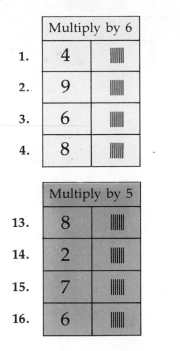

Multiply by 6	
1.	4	|||||
2.	9	|||||
3.	6	|||||
4.	8	|||||

Multiply by 8	
5.	6	|||||
6.	7	|||||
7.	8	|||||
8.	5	|||||

Multiply by 4	
9.	9	|||||
10.	3	|||||
11.	5	|||||
12.	7	|||||

Multiply by 5	
13.	8	|||||
14.	2	|||||
15.	7	|||||
16.	6	|||||

Multiply by 6	
17.	5	|||||
18.	3	|||||
19.	8	|||||
20.	9	|||||

Multiply by 7	
21.	9	|||||
22.	6	|||||
23.	8	|||||
24.	7	|||||

Copy each wheel. Find the products.

25. ×8 wheel: 64, 8, 6, 5, 4, 7, 2, 9, 3

26. ×7 wheel: 6, 8, 3, 5, 7, 2, 4, 9

27. ×9 wheel: 2, 5, 4, 9, 6, 8, 7, 3

28. ×6 wheel: 6, 2, 4, 8, 5, 9, 3, 7

Think!

What numbers should be under the counters a, b, c, e, and f?

1	10	19
2	11	20
3	12	21
4	13	22
5	14	23
6	15	24
7	16	25
8	17	26
9	18	27	a	b	c	63	e	f
d

Answers for Self-check   1. 72   2. 30   3. 18   4. 21   5. 32   6. 12   7. 49   8. 64   9. 24   10. 63   11. 56   12. 48   13. 54   14. 18   15. 40   16. 35   17. 0   18. 9   19. 24   20. 14   21. 56   22. 36   23. 28   24. 27

Find the products.

1. $\begin{array}{r} 9 \\ \times 8 \\ \hline \end{array}$	2. $\begin{array}{r} 5 \\ \times 6 \\ \hline \end{array}$	3. $\begin{array}{r} 2 \\ \times 9 \\ \hline \end{array}$	4. $\begin{array}{r} 3 \\ \times 7 \\ \hline \end{array}$	5. $\begin{array}{r} 4 \\ \times 8 \\ \hline \end{array}$	6. $\begin{array}{r} 2 \\ \times 6 \\ \hline \end{array}$
7. $\begin{array}{r} 7 \\ \times 7 \\ \hline \end{array}$	8. $\begin{array}{r} 8 \\ \times 8 \\ \hline \end{array}$	9. $\begin{array}{r} 4 \\ \times 6 \\ \hline \end{array}$	10. $\begin{array}{r} 7 \\ \times 9 \\ \hline \end{array}$	11. $\begin{array}{r} 8 \\ \times 7 \\ \hline \end{array}$	12. $\begin{array}{r} 6 \\ \times 8 \\ \hline \end{array}$

13. $9 \times 6 = \square$ 14. $6 \times 3 = \square$ 15. $8 \times 5 = \square$ 16. $7 \times 5 = \square$

17. $6 \times 0 = \square$ 18. $9 \times 1 = \square$ 19. $8 \times 3 = \square$ 20. $7 \times 2 = \square$

21. $8 \times 7 = \square$ 22. $6 \times 6 = \square$ 23. $7 \times 4 = \square$ 24. $9 \times 3 = \square$

Answers for Self-check—page 139

Test

1. $\begin{array}{r} 4 \\ \times 8 \\ \hline \end{array}$	2. $\begin{array}{r} 6 \\ \times 7 \\ \hline \end{array}$	3. $\begin{array}{r} 3 \\ \times 9 \\ \hline \end{array}$	4. $\begin{array}{r} 7 \\ \times 6 \\ \hline \end{array}$	5. $\begin{array}{r} 4 \\ \times 7 \\ \hline \end{array}$	6. $\begin{array}{r} 8 \\ \times 8 \\ \hline \end{array}$
7. $\begin{array}{r} 6 \\ \times 6 \\ \hline \end{array}$	8. $\begin{array}{r} 0 \\ \times 8 \\ \hline \end{array}$	9. $\begin{array}{r} 9 \\ \times 6 \\ \hline \end{array}$	10. $\begin{array}{r} 2 \\ \times 9 \\ \hline \end{array}$	11. $\begin{array}{r} 5 \\ \times 7 \\ \hline \end{array}$	12. $\begin{array}{r} 5 \\ \times 6 \\ \hline \end{array}$

13. $9 \times 6 = \square$ 14. $8 \times 2 = \square$ 15. $9 \times 5 = \square$ 16. $9 \times 4 = \square$

17. $7 \times 1 = \square$ 18. $6 \times 8 = \square$ 19. $7 \times 7 = \square$ 20. $8 \times 5 = \square$

21. $8 \times 7 = \square$ 22. $9 \times 9 = \square$ 23. $6 \times 4 = \square$ 24. $7 \times 8 = \square$

Breaking a Code

Copy each problem in order.
Work the problem.
Then put a letter under each answer.

Example:

9	3	33	5	7
− 8	× 1	− 18	× 3	+ 5
1	3	15	15	12
H	E	L	L	O

6	9	22		9	15	8	37
× 3	+ 6	− 7		+ 9	− 8	× 4	− 27
?	?	?		?	?	?	?

6	9	22		9	15	8	37
× 3	+ 6	− 7		+ 9	− 8	× 4	− 27
?	?	?		?	?	?	?

40	12	27	11	5	29	46
− 39	+ 6	+ 16	− 8	× 2	− 15	− 26
?	?	?	?	?	?	?

5	42	7	3
× 3	− 39	× 5	+ 7
?	?	?	?

Code

1	3	7	10	12	14	15	18	20	32	35	43
H	E	N	S	O	I	L	A	X	T	G	V

Problem Solving
Using Your Skills

1. How many cookies are in the boxes?

2. How many more cookies are on the large tray than on the small tray?

3. What other problems can you solve?

Solving Problems

1. Read carefully to find the facts.

2. Look for the question.

3. <u>Decide what to do.</u>

4. Find the answer.

5. Read again. Does your answer make sense?

What would you do to solve these problems?

1. Larry baked 25 cookies.
   Sam baked 18.
   How many in all?

   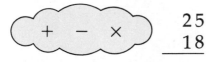
   $+ \quad - \quad \times$
   $$\begin{array}{r} 25 \\ 18 \\ \hline \end{array}$$

2. Michelle's tray had 3 rows of cookies. Each row had 5 cookies. How many cookies were on the tray?

   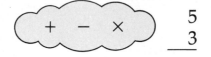
   $+ \quad - \quad \times$
   $$\begin{array}{r} 5 \\ 3 \\ \hline \end{array}$$

3. Rich baked 30 cookies.
   Sara baked 24.
   How many more did Rich bake?

   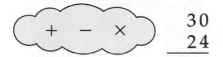
   $+ \quad - \quad \times$
   $$\begin{array}{r} 30 \\ 24 \\ \hline \end{array}$$

4. Judy baked 4 trays of cookies. There were 8 cookies on each tray. How many cookies did she bake?

   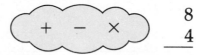
   $+ \quad - \quad \times$
   $$\begin{array}{r} 8 \\ 4 \\ \hline \end{array}$$

Now find the answers.

1. Softball:
   Won 15 games.
   Lost 8.
   Played how many?

2. Basketball:
   2 teams
   4 cheerleaders for each team
   How many cheerleaders?

3. Baseball:
   Played 162 games a year.
   Lost 73.
   Won how many?

4. Baseball:
   3 outs each inning
   9 innings
   How many outs?

5. Basketball:
   Winning team: 76 points
   Losing team: 59 points
   How many points in all?

6. Tennis:
   9 courts
   4 players on each court
   How many players?

7. Bowling:
   Sue's score: 102
   Jerry's score: 85
   How much greater
   was Sue's score?

8. Football:
   Jets: 35 points
   Tigers: 17 points
   Jets won by how many?

9. Hockey:
   Played 27 minutes one game.
   Played 34 minutes next game.
   How many minutes for both?

10. Softball:
    9 players on each team
    4 teams
    How many players?

11. Basketball:
    Winning team scored 53 points.
    Won by 18 points.
    How many points
    for the losing team?

12. Football:
    6 points for a touchdown
    5 touchdowns
    How many points?

13. Soccer:
    Team A—Starting players: 11
            Extra players: 7
    Team B—Starting players: 11
            Extra players: 8
    How many players in all?

Add.

1. $\begin{array}{r} 74 \\ + 13 \\ \hline \end{array}$
2. $\begin{array}{r} 22 \\ + 45 \\ \hline \end{array}$
3. $\begin{array}{r} 56 \\ + 27 \\ \hline \end{array}$
4. $\begin{array}{r} 35 \\ + 58 \\ \hline \end{array}$
5. $\begin{array}{r} 83 \\ + 68 \\ \hline \end{array}$

6. $\begin{array}{r} 265 \\ + 126 \\ \hline \end{array}$
7. $\begin{array}{r} 453 \\ + 287 \\ \hline \end{array}$
8. $\begin{array}{r} 506 \\ + 429 \\ \hline \end{array}$
9. $\begin{array}{r} 187 \\ + 945 \\ \hline \end{array}$
10. $\begin{array}{r} 293 \\ + 579 \\ \hline \end{array}$

11. $\begin{array}{r} 34 \\ 17 \\ + 88 \\ \hline \end{array}$
12. $\begin{array}{r} 19 \\ 63 \\ + 76 \\ \hline \end{array}$
13. $\begin{array}{r} 25 \\ 82 \\ + 95 \\ \hline \end{array}$
14. $\begin{array}{r} 43 \\ 61 \\ + 54 \\ \hline \end{array}$
15. $\begin{array}{r} 75 \\ 42 \\ + 93 \\ \hline \end{array}$

16. $\begin{array}{r} 928 \\ 714 \\ + 568 \\ \hline \end{array}$
17. $\begin{array}{r} 327 \\ 786 \\ + 269 \\ \hline \end{array}$
18. $\begin{array}{r} 159 \\ 138 \\ + 145 \\ \hline \end{array}$
19. $\begin{array}{r} 749 \\ 526 \\ + 734 \\ \hline \end{array}$
20. $\begin{array}{r} 263 \\ 451 \\ + 839 \\ \hline \end{array}$

Write each problem in columns. Find the sums.

Example: $35 + 78 = \square$ $\quad \begin{array}{r} 35 \\ + 78 \\ \hline 113 \end{array}$

21. $48 + 56 = \square$
22. $61 + 70 = \square$
23. $95 + 47 = \square$

24. $50 + 84 = \square$
25. $39 + 42 = \square$
26. $73 + 46 = \square$

27. $341 + 238 = \square$
28. $612 + 835 = \square$
29. $295 + 478 = \square$

30. $529 + 38 = \square$
31. $47 + 521 = \square$
32. $842 + 65 = \square$

Subtract.

1. $\begin{array}{r} 75 \\ -48 \\ \hline \end{array}$ 2. $\begin{array}{r} 51 \\ -32 \\ \hline \end{array}$ 3. $\begin{array}{r} 63 \\ -27 \\ \hline \end{array}$ 4. $\begin{array}{r} 94 \\ -48 \\ \hline \end{array}$ 5. $\begin{array}{r} 78 \\ -46 \\ \hline \end{array}$

6. $\begin{array}{r} 357 \\ -286 \\ \hline \end{array}$ 7. $\begin{array}{r} 841 \\ -429 \\ \hline \end{array}$ 8. $\begin{array}{r} 624 \\ -315 \\ \hline \end{array}$ 9. $\begin{array}{r} 577 \\ -298 \\ \hline \end{array}$ 10. $\begin{array}{r} 936 \\ -657 \\ \hline \end{array}$

11. $\begin{array}{r} 405 \\ -128 \\ \hline \end{array}$ 12. $\begin{array}{r} 608 \\ -442 \\ \hline \end{array}$ 13. $\begin{array}{r} 726 \\ -589 \\ \hline \end{array}$ 14. $\begin{array}{r} 800 \\ -536 \\ \hline \end{array}$ 15. $\begin{array}{r} 502 \\ -375 \\ \hline \end{array}$

16. $\begin{array}{r} 726 \\ -385 \\ \hline \end{array}$ 17. $\begin{array}{r} 513 \\ -289 \\ \hline \end{array}$ 18. $\begin{array}{r} 320 \\ -108 \\ \hline \end{array}$ 19. $\begin{array}{r} 468 \\ -275 \\ \hline \end{array}$ 20. $\begin{array}{r} 608 \\ -419 \\ \hline \end{array}$

Write each problem in columns. Subtract.

Example: $73 - 54 = \square$ $\quad \begin{array}{r} 73 \\ -54 \\ \hline 19 \end{array}$

21. $46 - 32 = \square$ 22. $81 - 53 = \square$

23. $65 - 29 = \square$ 24. $37 - 19 = \square$

25. $95 - 68 = \square$ 26. $54 - 21 = \square$

27. $347 - 189 = \square$ 28. $704 - 252 = \square$

29. $843 - 596 = \square$ 30. $601 - 425 = \square$

31. $824 - 674 = \square$ 32. $300 - 115 = \square$

Subtract 24 from me,
Or take me from 42.
Your answer is the same,
Whichever one you do.
Who am I?

People need plants to live. Much of our food comes from plants. They help make the air fresh. Plants are used to make our homes and schools more beautiful.

1. Plants need water.
   Judy puts 4 cups of water on her plants each week. How much is this in 5 weeks?

2. Plants need light.
   Bill's plant got 5 hours of sunlight each day for 7 days. How many hours of sunlight did the plant get in that week?

3. Plants like plant food.
   Lisa puts 6 drops of food on her plant 3 times each year. How many drops of food is this in one year?

4. Some plants grow fast. Tom's plant grew 56 cm in one year. It grew 83 cm in the next year. How much did it grow in all?

5. Some plants grow slowly. Mary's plant grew 27 cm one year. It grew 14 cm the next year. How much did it grow in all?

6. Some plants seem to like music. Jeff played music for his plant 2 hours each day. How many hours is this in 5 days?

7. Some plants have flowers. Jan's plant had 14 flowers one year. Joe's plant had only 9. How many more did Jan's plant have?

8. Some plants have fruit. Gina's plant had 45 pieces of fruit one year and 68 the next year. How many in all?

⊛ "PROPERTY OF DIGHTON ELEMENTARY SCHOOL"

Can you tell
what numbers
Bert is hiding?

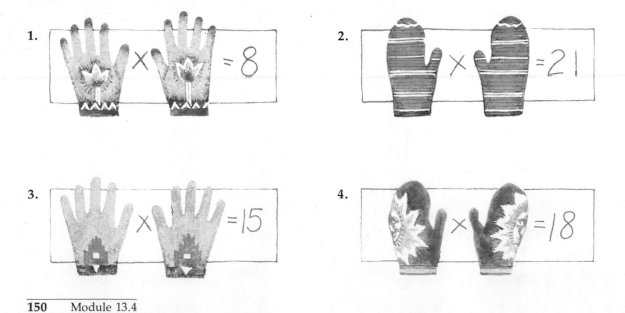

He could be hiding any of these.

| $3 \times 4 = 12$ | $2 \times 6 = 12$ | $1 \times 12 = 12$ |

These "hidden" numbers 3 and 4, 2 and 6, and 1 and 12
are called **factors** of 12.

What factors might be hidden?

1. $\square \times \square = 8$

2. $\square \times \square = 21$

3. $\square \times \square = 15$

4. $\square \times \square = 18$

Some numbers have only two factors.

"PROPERTY OF DIGHTON SCHOOL DEPARTMENT"

Examples:

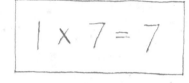

$$1 \times 7 = 7$$

$$1 \times 13 = 13$$

What factors might be hidden?

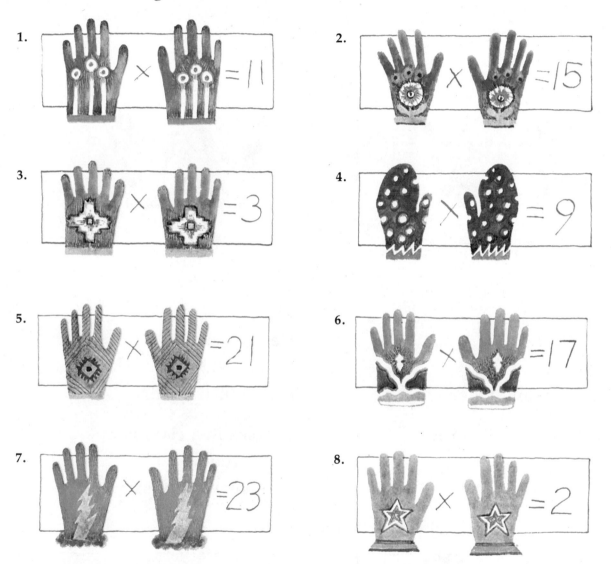

1. $\times$ $= 11$

2. $\times$ $= 15$

3. $\times$ $= 3$

4. $\times$ $= 9$

5. $\times$ $= 21$

6. $\times$ $= 17$

7. $\times$ $= 23$

8. $\times$ $= 2$

☆ 9. Numbers with only 2 factors are prime numbers.
       Which products above are prime numbers?

Answers for Self-check   1. 15.   2. 16   3. 20   4. 18   5. 1, 10; or 2, 5   6. 1, 18; 2, 9; or 3, 6

1. 3 engines on one plane
   5 planes in all
   How many engines?

2. 8 legs on a spider
   2 spiders
   How many legs?

3. 5 puppies
   4 legs on each puppy
   How many legs?

4. 6 legs on a ladybug
   3 ladybugs
   How many legs?

Name two factors that might be hidden.

5.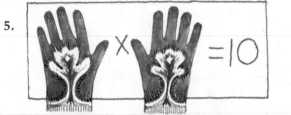

6.

Answers for Self-Check—page 151

Test

1. 4 wheels on a car
   6 cars
   How many wheels?

2. Had 3 nickels.
   5 cents each
   How much in all?

3. 4 chairs in each row
   3 rows
   How many chairs?

4. 5 tables in a classroom
   7 classrooms
   How many tables?

Name two factors that might be hidden.

5.

6.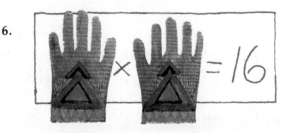

Horseshoe Game

Each player:

1. Make a list of these numbers: 2, 3, 4, 5, 6, 7, 8, 9.

2. Place a marker on start.

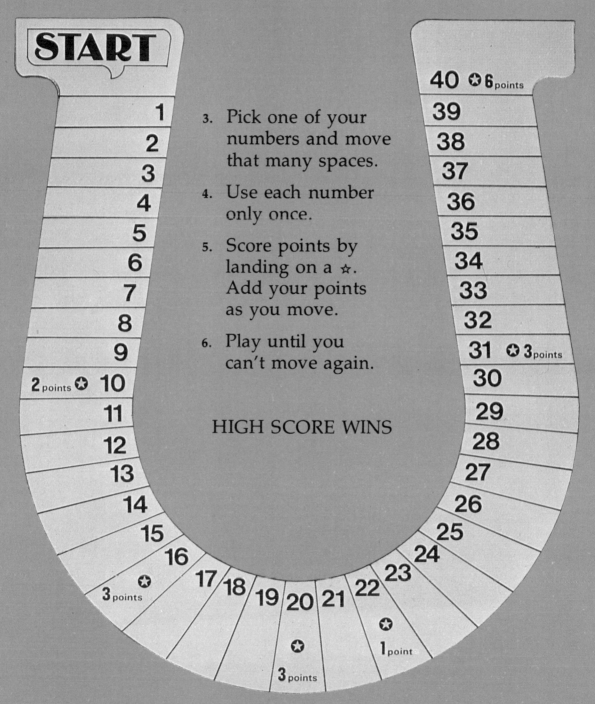

3. Pick one of your numbers and move that many spaces.

4. Use each number only once.

5. Score points by landing on a ☆. Add your points as you move.

6. Play until you can't move again.

HIGH SCORE WINS

Geometry 2

Getting started

The children are using 2 colors, 2 sizes, and 3 shapes.

Colors   Sizes   Shapes

large

small

circle

square

triangle

What pieces are missing below?

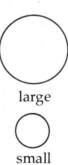

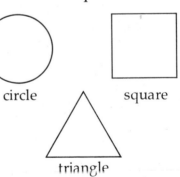

One piece is missing in each ring.

Which piece is it?

1. Same color

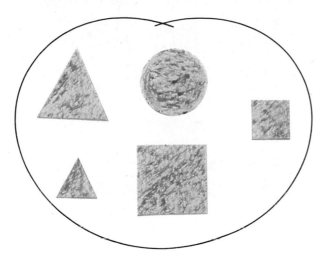

2. Same size

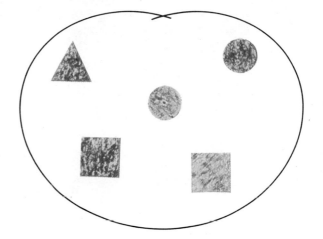

3. Same shape

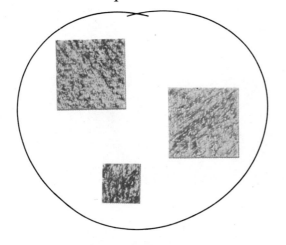

4. Same shape

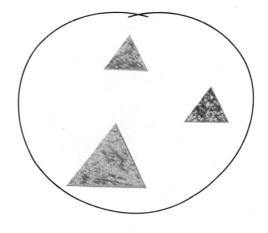

5. Same size and shape

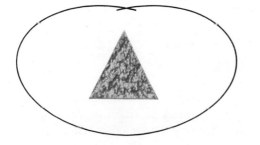

6. Same size and shape

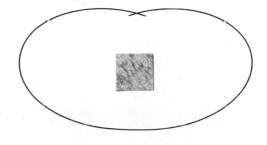

Similar figures

Two figures that have the same shape
are similar to each other.

These figures are similar.

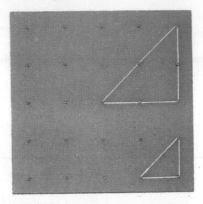

These figures are not similar.

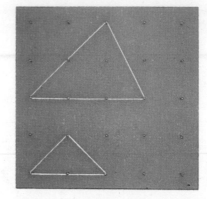

Which geoboards show similar figures?

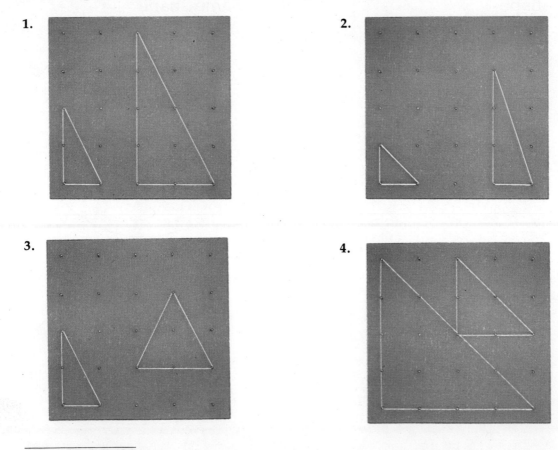

1.

2.

3.

4.

Which figure is similar to the first?

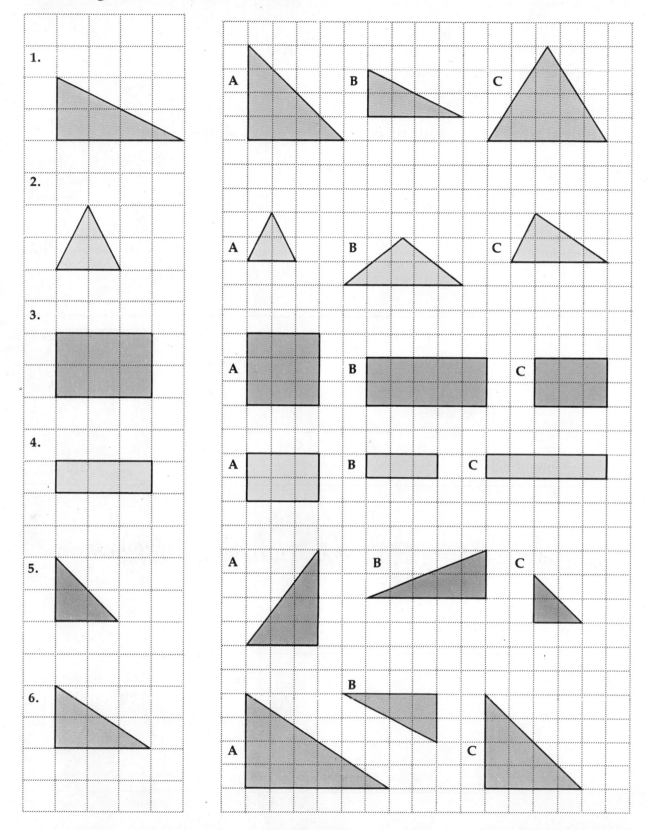

Congruent figures

Figures that have the same size and shape
are congruent to each other.
They will fit exactly on each other.

Which colored shape will fit on the geoboard shape?

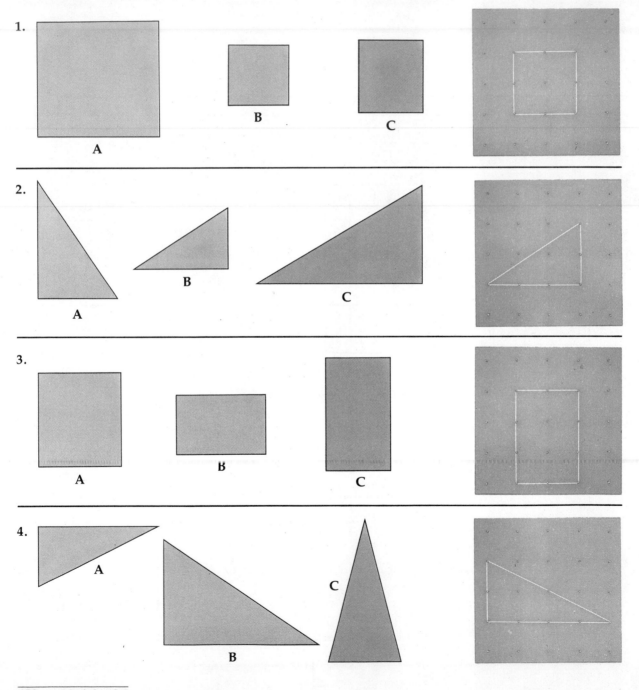

1. A   B   C

2. A   B   C

3. A   B   C

4. A   B   C

Which figure is congruent to the first?

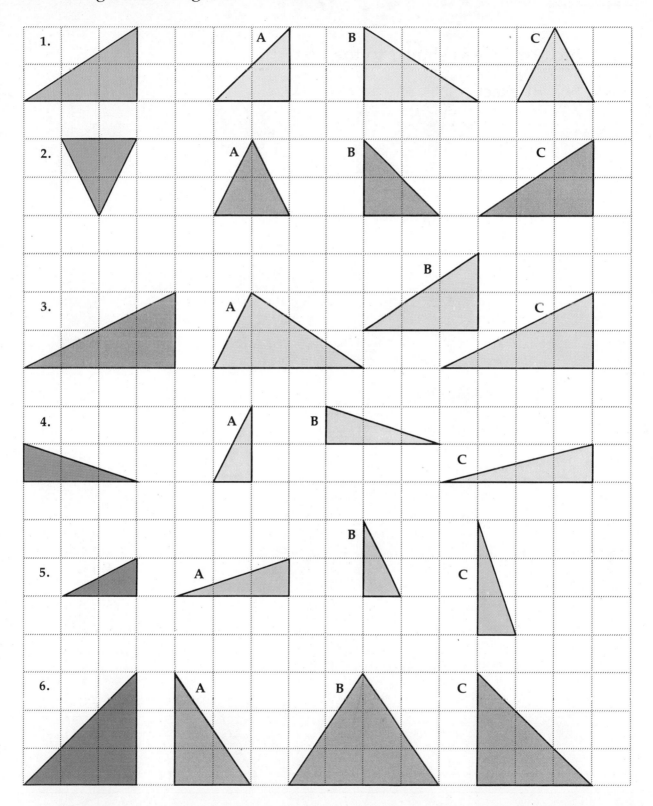

1. Which triangle is similar to the first?

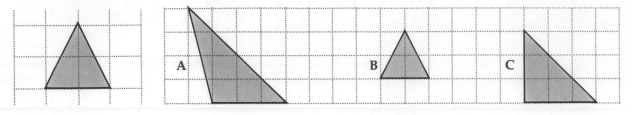

2. Which figure is congruent to the first?

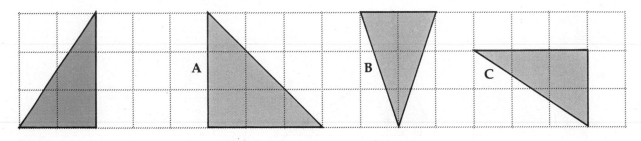

Answers for Self-check—page 159

Test

1. Which rectangle is similar to the first?

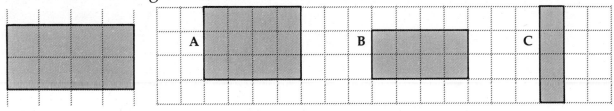

2. Which figure is congruent to the first?

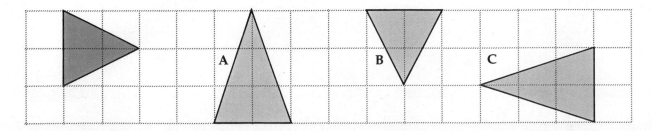

Triangle Puzzles

Trace these 4 triangles.
Cut them out.

Try to fit them
exactly on these shapes.

1.

2.

3.

4.

5.

1. $\begin{array}{r} 3 \\ \times 6 \\ \hline \end{array}$
2. $\begin{array}{r} 4 \\ \times 4 \\ \hline \end{array}$
3. $\begin{array}{r} 5 \\ \times 2 \\ \hline \end{array}$
4. $\begin{array}{r} 2 \\ \times 7 \\ \hline \end{array}$
5. $\begin{array}{r} 8 \\ \times 4 \\ \hline \end{array}$
6. $\begin{array}{r} 7 \\ \times 3 \\ \hline \end{array}$
7. $\begin{array}{r} 3 \\ \times 8 \\ \hline \end{array}$

8. $\begin{array}{r} 9 \\ \times 5 \\ \hline \end{array}$
9. $\begin{array}{r} 6 \\ \times 4 \\ \hline \end{array}$
10. $\begin{array}{r} 5 \\ \times 7 \\ \hline \end{array}$
11. $\begin{array}{r} 8 \\ \times 9 \\ \hline \end{array}$
12. $\begin{array}{r} 9 \\ \times 4 \\ \hline \end{array}$
13. $\begin{array}{r} 7 \\ \times 6 \\ \hline \end{array}$
14. $\begin{array}{r} 9 \\ \times 7 \\ \hline \end{array}$

15. $\begin{array}{r} 7 \\ \times 5 \\ \hline \end{array}$
16. $\begin{array}{r} 9 \\ \times 9 \\ \hline \end{array}$
17. $\begin{array}{r} 8 \\ \times 7 \\ \hline \end{array}$
18. $\begin{array}{r} 9 \\ \times 3 \\ \hline \end{array}$
19. $\begin{array}{r} 8 \\ \times 8 \\ \hline \end{array}$
20. $\begin{array}{r} 6 \\ \times 5 \\ \hline \end{array}$
21. $\begin{array}{r} 6 \\ \times 6 \\ \hline \end{array}$

22. $\begin{array}{r} 7 \\ \times 8 \\ \hline \end{array}$
23. $\begin{array}{r} 3 \\ \times 4 \\ \hline \end{array}$
24. $\begin{array}{r} 5 \\ \times 9 \\ \hline \end{array}$
25. $\begin{array}{r} 4 \\ \times 6 \\ \hline \end{array}$
26. $\begin{array}{r} 3 \\ \times 7 \\ \hline \end{array}$
27. $\begin{array}{r} 4 \\ \times 9 \\ \hline \end{array}$
28. $\begin{array}{r} 5 \\ \times 5 \\ \hline \end{array}$

29. $6 \times 9 = \square$
30. $2 \times 8 = \square$
31. $4 \times 7 = \square$
32. $5 \times 8 = \square$

33. $2 \times 6 = \square$
34. $7 \times 7 = \square$
35. $6 \times 8 = \square$
36. $4 \times 5 = \square$

37. $9 \times 7 = \square$
38. $8 \times 6 = \square$
39. $2 \times 9 = \square$
40. $9 \times 6 = \square$

41. $3 \times 8 = \square$
42. $5 \times 3 = \square$
43. $8 \times 9 = \square$
44. $2 \times 7 = \square$

45. 8 crayons in a box
3 boxes
How many crayons?

46. 7 books on a shelf
4 shelves
How many books?

47. 3 balloons for each child
5 children
How many balloons?

48. 2 flowers on each plant
6 plants
How many flowers?

Division
Fact Families and Division
Problem Solving—Using Your Skills
Graphs

Division

Getting started

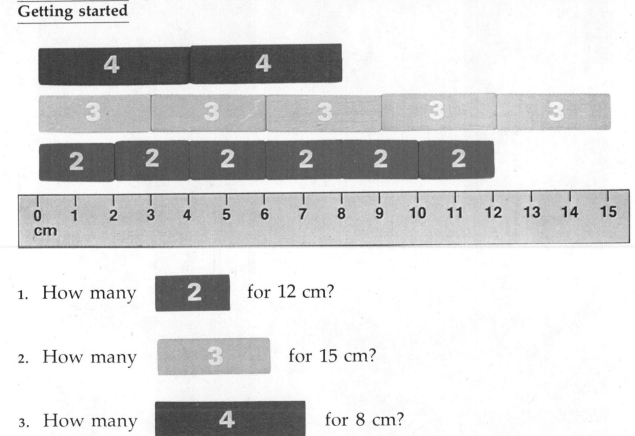

1. How many | 2 | for 12 cm?

2. How many | 3 | for 15 cm?

3. How many | 4 | for 8 cm?

We see:

We think: We write: We say:
3 twos $6 \div 2 = 3$ Six divided
in 6   by two equals
                                      three.

Solve.

1.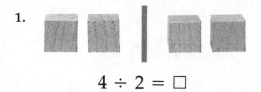

$$4 \div 2 = \square$$

2.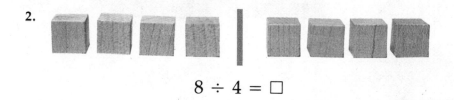

$$8 \div 4 = \square$$

3.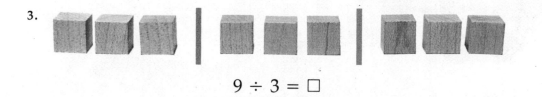

$$9 \div 3 = \square$$

4.

$$12 \div 4 = \square$$

5.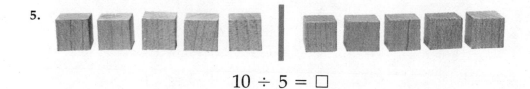

$$10 \div 5 = \square$$

Division and sets

Solve the equations.

1. $6 \div 2 = \square$

2. $12 \div 4 = \square$

3. $6 \div 3 = \square$

4. $16 \div 4 = \square$

5. $12 \div 3 = \square$

Solve the equations.

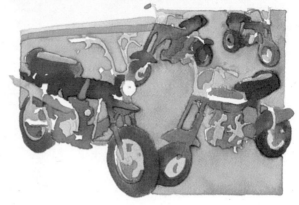

1. $8 \div 2 = \square$

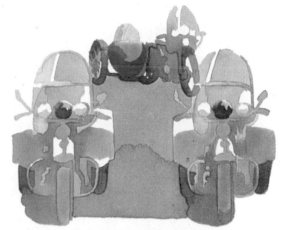

2. $8 \div 4 = \square$

3. $9 \div 3 = \square$

4. $20 \div 4 = \square$

5. $10 \div 2 = \square$

Finding the quotients

Jo Ann's party:
12 cookies
3 to each child
How many children?

$$12 \div 3 = 4$$

↑
quotient

Find the quotients.

1. $6 \div 3 = \square$

2. $6 \div 2 = \square$

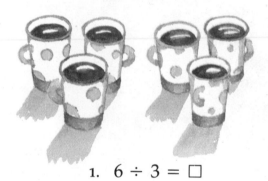

3. $8 \div 2 = \square$

4. $9 \div 3 = \square$

Find the quotients.

1. $8 \div 4 = \square$

2. $12 \div 4 = \square$

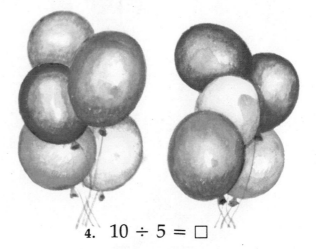

3. $4 \div 2 = \square$

4. $10 \div 5 = \square$

5. $15 \div 3 = \square$

Dave is three times as old as Sue.
In three years, he will be twice as old
as Sue. How old are Dave and Sue now?

Room C had 24 plants and some boxes.
The children wanted to put 6 plants in each box.
How many boxes do they need?

$$
\begin{array}{r}
24 \\
-\ 6 \\
\hline
\end{array}
$$

$$
\begin{array}{r}
18 \\
-\ 6 \\
\hline
\end{array}
$$

$$
\begin{array}{r}
12 \\
-\ 6 \\
\hline
\end{array}
$$

$$
\begin{array}{r}
6 \\
-\ 6 \\
\hline
\end{array}
$$

How many sixes in 24?

Solve. $24 \div 6 = \square$

1. How many fours in 24?

$$\begin{array}{r} 24 \\ -\ 4 \\ \hline \end{array} \qquad \begin{array}{r} 20 \\ -\ 4 \\ \hline \end{array} \qquad \begin{array}{r} 16 \\ -\ 4 \\ \hline \end{array} \qquad \begin{array}{r} 12 \\ -\ 4 \\ \hline \end{array} \qquad \begin{array}{r} 8 \\ -\ 4 \\ \hline \end{array} \qquad \begin{array}{r} 4 \\ -\ 4 \\ \hline \end{array}$$

Solve. $24 \div 4 = \square$

2. How many threes in 21?

$$\begin{array}{r} 21 \\ -\ 3 \\ \hline \end{array} \qquad \begin{array}{r} 18 \\ -\ 3 \\ \hline \end{array} \qquad \begin{array}{r} 15 \\ -\ 3 \\ \hline \end{array} \qquad \begin{array}{r} 12 \\ -\ 3 \\ \hline \end{array} \qquad \begin{array}{r} 9 \\ -\ 3 \\ \hline \end{array} \qquad \begin{array}{r} 6 \\ -\ 3 \\ \hline \end{array} \qquad \begin{array}{r} 3 \\ -\ 3 \\ \hline \end{array}$$

Solve. $21 \div 3 = \square$

3. How many fives in 30?

$$\begin{array}{r} 30 \\ -\ 5 \\ \hline \end{array} \qquad \begin{array}{r} 25 \\ -\ 5 \\ \hline \end{array} \qquad \begin{array}{r} 20 \\ -\ 5 \\ \hline \end{array} \qquad \begin{array}{r} 15 \\ -\ 5 \\ \hline \end{array} \qquad \begin{array}{r} 10 \\ -\ 5 \\ \hline \end{array} \qquad \begin{array}{r} 5 \\ -\ 5 \\ \hline \end{array}$$

Solve. $30 \div 5 = \square$

4. How many twos in 14?

$$\begin{array}{r} 14 \\ -\ 2 \\ \hline \end{array} \qquad \begin{array}{r} 12 \\ -\ 2 \\ \hline \end{array} \qquad \begin{array}{r} 10 \\ -\ 2 \\ \hline \end{array} \qquad \begin{array}{r} 8 \\ -\ 2 \\ \hline \end{array} \qquad \begin{array}{r} 6 \\ -\ 2 \\ \hline \end{array} \qquad \begin{array}{r} 4 \\ -\ 2 \\ \hline \end{array} \qquad \begin{array}{r} 2 \\ -\ 2 \\ \hline \end{array}$$

Solve. $14 \div 2 = \square$

Solve the equations.

5. $18 \div 3 = \square$ 6. $16 \div 2 = \square$ 7. $40 \div 5 = \square$

8. $28 \div 4 = \square$ 9. $24 \div 3 = \square$ 10. $18 \div 2 = \square$

Think!

1. Find the sum along each arrow.
2. Try this with any 3-by-3 square on a calendar.

NOVEMBER						
S	M	T	W	T	F	S
			1	2	3	4
5	6	7	8	9	10	11
12	13	14	15	16	17	18
19	20	21	22	23	24	25
26	27	28	29	30		

Answers for Self-check 1. 6   2. 5   3. 4   4. 3

Self-check

Solve the equations.

1.

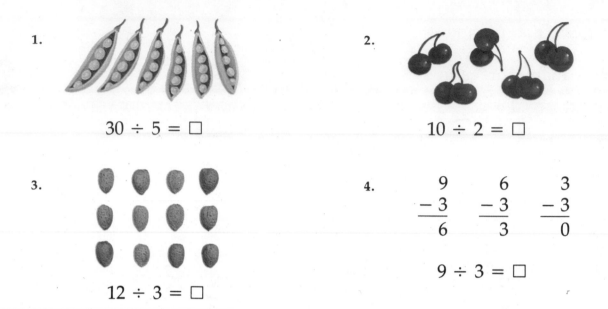

30 ÷ 5 = □

2.

10 ÷ 2 = □

3.

12 ÷ 3 = □

4.

$$
\begin{array}{r} 9 \\ -3 \\ \hline 6 \end{array} \qquad \begin{array}{r} 6 \\ -3 \\ \hline 3 \end{array} \qquad \begin{array}{r} 3 \\ -3 \\ \hline 0 \end{array}
$$

9 ÷ 3 = □

Answers for Self-check—page 171

Test

1.

12 ÷ 4 = □

2.

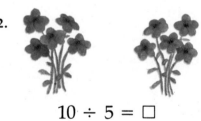

10 ÷ 5 = □

3.

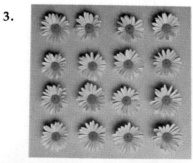

16 ÷ 4 = □

4.

$$
\begin{array}{r} 6 \\ -2 \\ \hline 4 \end{array} \qquad \begin{array}{r} 4 \\ -2 \\ \hline 2 \end{array} \qquad \begin{array}{r} 2 \\ -2 \\ \hline 0 \end{array}
$$

6 ÷ 2 = □

Square the Sticks

Make a square like this.
Use sticks or straws.

Try each of these. Start over each time.

1. Take away 4 sticks and have 1 square left.

2. Take away 2 sticks and have 3 squares left.

3. Take away 4 sticks and have 2 squares left.

Fact Families and Division

Getting started

Make one of these sets of cards.
Put the missing factor on the back.

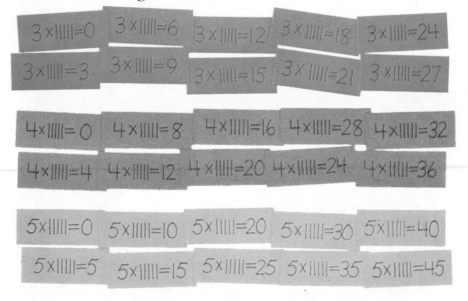

$3 \times |||||| = 0$ $3 \times |||||| = 6$ $3 \times |||||| = 12$ $3 \times |||||| = 18$ $3 \times |||||| = 24$

$3 \times |||||| = 3$ $3 \times |||||| = 9$ $3 \times |||||| = 15$ $3 \times |||||| = 21$ $3 \times |||||| = 27$

$4 \times |||||| = 0$ $4 \times |||||| = 8$ $4 \times |||||| = 16$ $4 \times |||||| = 28$ $4 \times |||||| = 32$

$4 \times |||||| = 4$ $4 \times |||||| = 12$ $4 \times |||||| = 20$ $4 \times |||||| = 24$ $4 \times |||||| = 36$

$5 \times |||||| = 0$ $5 \times |||||| = 10$ $5 \times |||||| = 20$ $5 \times |||||| = 30$ $5 \times |||||| = 40$

$5 \times |||||| = 5$ $5 \times |||||| = 15$ $5 \times |||||| = 25$ $5 \times |||||| = 35$ $5 \times |||||| = 45$

Mix up your cards.
Have a classmate show you the front of a card.
Try to give the missing factor.

The multiplication facts
will help you find quotients.

Read what each child is thinking.
Give each quotient.

$12 \div 4 = \square$ I think $4 \times 3 = 12$

$20 \div 5 = \square$ I think $5 \times 4 = 20$

$24 \div 3 = \square$ I think $3 \times 8 = 24$

$30 \div 5 = \square$ I think $5 \times 6 = 30$

$28 \div 4 = \square$ I think $4 \times 7 = 28$

Fact family numbers can help you solve equations.

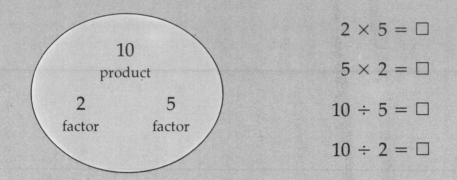

$2 \times 5 = \square$

$5 \times 2 = \square$

$10 \div 5 = \square$

$10 \div 2 = \square$

Find the quotients.

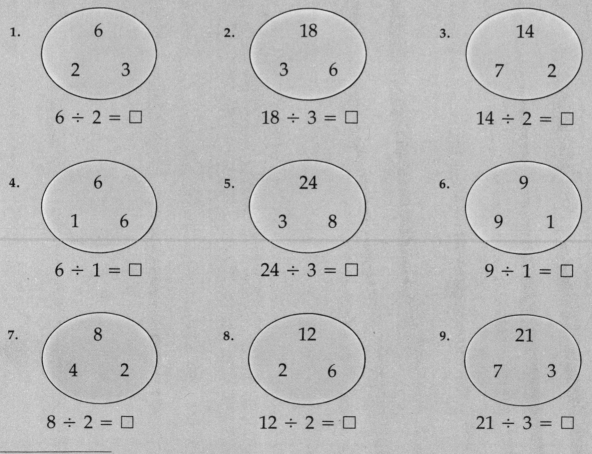

1. 6
    2   3
    $6 \div 2 = \square$

2. 18
    3   6
    $18 \div 3 = \square$

3. 14
    7   2
    $14 \div 2 = \square$

4. 6
    1   6
    $6 \div 1 = \square$

5. 24
    3   8
    $24 \div 3 = \square$

6. 9
    9   1
    $9 \div 1 = \square$

7. 8
    4   2
    $8 \div 2 = \square$

8. 12
    2   6
    $12 \div 2 = \square$

9. 21
    7   3
    $21 \div 3 = \square$

Find the quotients.

Dividing by 1

1. $6 \div 1 = \square$
2. $9 \div 1 = \square$
3. $8 \div 1 = \square$
4. $3 \div 1 = \square$
5. $4 \div 1 = \square$
6. $1 \div 1 = \square$
7. $5 \div 1 = \square$
8. $7 \div 1 = \square$

Dividing by 2

9. $8 \div 2 = \square$
10. $2 \div 2 = \square$
11. $12 \div 2 = \square$
12. $6 \div 2 = \square$
13. $4 \div 2 = \square$
14. $16 \div 2 = \square$
15. $0 \div 2 = \square$
16. $18 \div 2 = \square$

Dividing by 3

17. $12 \div 3 = \square$
18. $24 \div 3 = \square$
19. $15 \div 3 = \square$
20. $3 \div 3 = \square$
21. $18 \div 3 = \square$
22. $6 \div 3 = \square$
23. $9 \div 3 = \square$
24. $21 \div 3 = \square$

Dividing by 1, 2, or 3

25. $8 \div 2 = \square$
26. $14 \div 2 = \square$
27. $12 \div 2 = \square$
28. $15 \div 3 = \square$
29. $6 \div 2 = \square$
30. $6 \div 3 = \square$
31. $9 \div 3 = \square$
32. $1 \div 1 = \square$
33. $16 \div 2 = \square$
34. $21 \div 3 = \square$
35. $4 \div 2 = \square$
36. $7 \div 1 = \square$
37. $0 \div 2 = \square$
38. $3 \div 3 = \square$
39. $3 \div 1 = \square$
40. $24 \div 3 = \square$
41. $18 \div 3 = \square$
42. $2 \div 1 = \square$
43. $2 \div 2 = \square$
44. $0 \div 3 = \square$
45. $27 \div 3 = \square$
46. $18 \div 2 = \square$
47. $12 \div 3 = \square$
48. $6 \div 1 = \square$
49. $0 \div 1 = \square$
50. $21 \div 3 = \square$
51. $10 \div 2 = \square$
52. $8 \div 1 = \square$

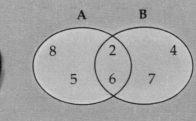

Find the sum of
1. the numbers in A
2. the numbers in B but not A
3. the numbers in both A and B
4. the numbers in A or B

Dividing by 4

The clip has
landed on 28.

What is the score?

$28 \div 4 = 7$

The score is 7.

Score: Divide
your number
by 4.

These are some
fact family numbers for 4.

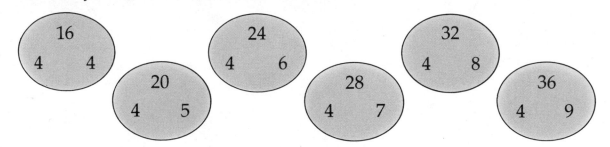

Find the quotients.

1. $16 \div 4 = \square$
2. $0 \div 4 = \square$
3. $36 \div 4 = \square$
4. $20 \div 4 = \square$

5. $28 \div 4 = \square$
6. $32 \div 4 = \square$
7. $12 \div 4 = \square$
8. $24 \div 4 = \square$

9. $20 \div 4 = \square$
10. $8 \div 4 = \square$
11. $4 \div 4 = \square$
12. $28 \div 4 = \square$

13. $36 \div 4 = \square$
14. $24 \div 4 = \square$
15. $32 \div 4 = \square$
16. $12 \div 4 = \square$

17. $16 \div 4 = \square$
18. $0 \div 4 = \square$
19. $4 \div 4 = \square$
20. $8 \div 4 = \square$

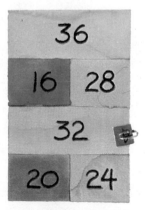

Dividing by 3 or 4

1. $9 \div 3 = \square$ 2. $20 \div 4 = \square$ 3. $21 \div 3 = \square$

4. $24 \div 4 = \square$ 5. $12 \div 4 = \square$ 6. $3 \div 3 = \square$

7. $8 \div 4 = \square$ 8. $21 \div 3 = \square$ 9. $28 \div 4 = \square$

10. $18 \div 3 = \square$ 11. $0 \div 4 = \square$ 12. $0 \div 3 = \square$

13. $27 \div 3 = \square$ 14. $4 \div 4 = \square$ 15. $12 \div 3 = \square$ 16. $16 \div 4 = \square$

17. $6 \div 3 = \square$ 18. $36 \div 4 = \square$ 19. $24 \div 3 = \square$ 20. $32 \div 4 = \square$

Dividing by 1, 2, 3, or 4

21. $20 \div 4 = \square$ 22. $12 \div 2 = \square$ 23. $8 \div 4 = \square$ 24. $15 \div 3 = \square$

25. $18 \div 3 = \square$ 26. $6 \div 3 = \square$ 27. $7 \div 1 = \square$ 28. $12 \div 4 = \square$

29. $8 \div 1 = \square$ 30. $4 \div 4 = \square$ 31. $24 \div 4 = \square$ 32. $21 \div 3 = \square$

33. $16 \div 2 = \square$ 34. $27 \div 3 = \square$ 35. $0 \div 4 = \square$ 36. $8 \div 2 = \square$

37. $10 \div 2 = \square$ 38. $14 \div 2 = \square$ 39. $28 \div 4 = \square$ 40. $16 \div 4 = \square$

41.

36

16   28

32

20   24

Find the score.
Divide by 4.

☆ 42. Try the 4-clip game
with a friend.
The player with
the highest total
after 5 tosses wins.

Jack started with a
number and multiplied
it by 4. Then he added
25, subtracted 25,
and divided by 4.
Jack's answer was 6.
What number did Jack
start with?

The spinner stopped on 40.

Divide the number by 5.

What is the score?

$40 \div 5 = 8$

The score is 8.

These are some fact family numbers for 5.

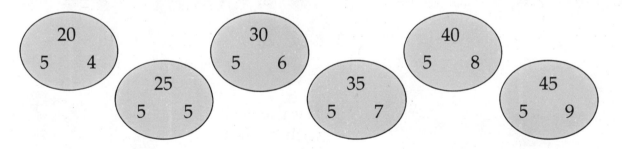

Find the quotients.

1. $30 \div 5 = \square$
2. $45 \div 5 = \square$
3. $0 \div 5 = \square$
4. $35 \div 5 = \square$

5. $5 \div 5 = \square$
6. $10 \div 5 = \square$
7. $15 \div 5 = \square$
8. $25 \div 5 = \square$

9. $20 \div 5 = \square$
10. $25 \div 5 = \square$
11. $40 \div 5 = \square$
12. $0 \div 5 = \square$

13. $40 \div 5 = \square$
14. $20 \div 5 = \square$
15. $10 \div 5 = \square$
16. $30 \div 5 = \square$

17. $15 \div 5 = \square$
18. $35 \div 5 = \square$
19. $45 \div 5 = \square$
20. $5 \div 5 = \square$

Dividing by 4 or 5

1. $10 \div 5 = \square$ 2. $24 \div 4 = \square$ 3. $40 \div 5 = \square$ 4. $8 \div 4 = \square$

5. $12 \div 4 = \square$ 6. $35 \div 5 = \square$ 7. $16 \div 4 = \square$ 8. $0 \div 5 = \square$

9. $28 \div 4 = \square$ 10. $30 \div 5 = \square$ 11. $0 \div 4 = \square$ 12. $5 \div 5 = \square$

13. $25 \div 5 = \square$ 14. $20 \div 5 = \square$ 15. $45 \div 5 = \square$ 16. $20 \div 4 = \square$

17. $4 \div 4 = \square$ 18. $32 \div 4 = \square$ 19. $15 \div 5 = \square$ 20. $36 \div 4 = \square$

Dividing by 1, 2, 3, 4, or 5

21. $18 \div 3 = \square$ 22. $10 \div 5 = \square$ 23. $8 \div 4 = \square$ 24. $28 \div 4 = \square$

25. $15 \div 3 = \square$ 26. $0 \div 5 = \square$ 27. $25 \div 5 = \square$ 28. $35 \div 5 = \square$

29. $27 \div 3 = \square$ 30. $7 \div 1 = \square$ 31. $36 \div 4 = \square$ 32. $12 \div 2 = \square$

33. $8 \div 2 = \square$ 34. $45 \div 5 = \square$ 35. $40 \div 5 = \square$ 36. $20 \div 4 = \square$

37. $6 \div 2 = \square$ 38. $32 \div 4 = \square$ 39. $20 \div 5 = \square$ 40. $15 \div 5 = \square$

41. Divide by 5.

Find the score.

Find the missing
fact family numbers.

Both even — 12, ?, ?

One odd — 18, ?, ?

Both even — 24, ?, ?

One odd — 24, ?, ?

☆ 42. Make a spinner.
Take turns with a friend.
The player with the highest
total after 5 turns wins.

A new sign for division

$$20 \div 5 = 4 \text{ may be written } 5\overline{)20}^{\,4}$$

Find the quotients.

1. $3\overline{)15}$ — 5

2. $4\overline{)12}$ — 3

3. $5\overline{)10}$ — 2

4. $2\overline{)12}$ — 6

5. $2\overline{)18}$ — 9

6. $1\overline{)6}$ — 6

7. $5\overline{)30}$ — 0

8. $3\overline{)9}$ — 3

9. $4\overline{)28}$ — 7

10. $5\overline{)20}$ — 4

11. $4\overline{)24}$ — 6

12. $1\overline{)9}$ — 9

13. $3\overline{)21}$ — 7

14. $5\overline{)35}$ — 7

15. $2\overline{)16}$ — 8

16. $3\overline{)6}$ — 2

17. $5\overline{)5}$ — 1

18. $2\overline{)10}$ — 5

19. $3\overline{)24}$ — 8

20. $4\overline{)8}$ — 2

21. $5\overline{)25}$ — 7

22. $3\overline{)27}$ — 9

23. $4\overline{)4}$ — 1

24. $5\overline{)45}$ — 9

25. $2\overline{)6}$ — 3

26. $4\overline{)20}$ — 5

27. $5\overline{)15}$ — 3

28. $4\overline{)16}$ — 4

29. $4\overline{)32}$ — 8

30. $3\overline{)18}$ — 6

More practice, page 336, Set A

Solve the fact family equations.

1. $3 \times 4 = \square$

   $4 \times 3 = \square$

   $12 \div 4 = \square$

   $12 \div 3 = \square$

2. $4 \times 7 = \square$

   $7 \times 4 = \square$

   $28 \div 7 = \square$

   $28 \div 4 = \square$

3. $5 \times 6 = \square$

   $6 \times 5 = \square$

   $30 \div 6 = \square$

   $30 \div 5 = \square$

4. $5 \times 9 = \square$

   $9 \times 5 = \square$

   $45 \div 9 = \square$

   $45 \div 5 = \square$

5. $8 \times 4 = \square$

   $4 \times 8 = \square$

   $32 \div 4 = \square$

   $32 \div 8 = \square$

6. $3 \times 9 = \square$

   $9 \times 3 = \square$

   $27 \div 9 = \square$

   $27 \div 3 = \square$

7. $9 \times 4 = \square$

   $4 \times 9 = \square$

   $36 \div 4 = \square$

   $36 \div 9 = \square$

8. $7 \times 5 = \square$

   $5 \times 7 = \square$

   $35 \div 5 = \square$

   $35 \div 7 = \square$

9. $5 \times 8 = \square$

   $8 \times 5 = \square$

   $40 \div 8 = \square$

   $40 \div 5 = \square$

Find the quotients.

10. $5\overline{)30}$

11. $4\overline{)32}$

12. $5\overline{)40}$

13. $3\overline{)12}$

14. $4\overline{)24}$

15. $5\overline{)35}$

16. $5\overline{)45}$

17. $4\overline{)36}$

18. $4\overline{)28}$

19. $3\overline{)27}$

20. $5\overline{)25}$

21. $3\overline{)21}$

Think!

18 is a number
In my fact family.
The other number
Is exactly 2 times me.

Who am I?

Answers for Self-check 1. 5 2. 5 3. 6 4. 4 5. 7 6. 5 7. 9 8. 2 9. 8 10. 7 11. 6
12. 7 13. 4 14. 7 15. 5 16. 7 17. 3 18. 6 19. 9 20. 9 21. 8 22. 6 23. 5 24. 3
25. 4 26. 8 27. 9 28. 8 29. 7 30. 7

Divide.

1. $5 \div 1 = \square$ 2. $10 \div 2 = \square$ 3. $18 \div 3 = \square$ 4. $8 \div 2 = \square$

5. $21 \div 3 = \square$ 6. $15 \div 3 = \square$ 7. $9 \div 1 = \square$ 8. $6 \div 3 = \square$

9. $24 \div 3 = \square$ 10. $7 \div 1 = \square$ 11. $12 \div 2 = \square$ 12. $14 \div 2 = \square$

13. $16 \div 4 = \square$ 14. $35 \div 5 = \square$ 15. $25 \div 5 = \square$ 16. $28 \div 4 = \square$

17. $12 \div 4 = \square$ 18. $24 \div 4 = \square$ 19. $36 \div 4 = \square$ 20. $45 \div 5 = \square$

21. $5\overline{)40}$ 22. $3\overline{)18}$ 23. $4\overline{)20}$ 24. $5\overline{)15}$ 25. $4\overline{)16}$

26. $4\overline{)32}$ 27. $4\overline{)36}$ 28. $2\overline{)16}$ 29. $3\overline{)21}$ 30. $5\overline{)35}$

Answers for Self-check—page 183

Test

Divide.

1. $6 \div 3 = \square$ 2. $4 \div 2 = \square$ 3. $10 \div 5 = \square$ 4. $12 \div 3 = \square$

5. $10 \div 2 = \square$ 6. $9 \div 3 = \square$ 7. $12 \div 2 = \square$ 8. $8 \div 4 = \square$

9. $12 \div 1 = \square$ 10. $14 \div 2 = \square$ 11. $21 \div 3 = \square$ 12. $12 \div 4 = \square$

13. $16 \div 2 = \square$ 14. $24 \div 4 = \square$ 15. $20 \div 4 = \square$ 16. $18 \div 3 = \square$

17. $20 \div 5 = \square$ 18. $18 \div 2 = \square$ 19. $16 \div 4 = \square$ 20. $15 \div 5 = \square$

21. $4\overline{)36}$ 22. $3\overline{)15}$ 23. $5\overline{)45}$ 24. $3\overline{)24}$ 25. $5\overline{)30}$

26. $3\overline{)27}$ 27. $5\overline{)25}$ 28. $4\overline{)32}$ 29. $4\overline{)28}$ 30. $5\overline{)40}$

Hidden Shapes

Each of these shapes is hidden below.

Give a letter for each one you find.

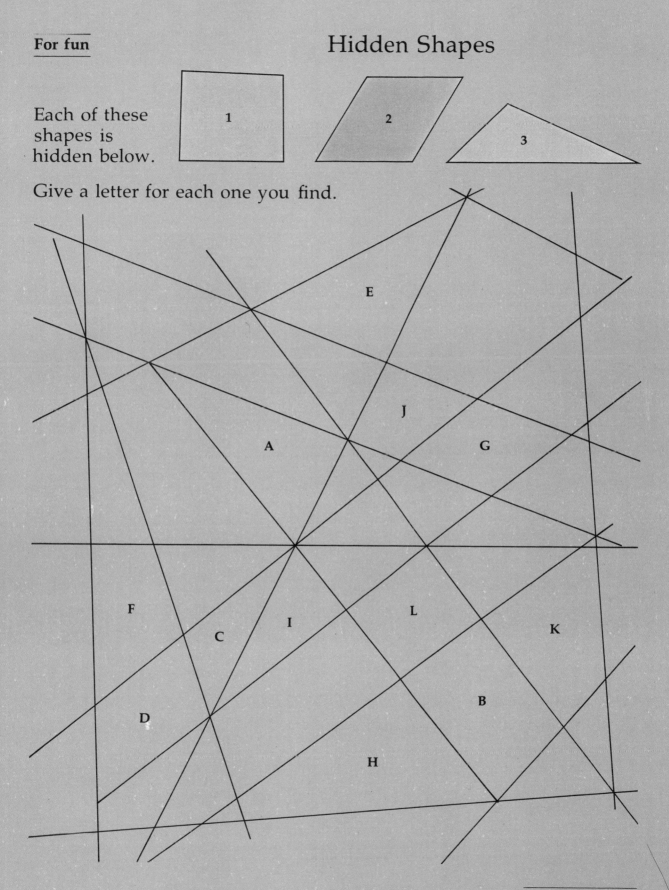

Problem Solving
Using Your Skills

1. What would the scale show if 2 yellow bricks were in the pan?

2. What is the mass of the 6 yellow bricks?

3. What other problems can you solve?

Solving Problems

1. Read carefully to find the facts.

2. Look for the question.

3. Decide what to do.

4. Find the answer.

5. Read again. Does your answer make sense?

Now you have 4 things to think about:

+ Add
− Subtract
× Multiply
÷ Divide

What would you do to solve these problems?

1. Had 15 cents.
   Found 25 cents.
   Have how much now?

2. 15 cookies
   3 to each child
   How many children get cookies?

3. 7 days a week
   4 weeks
   How many days?

4. 4 teams
   20 players in all
   How many players on each team?

Now find the answers.

After school

1. Linda took 15 minutes to walk home. She took 8 minutes to change her clothes. How many minutes did she take in all?

2. Ben took 18 minutes to walk home. Then he played the piano for 45 minutes. How many minutes did he take in all?

4. Ron spent 25 minutes cleaning his fish bowl. Karen spent 40 minutes walking and brushing her dog. How much longer did Karen take than Ron?

3. Jan played softball. There were 36 children on 4 teams. How many players were on each team?

5. Jim played basketball. There were 6 teams with 5 children on each team. How many children were there?

7. Julie walks a total of 8 blocks to and from school each day. How many blocks does she walk in 5 days?

8. Jack bought 4 oranges for 36 cents. How much did he pay for each orange?

9. Rick cleaned his room for 35 minutes. Then he skated for 45 minutes. How many minutes was this in all?

6. Karen baked 27 cookies in the first batch. In the second batch she baked 32 cookies. How many more cookies did she bake in the second batch?

10. Ruth put 28 stamps in her stamp book. She put 7 stamps on each page. How many pages did she use?

Practicing your skills

Add or subtract.

1. 7 $\underline{+8}$	2. 12 $\underline{-4}$	3. 9 $\underline{+7}$	4. 13 $\underline{-6}$	5. 6 $\underline{+5}$	6. 15 $\underline{-8}$
7. 9 $\underline{+9}$	8. 14 $\underline{-7}$	9. 8 $\underline{+6}$	10. 10 $\underline{-4}$	11. 8 $\underline{+8}$	12. 17 $\underline{-9}$
13. 16 $\underline{-8}$	14. 7 $\underline{+4}$	15. 15 $\underline{-9}$	16. 9 $\underline{+2}$	17. 13 $\underline{-4}$	18. 3 $\underline{+7}$
19. 6 $\underline{+7}$	20. 18 $\underline{-9}$	21. 5 $\underline{+9}$	22. 12 $\underline{-5}$	23. 6 $\underline{+6}$	24. 11 $\underline{-8}$

Add.

25. 3 4 $\underline{+3}$	26. 8 5 $\underline{+6}$	27. 7 2 $\underline{+4}$	28. 9 8 $\underline{+7}$	29. 5 9 $\underline{+4}$	30. 6 4 $\underline{+7}$
31. 9 1 $\underline{+8}$	32. 5 8 $\underline{+3}$	33. 6 9 $\underline{+4}$	34. 7 6 $\underline{+3}$	35. 8 8 $\underline{+7}$	36. 5 9 $\underline{+6}$
37. 5 4 8 $\underline{+5}$	38. 7 2 4 $\underline{+6}$	39. 8 6 7 $\underline{+9}$	40. 5 8 9 $\underline{+4}$	41. 9 3 6 $\underline{+5}$	42. 7 5 8 $\underline{+2}$

Add.

1.
$$\begin{array}{r} 43 \\ + 52 \\ \hline \end{array}$$

2.
$$\begin{array}{r} 71 \\ + 29 \\ \hline \end{array}$$

3.
$$\begin{array}{r} 66 \\ + 35 \\ \hline \end{array}$$

4.
$$\begin{array}{r} 87 \\ + 51 \\ \hline \end{array}$$

5.
$$\begin{array}{r} 56 \\ + 97 \\ \hline \end{array}$$

6.
$$\begin{array}{r} 39 \\ + 48 \\ \hline \end{array}$$

7.
$$\begin{array}{r} 59 \\ + 48 \\ \hline \end{array}$$

8.
$$\begin{array}{r} 93 \\ + 67 \\ \hline \end{array}$$

9.
$$\begin{array}{r} 75 \\ + 28 \\ \hline \end{array}$$

10.
$$\begin{array}{r} 65 \\ + 87 \\ \hline \end{array}$$

11.
$$\begin{array}{r} 98 \\ + 74 \\ \hline \end{array}$$

12.
$$\begin{array}{r} 46 \\ + 85 \\ \hline \end{array}$$

13.
$$\begin{array}{r} 38 \\ 74 \\ + 56 \\ \hline \end{array}$$

14.
$$\begin{array}{r} 29 \\ 54 \\ + 68 \\ \hline \end{array}$$

15.
$$\begin{array}{r} 73 \\ 96 \\ + 58 \\ \hline \end{array}$$

16.
$$\begin{array}{r} 45 \\ 37 \\ + 61 \\ \hline \end{array}$$

17.
$$\begin{array}{r} 27 \\ 59 \\ + 84 \\ \hline \end{array}$$

18.
$$\begin{array}{r} 68 \\ 74 \\ + 59 \\ \hline \end{array}$$

Subtract.

19.
$$\begin{array}{r} 72 \\ - 46 \\ \hline \end{array}$$

20.
$$\begin{array}{r} 51 \\ - 27 \\ \hline \end{array}$$

21.
$$\begin{array}{r} 36 \\ - 18 \\ \hline \end{array}$$

22.
$$\begin{array}{r} 44 \\ - 29 \\ \hline \end{array}$$

23.
$$\begin{array}{r} 62 \\ - 35 \\ \hline \end{array}$$

24.
$$\begin{array}{r} 81 \\ - 59 \\ \hline \end{array}$$

25.
$$\begin{array}{r} 215 \\ - 162 \\ \hline \end{array}$$

26.
$$\begin{array}{r} 758 \\ - 399 \\ \hline \end{array}$$

27.
$$\begin{array}{r} 501 \\ - 256 \\ \hline \end{array}$$

28.
$$\begin{array}{r} 829 \\ - 364 \\ \hline \end{array}$$

29.
$$\begin{array}{r} 637 \\ - 288 \\ \hline \end{array}$$

30.
$$\begin{array}{r} 908 \\ - 647 \\ \hline \end{array}$$

31.
$$\begin{array}{r} 852 \\ - 494 \\ \hline \end{array}$$

32.
$$\begin{array}{r} 613 \\ - 275 \\ \hline \end{array}$$

33.
$$\begin{array}{r} 405 \\ - 267 \\ \hline \end{array}$$

34.
$$\begin{array}{r} 700 \\ - 528 \\ \hline \end{array}$$

35.
$$\begin{array}{r} 521 \\ - 368 \\ \hline \end{array}$$

36.
$$\begin{array}{r} 905 \\ - 617 \\ \hline \end{array}$$

Find the missing digits.

1.
$$\begin{array}{r} 2\,▓ \\ - \quad 8 \\ \hline 1\,9 \end{array}$$

2.
$$\begin{array}{r} 2\,▓ \\ - \quad 8 \\ \hline 1\,3 \end{array}$$

3.
$$\begin{array}{r} 3\,▓ \\ + 5\,6 \\ \hline 9\,4 \end{array}$$

4.
$$\begin{array}{r} 3\,▓ \\ + 5\,6 \\ \hline 8\,8 \end{array}$$

5.
$$\begin{array}{r} 5\,▓ \\ + ▓\,6 \\ \hline 9\,3 \end{array}$$

Chimpanzees

Chimpanzees live deep in the rain forests of Africa. There they eat fruit and leaves. They are sometimes called chimps. Chimps are smart enough to use rocks and sticks as tools.

Solve these problems about chimps.

1. Two chimps ate a total of 13 bananas. One of them ate 6. How many did the other eat?

2. One young chimp played for 18 minutes. Then she rested for 35 minutes. How many minutes in all?

3. One chimp slept 9 hours a night for 4 nights. How many hours is this?

4. One young chimp was 3 years old. His mother was 5 times as old. How old was his mother?

5. A mother chimp found 18 pieces of fruit. She divided them equally among 3 young chimps. How many pieces of fruit did each chimp get?

6. A father chimp was 135 cm tall. A mother chimp was 118 cm tall. How much taller was the father chimp?

7. One chimp made 7 jumps from one tree to another. The trees were 3 m apart. How many meters did the chimp jump?

8. In one forest 20 chimps lived together. One day there were 4 chimps in each tree. How many trees had chimps in them?

Finding missing numbers

Copy these practice wheels.
Give the sums or products.

1.

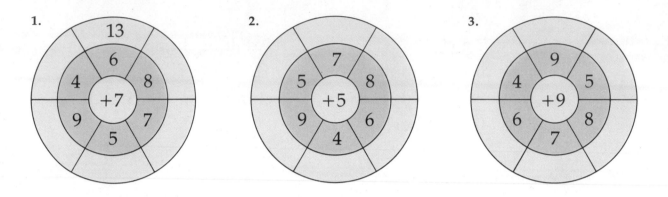

2.

3.

4.

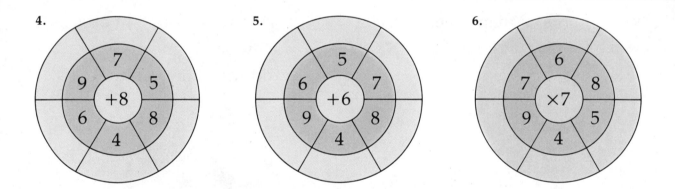

5.

6.

7.

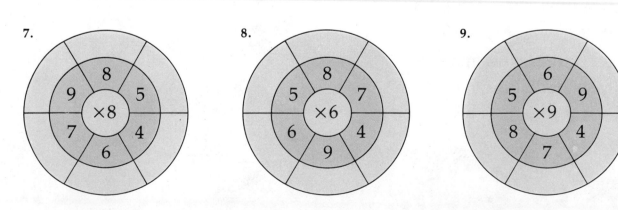

8.

9.

Study this figure.

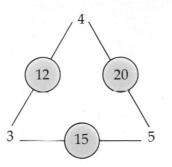

Find the missing numbers.

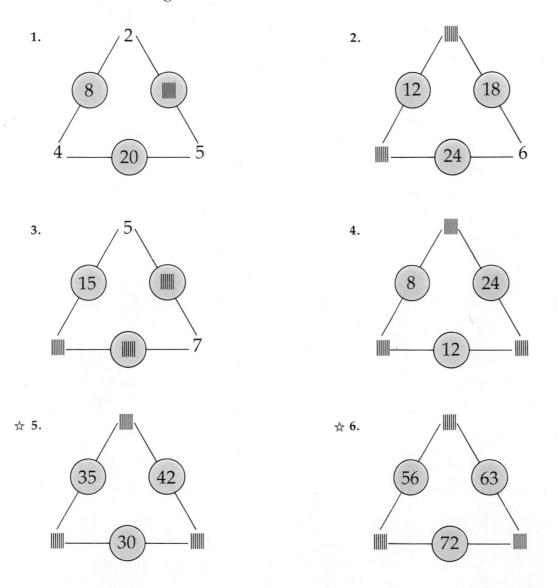

1.

2.

3.

4.

☆ 5.

☆ 6.

Answers for Self-check   1. 6   2. 15   3. 30   4. 7

1. 18 marbles
   3 in each bag
   How many bags?

2. 3 cars
   5 children in each car
   How many children?

3. Room M had 5 tables.
   Each table had 6 chairs.
   How many chairs in all?

4. Susan held 14 pencils in
   her hands. Each hand held
   the same number.
   How many pencils
   in each hand?

Answers for Self-check—page 195

Test

1. 20 players
   5 on each team
   How many teams?

2. 4 boxes
   6 books in each box
   How many books?

3. Robin had 3 fishbowls.
   Each fishbowl had 4 fish.
   How many fish in all?

4. Andy had 20 marbles
   and 5 bags. He put
   the same number of
   marbles in each bag.
   How many marbles did
   he put in each bag?

Cover the Strip

Try this 10-unit game
with a classmate.

Make 8 of these pieces.

1-unit

Make 5 of these pieces.

2-unit

Take turns placing one of the
13 pieces on a 10-unit strip.

Start at the left.

Place the pieces side by side until
the strip is exactly covered.

The last player to put down
a piece is the winner.

Winner

Graphs

BIRTHDAYS IN OUR CLASS—ROOM 17

NUMBER OF CHILDREN

JAN. FEB. MAR. APR. MAY JUNE JULY AUG. Sept. OCT. NOV. DEC.

Getting started

The children in Room 17 made this
birthday graph. Each child put up
one square to show the month
of his or her birthday.

1. Are there more birthdays
   in July or September?

2. Which month has the most birthdays?

3. Make a graph to show birthdays in your class.

	1	2	3	4	5	6	7	8
CARLA	★	★	★					
TOM	★	★	★	★	★			
FRAN	★	★	★	★	★	★	★	
JOE	★	★						
NITA	★	★	★	★	★	★		
JOSE	★	★	★	★	★	★		

SELLING TICKETS FOR THE PLAY

NUMBER SOLD

Room 17 put on a class play. Six children sold tickets.
They put up one star for each ticket they sold.

1. Who sold the most tickets?
2. Who sold the fewest tickets?
3. Which two children sold the same number of tickets?
4. How many tickets would Tom need to sell to pass Fran?
5. How many tickets were sold in all?

Bar graphs

The children in Katy's class made this graph to show the kinds of pets they have. They colored a square for each child who had that kind of pet.

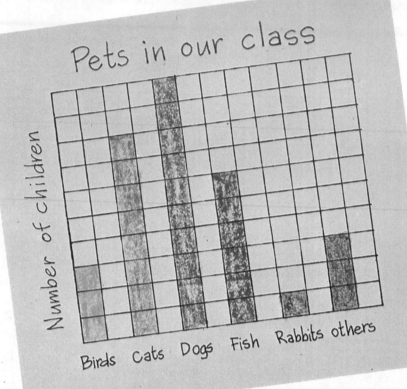

Pets in our class

Number of children

Birds   Cats   Dogs   Fish   Rabbits   others

1. How many children had dogs?
2. How many had fish?
3. Katy had a pet turtle. Where did she color her square?

☆ 4. Make a graph for the kinds of pets the children in your class have.

Jack made this graph to show
his spelling scores for six weeks.
Each test had ten words.

My spelling scores Jack

Number right

first second third fourth fifth sixth
week

1. In what week did Jack
   get all the words right?

2. When did Jack miss only one word?

3. Was Jack's spelling score better by
   the sixth week than when he started?

☆ 4. Study these words.
   Take a test on them
   with some friends.
   Make a graph to show
   all of your scores.

Spelling Words	
triangle	subtract
add	rectangle
square	multiply
divide	circle
product	equal

Reading graphs

Some children measured to see how much water some things would hold. A cup was used as the unit. The children made a picture graph to show what they found out.

How many cups?

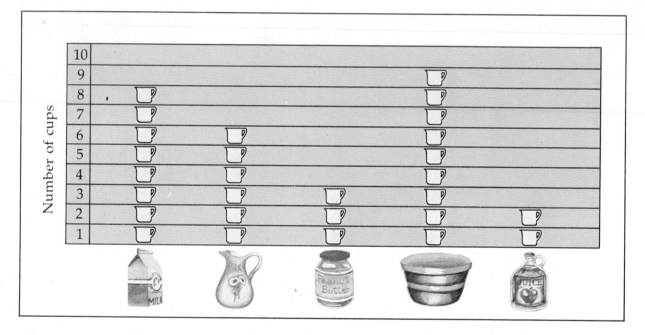

Study the graph. How many cups does each of these hold?

1.　2.　3.　4.　5.

☆ 6. Find out how many cups of water something holds. How would you show it on the graph?

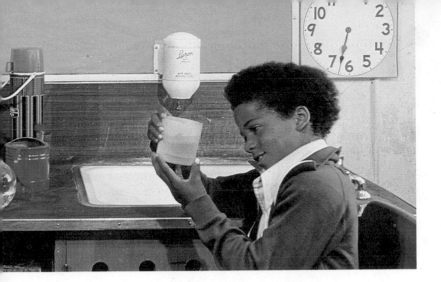

Some children found how many liters some things hold. They made this picture graph to record their findings.

How many liters?

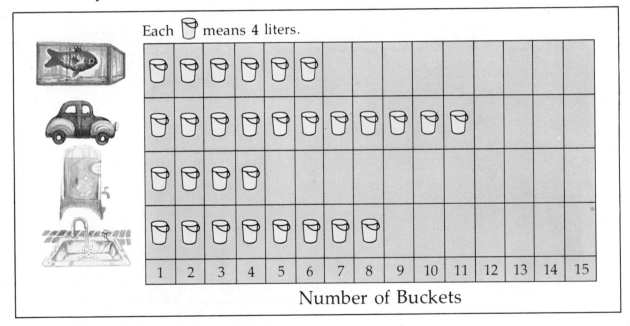

Each 🪣 means 4 liters.

	1	2	3	4	5	6	7	8	9	10	11	12	13	14	15

Number of Buckets

Study the graph. How much does each hold?
(Remember: each 🪣 holds 4 liters.)

1. Fish tank
2. Gas tank in small car
3. Water cooler
4. Sink

☆ 5. Find out how many liters something holds.
How many buckets would you show on the graph?

Answers for Self-check   1. 10   2. 7   3. 9   4. 2   5. more walk; 1

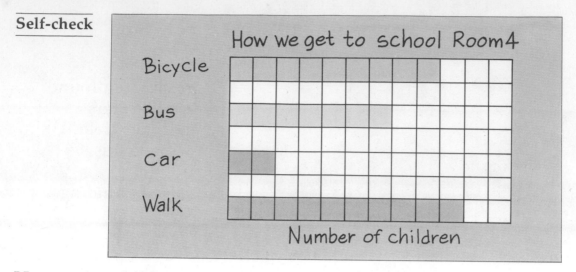

How many children come to school

1. by walking. 2. by bus. 3. by bicycle. 4. by car.

5. Do more children walk or ride their bikes? How many more?

Answers for Self-check—page 203

Answers for Self-check—page 203

Test

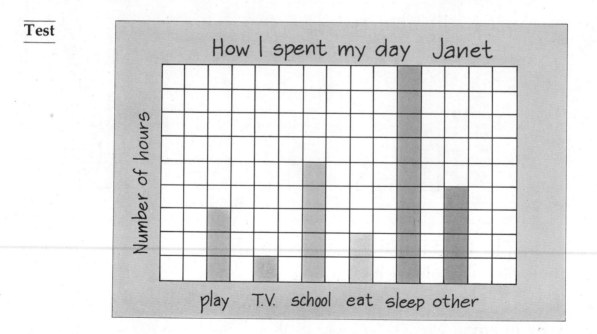

How many hours does Janet spend

1. eating. 2. playing. 3. in school. 4. sleeping.

5. Does Janet spend more time playing or more time in school? How much more?

A Roman Numeral Puzzle

The tables show what the Romans wrote for some numbers.
Study the table.
Then copy and fill in the puzzle.

I	1
II	2
III	3
IV	4
V	5
VI	6

VII	7
VIII	8
IX	9
X	10
XI	11
XII	12

XIV	14
XV	15
XVI	16
XIX	19
XX	20
XXI	21

XXXV	35
XL	40
XLIX	49
L	50
XC	90
C	100

Puzzle

Across

1. XII
2. XV
3. C
4. CCIII
5. CCCLI
7. CXXVI
8. XXIV
9. XXXIX

Down

1. CXII
2. X
3. XIII
5. XXXVI
6. CXIX
7. XIV

Solve the equations.

1.
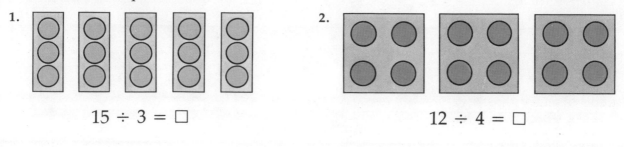

$$15 \div 3 = \square$$

2.

$$12 \div 4 = \square$$

Find the quotients.

3. $10 \div 2 = \square$ 4. $12 \div 3 = \square$ 5. $15 \div 3 = \square$ 6. $27 \div 3 = \square$

7. $18 \div 3 = \square$ 8. $14 \div 2 = \square$ 9. $16 \div 2 = \square$ 10. $9 \div 1 = \square$

11. $4 \div 1 = \square$ 12. $6 \div 1 = \square$ 13. $7 \div 1 = \square$ 14. $12 \div 2 = \square$

15. $6 \div 2 = \square$ 16. $24 \div 3 = \square$ 17. $8 \div 2 = \square$ 18. $21 \div 3 = \square$

19. $16 \div 4 = \square$ 20. $15 \div 5 = \square$ 21. $20 \div 4 = \square$ 22. $40 \div 5 = \square$

23. $25 \div 5 = \square$ 24. $8 \div 4 = \square$ 25. $30 \div 5 = \square$ 26. $4 \div 4 = \square$

27. $28 \div 4 = \square$ 28. $45 \div 5 = \square$ 29. $10 \div 5 = \square$ 30. $32 \div 4 = \square$

31. $35 \div 5 = \square$ 32. $24 \div 4 = \square$ 33. $12 \div 4 = \square$ 34. $20 \div 5 = \square$

35. Bought 3 oranges.
Spent 24 cents.
How much for each one?

36. 36 legs
4 on each dog
How many dogs?

37. Twenty-four people
4 cars
Same number in each car
How many were in each car?

38. Five children divided
35 tickets equally among
themselves. How many
tickets did each child get?

Special Products
Multiplying
Problem Solving—Using Your Skills
Measurement 2

Special Products

10, 20, 30, 40, 50

Getting started

How many?

1.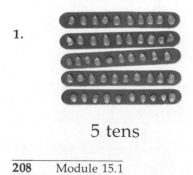

5 tens

2.

4 hundreds

5.

$$3 \times 10 = \square$$

6.

$$6 \times 10 = \square$$

7.

$$4 \times 100 = \square$$

Solve the equations.

3.

$$2 \times 100 = \square$$

4.

$$2 \times 10 = \square$$

8.

$$3 \times 100 = \square$$

Peter and Cindy collect pennies.

Peter has 16 dimes.
How many pennies can
he get for his dimes?

Cindy has 7 dollars.
How many pennies can
she get?

Finding the answer

Write 16
followed by 0.

Write 7
followed by 00.

$16 \times 10 = 160$

$7 \times 100 = 700$

Peter can get 160 pennies.

Cindy can get 700 pennies.

Find the products.

1. $6 \times 10 = \square$ 2. $8 \times 10 = \square$ 3. $27 \times 10 = \square$

4. $18 \times 10 = \square$ 5. $11 \times 10 = \square$ 6. $24 \times 10 = \square$

7. $9 \times 10 = \square$ 8. $4 \times 10 = \square$ 9. $7 \times 10 = \square$

10. $36 \times 10 = \square$ 11. $48 \times 10 = \square$ 12. $10 \times 10 = \square$

13. $3 \times 10 = \square$ 14. $15 \times 10 = \square$ 15. $32 \times 10 = \square$

16. $5 \times 100 = \square$ 17. $8 \times 100 = \square$ 18. $3 \times 100 = \square$

19. $2 \times 100 = \square$ 20. $1 \times 100 = \square$ 21. $9 \times 100 = \square$

22. $7 \times 100 = \square$ 23. $4 \times 100 = \square$ 24. $6 \times 100 = \square$

Solve the equations.

1. $12 \times 10 = \square$ 2. $49 \times 10 = \square$ 3. $4 \times 10 = \square$

4. $4 \times 100 = \square$ 5. $32 \times 10 = \square$ 6. $8 \times 100 = \square$

7. $7 \times 10 = \square$ 8. $9 \times 100 = \square$ 9. $14 \times 10 = \square$

10. $28 \times 10 = \square$ 11. $8 \times 10 = \square$ 12. $2 \times 10 = \square$

13. $12 \times 100 = \square$ 14. $35 \times 100 = \square$ 15. $11 \times 100 = \square$

16. $81 \times 10 = \square$ 17. $18 \times 10 = \square$ 18. $10 \times 100 = \square$

19. $20 \times 10 = \square$ 20. $15 \times 100 = \square$ 21. $54 \times 10 = \square$

22. $23 \times 100 = \square$ 23. $79 \times 10 = \square$ 24. $24 \times 10 = \square$

25. $7 \times 100 = \square$ 26. $1 \times 100 = \square$ 27. $6 \times 10 = \square$

Find the products.

☆ 28. $4 \times 3 \times 10 = \square$ ☆ 29. $2 \times 8 \times 10 = \square$

☆ 30. $5 \times 6 \times 10 = \square$ ☆ 31. $7 \times 4 \times 10 = \square$

☆ 32. $8 \times 3 \times 10 = \square$ ☆ 33. $9 \times 6 \times 10 = \square$

34. Maria traded 12 dimes for pennies. How many pennies did she get?

35. How many pennies should Ted get for 3 dollars?

Think!

How many squares can you find?

Finding special products

Blue cube: 2, 3, 4, 5, 6, 7
Red cube: 20, 30, 40, 50, 60, 70
Your score is the product of the top numbers on the cubes.

Blue: 3
Red: 40

What is the score?

Finding the answer

3 × 4 tens is 12 tens

$3 \times 40 = 12 \times 10$
$3 \times 40 = 120$

The score is 120.

Other examples

$6 \times 30 = 180$ $5 \times 700 = 3500$
$5 \times 80 = 400$ $4 \times 600 = 2400$

Find the products.

1. $6 \times 40 = \square$ 2. $7 \times 20 = \square$ 3. $5 \times 20 = \square$ 4. $7 \times 30 = \square$

5. $3 \times 40 = \square$ 6. $7 \times 60 = \square$ 7. $7 \times 80 = \square$ 8. $9 \times 30 = \square$

9. $2 \times 90 = \square$ 10. $6 \times 50 = \square$ 11. $8 \times 70 = \square$ 12. $6 \times 30 = \square$

13. $3 \times 90 = \square$ 14. $8 \times 60 = \square$ 15. $3 \times 80 = \square$ 16. $5 \times 50 = \square$

17. $7 \times 70 = \square$ 18. $5 \times 60 = \square$ 19. $8 \times 80 = \square$ 20. $5 \times 90 = \square$

21. $9 \times 40 = \square$ 22. $4 \times 70 = \square$ 23. $7 \times 50 = \square$ 24. $6 \times 70 = \square$

25. $2 \times 60 = \square$ 26. $4 \times 90 = \square$ 27. $8 \times 50 = \square$ 28. $9 \times 60 = \square$

29. $2 \times 80 = \square$ 30. $4 \times 30 = \square$ 31. $7 \times 90 = \square$ 32. $9 \times 80 = \square$

Find the products.

1. $6 \times 300 = \square$
2. $9 \times 200 = \square$
3. $6 \times 400 = \square$
4. $2 \times 700 = \square$
5. $4 \times 800 = \square$
6. $3 \times 500 = \square$
7. $3 \times 400 = \square$
8. $7 \times 300 = \square$
9. $5 \times 100 = \square$
10. $5 \times 300 = \square$
11. $2 \times 600 = \square$
12. $8 \times 300 = \square$

Multiply.

13. $6 \times 50 = \square$
14. $2 \times 70 = \square$
15. $7 \times 80 = \square$
16. $8 \times 30 = \square$
17. $4 \times 70 = \square$
18. $6 \times 200 = \square$
19. $4 \times 50 = \square$
20. $3 \times 200 = \square$
21. $7 \times 800 = \square$
22. $5 \times 70 = \square$
23. $6 \times 900 = \square$
24. $7 \times 70 = \square$
25. $9 \times 40 = \square$
26. $2 \times 400 = \square$
27. $2 \times 60 = \square$
28. $5 \times 80 = \square$
29. $2 \times 800 = \square$
30. $4 \times 60 = \square$

31.

Blue times red.

What is the score?

☆ 32. Play a cube game with a friend.

Now here's a simple rule
That should always be
your friend.
When you multiply by me,
Put two zeros on the end.

Who am I?

Answers for Self-check 1. 30 2. 400 3. 240 4. 1200 5. 80 6. 300 7. 360 8. 600 9. 4200 10. 240 11. 120 12. 480 13. 1800 14. 5600 15. 2700 16. 350 17. 150 18. 320 19. 160 20. 450 21. 4900

Self-check

Find the products.

1. $3 \times 10 = \square$
2. $4 \times 100 = \square$
3. $24 \times 10 = \square$

4. $12 \times 100 = \square$
5. $8 \times 10 = \square$
6. $3 \times 100 = \square$

7. $36 \times 10 = \square$
8. $6 \times 100 = \square$
9. $42 \times 100 = \square$

10. $4 \times 60 = \square$
11. $2 \times 60 = \square$
12. $6 \times 80 = \square$

13. $6 \times 300 = \square$
14. $8 \times 700 = \square$
15. $9 \times 300 = \square$

16. $5 \times 70 = \square$
17. $5 \times 30 = \square$
18. $4 \times 80 = \square$

19. $8 \times 20 = \square$
20. $9 \times 50 = \square$
21. $7 \times 700 = \square$

Answers for Self-check—page 213

Test

Find the products.

1. $28 \times 10 = \square$
2. $72 \times 10 = \square$
3. $4 \times 100 = \square$

4. $6 \times 10 = \square$
5. $7 \times 100 = \square$
6. $9 \times 10 = \square$

7. $3 \times 100 = \square$
8. $45 \times 100 = \square$
9. $16 \times 100 = \square$

10. $5 \times 50 = \square$
11. $7 \times 60 = \square$
12. $7 \times 500 = \square$

13. $3 \times 600 = \square$
14. $2 \times 300 = \square$
15. $5 \times 80 = \square$

16. $6 \times 60 = \square$
17. $9 \times 50 = \square$
18. $3 \times 90 = \square$

19. $5 \times 700 = \square$
20. $6 \times 800 = \square$
21. $8 \times 400 = \square$

What Does It Say?

Code:

S	E	N
I	U	H
W	T	R

Example

W I N T E R

What does this say?

Multiplying

Getting started

Example

$4 \times 3 = 12$
$4 \times 60 = 240$
Score: $\overline{252}$

Score: Find the product of the
blue number times each red number.
Add the products.

1. How much is 2 × 3?
   How much is 2 × 40?
   What is the score?

2. How much is 3 × 4?
   How much is 3 × 50?
   What is the score?

3. Find the score for each toss.

First toss

Second toss

Third toss

Numbers for making
your own cubes:

Blue: 2, 3, 4, 5, 6, 7

Red: 2, 3, 4, 5, 6, 7

Red: 20, 30, 40, 50, 60, 70

Multiplying without regrouping

There are 12 flowers in each dozen. How many flowers are in 4 dozen?

Finding the answer

Multiply the ones	→	Multiply the tens

$$\begin{array}{r} 12 \\ \times\ 4 \\ \hline 8 \end{array} \qquad \begin{array}{r} 12 \\ \times\ 4 \\ \hline 48 \end{array}$$

There are 48 flowers.

Other examples

$$\begin{array}{r} 23 \\ \times\ 2 \\ \hline 46 \end{array} \qquad \begin{array}{r} 42 \\ \times\ 3 \\ \hline 126 \end{array} \qquad \begin{array}{r} 50 \\ \times\ 3 \\ \hline 150 \end{array} \qquad \begin{array}{r} 321 \\ \times\ 4 \\ \hline 1284 \end{array}$$

Multiply.

1. $\begin{array}{r} 13 \\ \times\ 2 \\ \hline \end{array}$ 2. $\begin{array}{r} 12 \\ \times\ 3 \\ \hline \end{array}$ 3. $\begin{array}{r} 21 \\ \times\ 4 \\ \hline \end{array}$ 4. $\begin{array}{r} 52 \\ \times\ 3 \\ \hline \end{array}$ 5. $\begin{array}{r} 63 \\ \times\ 2 \\ \hline \end{array}$ 6. $\begin{array}{r} 14 \\ \times\ 2 \\ \hline \end{array}$

7. $\begin{array}{r} 51 \\ \times\ 4 \\ \hline \end{array}$ 8. $\begin{array}{r} 33 \\ \times\ 2 \\ \hline \end{array}$ 9. $\begin{array}{r} 32 \\ \times\ 4 \\ \hline \end{array}$ 10. $\begin{array}{r} 40 \\ \times\ 2 \\ \hline \end{array}$ 11. $\begin{array}{r} 42 \\ \times\ 4 \\ \hline \end{array}$ 12. $\begin{array}{r} 60 \\ \times\ 3 \\ \hline \end{array}$

13. $\begin{array}{r} 62 \\ \times\ 3 \\ \hline \end{array}$ 14. $\begin{array}{r} 72 \\ \times\ 4 \\ \hline \end{array}$ 15. $\begin{array}{r} 31 \\ \times\ 6 \\ \hline \end{array}$ 16. $\begin{array}{r} 43 \\ \times\ 3 \\ \hline \end{array}$ 17. $\begin{array}{r} 82 \\ \times\ 4 \\ \hline \end{array}$ 18. $\begin{array}{r} 74 \\ \times\ 2 \\ \hline \end{array}$

Find the products.

1. $\begin{array}{r} 213 \\ \times\ \ \ 3 \\ \hline \end{array}$	2. $\begin{array}{r} 341 \\ \times\ \ \ 2 \\ \hline \end{array}$	3. $\begin{array}{r} 212 \\ \times\ \ \ 4 \\ \hline \end{array}$	4. $\begin{array}{r} 311 \\ \times\ \ \ 5 \\ \hline \end{array}$	5. $\begin{array}{r} 642 \\ \times\ \ \ 2 \\ \hline \end{array}$
	6. $\begin{array}{r} 612 \\ \times\ \ \ 3 \\ \hline \end{array}$	7. $\begin{array}{r} 322 \\ \times\ \ \ 2 \\ \hline \end{array}$	8. $\begin{array}{r} 521 \\ \times\ \ \ 3 \\ \hline \end{array}$	9. $\begin{array}{r} 714 \\ \times\ \ \ 2 \\ \hline \end{array}$
	10. $\begin{array}{r} 312 \\ \times\ \ \ 4 \\ \hline \end{array}$	11. $\begin{array}{r} 422 \\ \times\ \ \ 3 \\ \hline \end{array}$	12. $\begin{array}{r} 430 \\ \times\ \ \ 2 \\ \hline \end{array}$	13. $\begin{array}{r} 410 \\ \times\ \ \ 5 \\ \hline \end{array}$
		14. $\begin{array}{r} 304 \\ \times\ \ \ 2 \\ \hline \end{array}$	15. $\begin{array}{r} 721 \\ \times\ \ \ 3 \\ \hline \end{array}$	16. $\begin{array}{r} 52 \\ \times\ \ \ 3 \\ \hline \end{array}$
		17. $\begin{array}{r} 41 \\ \times\ \ \ 4 \\ \hline \end{array}$	18. $\begin{array}{r} 34 \\ \times\ \ \ 2 \\ \hline \end{array}$	19. $\begin{array}{r} 71 \\ \times\ \ \ 5 \\ \hline \end{array}$
		20. $\begin{array}{r} 53 \\ \times\ \ \ 2 \\ \hline \end{array}$	21. $\begin{array}{r} 23 \\ \times\ \ \ 3 \\ \hline \end{array}$	22. $\begin{array}{r} 44 \\ \times\ \ \ 2 \\ \hline \end{array}$
	23. $\begin{array}{r} 52 \\ \times\ \ \ 3 \\ \hline \end{array}$	24. $\begin{array}{r} 30 \\ \times\ \ \ 4 \\ \hline \end{array}$	25. $\begin{array}{r} 62 \\ \times\ \ \ 3 \\ \hline \end{array}$	26. $\begin{array}{r} 41 \\ \times\ \ \ 5 \\ \hline \end{array}$

27.

How many flowers?

28.

How many flowers?

The sum of two numbers and 13 is 70. One of the numbers is 25. What is the other?

More practice, page 337, Set A

Multiplying: 1 digit × 2 digits

Don cut out a piece 7 squares
wide and 24 squares long.
How many squares?

Finding the answer

Multiply the ones		Multiply the tens Add the extra tens

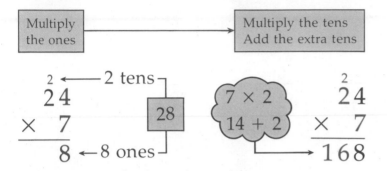

Don's piece has 168 squares.

Other examples

$$\begin{array}{r} \overset{1}{2}5 \\ \times\ 3 \\ \hline 75 \end{array}\qquad \begin{array}{r} \overset{3}{5}8 \\ \times\ 4 \\ \hline 232 \end{array}\qquad \begin{array}{r} \overset{2}{3}5 \\ \times\ 5 \\ \hline 175 \end{array}$$

Multiply.

1. $\begin{array}{r} 13 \\ \times\ 4 \\ \hline \end{array}$
2. $\begin{array}{r} 25 \\ \times\ 5 \\ \hline \end{array}$
3. $\begin{array}{r} 17 \\ \times\ 3 \\ \hline \end{array}$
4. $\begin{array}{r} 36 \\ \times\ 4 \\ \hline \end{array}$
5. $\begin{array}{r} 27 \\ \times\ 6 \\ \hline \end{array}$
6. $\begin{array}{r} 32 \\ \times\ 5 \\ \hline \end{array}$

7. $\begin{array}{r} 37 \\ \times\ 5 \\ \hline \end{array}$
8. $\begin{array}{r} 58 \\ \times\ 4 \\ \hline \end{array}$
9. $\begin{array}{r} 47 \\ \times\ 3 \\ \hline \end{array}$
10. $\begin{array}{r} 12 \\ \times\ 5 \\ \hline \end{array}$
11. $\begin{array}{r} 94 \\ \times\ 3 \\ \hline \end{array}$
12. $\begin{array}{r} 58 \\ \times\ 5 \\ \hline \end{array}$

13. $\begin{array}{r} 24 \\ \times\ 9 \\ \hline \end{array}$
14. $\begin{array}{r} 84 \\ \times\ 4 \\ \hline \end{array}$
15. $\begin{array}{r} 35 \\ \times\ 7 \\ \hline \end{array}$
16. $\begin{array}{r} 65 \\ \times\ 7 \\ \hline \end{array}$
17. $\begin{array}{r} 48 \\ \times\ 6 \\ \hline \end{array}$
18. $\begin{array}{r} 54 \\ \times\ 8 \\ \hline \end{array}$

Find the products.

1.	24 × 3	2.	19 × 5	3.	22 × 6	4.	17 × 4	5.	32 × 3
6.	75 × 2	7.	16 × 5	8.	48 × 3	9.	56 × 6	10.	27 × 5
11.	45 × 4	12.	94 × 3	13.	83 × 5	14.	26 × 7	15.	14 × 4
		16.	33 × 5	17.	28 × 8	18.	63 × 9	19.	66 × 6

20. 7 squares wide
43 squares long
How many squares in all?

├────── 43 ──────→

7

☆ 21. Carlos used a different way to find products. Can you use his way to find these products?

$$\begin{array}{r} 24 \\ \times\ 6 \\ \hline 24 \\ 120 \\ \hline 144 \end{array}$$

A   38 × 4   B   54 × 7   C   43 × 5

☆ 22. Cut a strip 5 squares wide and more than 20 squares long. How many squares did you cut out?

Think!

Copy this picture.

Put different numbers in each circle so the sum across is 13 and the sum down is 13.

Multiplying with money

1 ticket costs 25¢.
How much will 7 tickets cost?

Finding the answer

Multiply	→	Show cents or dollars

$$\begin{array}{r} 25¢ \\ \times\ 7 \\ \hline 175 \end{array} \qquad \begin{array}{r} 25¢ \\ \times\ 7 \\ \hline 175¢ \end{array} \text{ or } \$1.75$$

The cost for 7 tickets is $1.75.

Other examples

$$\begin{array}{r} 14¢ \\ \times\ 4 \\ \hline 56¢ \end{array} \qquad \begin{array}{r} 65¢ \\ \times\ 4 \\ \hline 260¢ \end{array} \qquad \begin{array}{r} 38¢ \\ \times\ 2 \\ \hline 76¢ \end{array}$$

$$\$0.56 \qquad \$2.60 \qquad \$0.76$$

Find the amounts. Show the answers in dollars and cents.

1. $\begin{array}{r} 19¢ \\ \times\ 4 \\ \hline \end{array}$
2. $\begin{array}{r} 28¢ \\ \times\ 3 \\ \hline \end{array}$
3. $\begin{array}{r} 39¢ \\ \times\ 2 \\ \hline \end{array}$
4. $\begin{array}{r} 13¢ \\ \times\ 4 \\ \hline \end{array}$
5. $\begin{array}{r} 18¢ \\ \times\ 5 \\ \hline \end{array}$

6. $\begin{array}{r} 46¢ \\ \times\ 5 \\ \hline \end{array}$
7. $\begin{array}{r} 81¢ \\ \times\ 4 \\ \hline \end{array}$
8. $\begin{array}{r} 32¢ \\ \times\ 5 \\ \hline \end{array}$
9. $\begin{array}{r} 75¢ \\ \times\ 3 \\ \hline \end{array}$
10. $\begin{array}{r} 24¢ \\ \times\ 2 \\ \hline \end{array}$

11. $\begin{array}{r} 15¢ \\ \times\ 6 \\ \hline \end{array}$
12. $\begin{array}{r} 31¢ \\ \times\ 5 \\ \hline \end{array}$
13. $\begin{array}{r} 48¢ \\ \times\ 9 \\ \hline \end{array}$
14. $\begin{array}{r} 25¢ \\ \times\ 6 \\ \hline \end{array}$
15. $\begin{array}{r} 50¢ \\ \times\ 8 \\ \hline \end{array}$

Find the amounts.
Show the answers in dollars and cents.

1. 12¢
    × 3

2. 18¢
    × 4

3. 34¢
    × 2

4. 41¢
    × 2

5. 21¢
    × 4

6. 28¢
    × 2

7. 16¢
    × 3

8. 47¢
    × 2

9. 25¢
    × 3

10. 17¢
     × 4

11. 54¢
     × 3

12. 64¢
     × 5

13. 71¢
     × 4

14. 40¢
     × 3

15. 29¢
     × 4

16. 75¢
     × 6

17. 29¢
     × 8

18. 36¢
     × 9

19. 52¢
     × 7

20. 42¢
     × 5

Solve.

21. Balloons: 12¢ each
    How much for 8 balloons?

22. Frozen bananas: 35¢ each
    How much for 6?

23. Orange drink: 15¢ each
    How much for 4 drinks?

24. Popcorn: 20¢ a bag
    How much for 9 bags?

25. Tickets: 25¢ each
    How much for 3?

Bart sells 114 papers each day.
How many does he sell in 6 days?

Finding the answer

Multiply the ones	Multiply the tens Add the extra tens	Multiply the hundreds

$$
\begin{array}{r}
\overset{2}{1}14 \\
\times\quad 6 \\
\hline
4
\end{array}
\qquad
\begin{array}{r}
\overset{2}{1}14 \\
\times\quad 6 \\
\hline
84
\end{array}
\qquad
\begin{array}{r}
\overset{2}{1}14 \\
\times\quad 6 \\
\hline
684
\end{array}
$$

Bart sells 684 papers in 6 days.

Other examples

$$
\begin{array}{r}
4\overset{2}{2}8 \\
\times\quad 3 \\
\hline
1284
\end{array}
\qquad
\begin{array}{r}
8\overset{1}{0}2 \\
\times\quad 7 \\
\hline
5614
\end{array}
\qquad
\begin{array}{r}
3\overset{2}{6}2 \\
\times\quad 4 \\
\hline
1448
\end{array}
$$

Multiply.

1. $\begin{array}{r} 125 \\ \times\quad 3 \\ \hline \end{array}$ 2. $\begin{array}{r} 346 \\ \times\quad 2 \\ \hline \end{array}$ 3. $\begin{array}{r} 215 \\ \times\quad 4 \\ \hline \end{array}$ 4. $\begin{array}{r} 415 \\ \times\quad 5 \\ \hline \end{array}$

5. $\begin{array}{r} 618 \\ \times\quad 3 \\ \hline \end{array}$ 6. $\begin{array}{r} 547 \\ \times\quad 2 \\ \hline \end{array}$ 7. $\begin{array}{r} 313 \\ \times\quad 5 \\ \hline \end{array}$ 8. $\begin{array}{r} 926 \\ \times\quad 2 \\ \hline \end{array}$ 9. $\begin{array}{r} 306 \\ \times\quad 3 \\ \hline \end{array}$

10. $\begin{array}{r} 214 \\ \times\quad 6 \\ \hline \end{array}$ 11. $\begin{array}{r} 738 \\ \times\quad 2 \\ \hline \end{array}$ 12. $\begin{array}{r} 423 \\ \times\quad 4 \\ \hline \end{array}$ 13. $\begin{array}{r} 516 \\ \times\quad 3 \\ \hline \end{array}$ 14. $\begin{array}{r} 804 \\ \times\quad 5 \\ \hline \end{array}$

Find the products.

1. 252
× 3

2. 736
× 2

3. 532
× 4

4. 642
× 3

5. 271
× 4

6. 223
× 4

7. 141
× 5

8. 114
× 3

9. 306
× 4

10. 763
× 2

11. 103
× 6

12. 131
× 5

13. 102
× 7

14. 504
× 4

15. 341
× 5

16. 150
× 8

17. 220
× 7

18. 140
× 6

19. 121 papers a day
6 days
How many papers?

20. 132 papers a day
How many papers
in 4 days?

☆ 21. Angie multiplies like this.
Can you use her method
to find these products?

```
    232
  ×   4
      8
    120
    800
    928
```

```
  392          624
×   3        ×   4
```

Together, a doll and a
dress cost $11. The doll
cost $10 more than the dress.
How much was the doll?

More practice, page 338, Set A

✳ More about multiplying

How many days in 3 years?
(Use 365 days for 1 year.)

Finding the answer

Multiply the ones	→	Multiply the tens Add the extra tens	→	Multiply the hundreds Add the extra hundreds

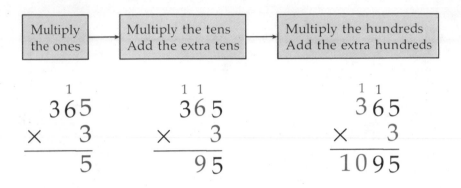

$$
\begin{array}{r}
{}^{1} \\
3\,6\,5 \\
\times \quad 3 \\
\hline
5
\end{array}
\qquad
\begin{array}{r}
{}^{1}\,{}^{1} \\
3\,6\,5 \\
\times \quad 3 \\
\hline
9\,5
\end{array}
\qquad
\begin{array}{r}
{}^{1}\,{}^{1} \\
3\,6\,5 \\
\times \quad 3 \\
\hline
1\,0\,9\,5
\end{array}
$$

There are 1095 days in 3 years.

Other examples

$$
\begin{array}{r}
{}^{3}\,{}^{2} \\
3\,7\,6 \\
\times \quad 4 \\
\hline
1\,5\,0\,4
\end{array}
\qquad
\begin{array}{r}
{}^{5}\,{}^{3} \\
1\,8\,5 \\
\times \quad 6 \\
\hline
1\,1\,1\,0
\end{array}
\qquad
\begin{array}{r}
{}^{2}\,{}^{1} \\
6\,7\,4 \\
\times \quad 3 \\
\hline
2\,0\,2\,2
\end{array}
$$

Multiply.

1. $\begin{array}{r} 276 \\ \times \quad 2 \\ \hline \end{array}$
2. $\begin{array}{r} 358 \\ \times \quad 4 \\ \hline \end{array}$
3. $\begin{array}{r} 275 \\ \times \quad 6 \\ \hline \end{array}$
4. $\begin{array}{r} 346 \\ \times \quad 5 \\ \hline \end{array}$
5. $\begin{array}{r} 294 \\ \times \quad 4 \\ \hline \end{array}$

6. $\begin{array}{r} 375 \\ \times \quad 6 \\ \hline \end{array}$
7. $\begin{array}{r} 182 \\ \times \quad 3 \\ \hline \end{array}$
8. $\begin{array}{r} 243 \\ \times \quad 8 \\ \hline \end{array}$
9. $\begin{array}{r} 372 \\ \times \quad 7 \\ \hline \end{array}$
10. $\begin{array}{r} 317 \\ \times \quad 4 \\ \hline \end{array}$

11. $\begin{array}{r} 165 \\ \times \quad 9 \\ \hline \end{array}$
12. $\begin{array}{r} 347 \\ \times \quad 5 \\ \hline \end{array}$
13. $\begin{array}{r} 472 \\ \times \quad 6 \\ \hline \end{array}$
14. $\begin{array}{r} 834 \\ \times \quad 8 \\ \hline \end{array}$
15. $\begin{array}{r} 952 \\ \times \quad 7 \\ \hline \end{array}$

Find the products.

1.	294 × 3	2.	233 × 4	3.	457 × 2	4.	826 × 5
5.	305 × 4	6.	726 × 3	7.	837 × 5	8.	506 × 4
9.	765 × 3	10.	832 × 4	11.	954 × 5	12.	650 × 8
13.	727 × 6	14.	816 × 7	15.	923 × 6	16.	456 × 9
17.	327 × 5	18.	842 × 8	19.	654 × 6	20.	329 × 7

Now find these products.

☆ 21.	2346 × 4	☆ 22.	5176 × 3	☆ 23.	3843 × 6
☆ 24.	7506 × 5	☆ 25.	2304 × 8	☆ 26.	5263 × 7

☆ 27. 365 days in a year
How many days old
will you be on
your next birthday?

Think!

The bug went around
one time. He traveled
12 units. About how
long is this segment?

Answers for Self-check   1. 48   2. 128   3. 936   4. 369   5. 2484   6. 112   7. 108   8. 324   9. 336
10. 320   11. $0.42   12. $1.25   13. $0.74   14. $3.84   15. $3.36   16. 972   17. 2064   18. 1396   19. 2850
20. 5936

More practice, page 338, Set B

Self-check

1. $\begin{array}{r} 24 \\ \times\ 2 \\ \hline \end{array}$	2. $\begin{array}{r} 32 \\ \times\ 4 \\ \hline \end{array}$	3. $\begin{array}{r} 312 \\ \times\ \ 3 \\ \hline \end{array}$	4. $\begin{array}{r} 123 \\ \times\ \ 3 \\ \hline \end{array}$	5. $\begin{array}{r} 621 \\ \times\ \ 4 \\ \hline \end{array}$
6. $\begin{array}{r} 28 \\ \times\ 4 \\ \hline \end{array}$	7. $\begin{array}{r} 36 \\ \times\ 3 \\ \hline \end{array}$	8. $\begin{array}{r} 54 \\ \times\ 6 \\ \hline \end{array}$	9. $\begin{array}{r} 48 \\ \times\ 7 \\ \hline \end{array}$	10. $\begin{array}{r} 64 \\ \times\ 5 \\ \hline \end{array}$
11. $\begin{array}{r} 14¢ \\ \times\ 3 \\ \hline \end{array}$	12. $\begin{array}{r} 25¢ \\ \times\ 5 \\ \hline \end{array}$	13. $\begin{array}{r} 37¢ \\ \times\ 2 \\ \hline \end{array}$	14. $\begin{array}{r} 48¢ \\ \times\ 8 \\ \hline \end{array}$	15. $\begin{array}{r} 56¢ \\ \times\ 6 \\ \hline \end{array}$
☆ 16. $\begin{array}{r} 324 \\ \times\ \ 3 \\ \hline \end{array}$	☆ 17. $\begin{array}{r} 516 \\ \times\ \ 4 \\ \hline \end{array}$	☆ 18. $\begin{array}{r} 698 \\ \times\ \ 2 \\ \hline \end{array}$	☆ 19. $\begin{array}{r} 475 \\ \times\ \ 6 \\ \hline \end{array}$	☆ 20. $\begin{array}{r} 742 \\ \times\ \ 8 \\ \hline \end{array}$

Answers for Self-check—page 227

Test

1. $\begin{array}{r} 31 \\ \times\ 3 \\ \hline \end{array}$	2. $\begin{array}{r} 25 \\ \times\ 2 \\ \hline \end{array}$	3. $\begin{array}{r} 313 \\ \times\ \ 3 \\ \hline \end{array}$	4. $\begin{array}{r} 421 \\ \times\ \ 4 \\ \hline \end{array}$	5. $\begin{array}{r} 223 \\ \times\ \ 3 \\ \hline \end{array}$
6. $\begin{array}{r} 35 \\ \times\ 4 \\ \hline \end{array}$	7. $\begin{array}{r} 56 \\ \times\ 3 \\ \hline \end{array}$	8. $\begin{array}{r} 82 \\ \times\ 6 \\ \hline \end{array}$	9. $\begin{array}{r} 74 \\ \times\ 8 \\ \hline \end{array}$	10. $\begin{array}{r} 46 \\ \times\ 9 \\ \hline \end{array}$
11. $\begin{array}{r} 12¢ \\ \times\ 4 \\ \hline \end{array}$	12. $\begin{array}{r} 35¢ \\ \times\ 2 \\ \hline \end{array}$	13. $\begin{array}{r} 48¢ \\ \times\ 5 \\ \hline \end{array}$	14. $\begin{array}{r} 75¢ \\ \times\ 9 \\ \hline \end{array}$	15. $\begin{array}{r} 68¢ \\ \times\ 8 \\ \hline \end{array}$
☆ 16. $\begin{array}{r} 415 \\ \times\ \ 3 \\ \hline \end{array}$	☆ 17. $\begin{array}{r} 638 \\ \times\ \ 5 \\ \hline \end{array}$	☆ 18. $\begin{array}{r} 513 \\ \times\ \ 4 \\ \hline \end{array}$	☆ 19. $\begin{array}{r} 842 \\ \times\ \ 9 \\ \hline \end{array}$	☆ 20. $\begin{array}{r} 785 \\ \times\ \ 7 \\ \hline \end{array}$

Magic Trains

Try these yourself.

Then try them on a friend.

Number back train

Choose a number between 1 and 10 — Add 10 — Multiply by 4 — Subtract 40 — Divide by 4 — Answer?

A Two train

Choose a number between 1 and 10 — Add 8 — Multiply by 3 — Subtract 18 — Divide by 3 — Subtract the number you choose — Answer?

Age Family train

Your age — Multiply by 5 — Add 9 — Multiply by 2 — Add the number in your family — Subtract 18 — Answer?

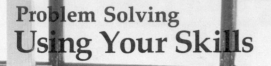

Problem Solving
Using Your Skills

THE YUM YUM TRE

ROOM 16

GOLDFISH - 19¢

PAINTED ROCKS
35¢ EACH

ANIMALS -
39¢ EACH

SHELLS
LARGE - 79¢
MEDIUM - 45¢
SMALL - 29¢

89¢ EACH

25¢ EACH

Getting started

How much money would you need to buy

1. 1 rock and 1 goldfish?   2. 3 animals?

What other problems can you solve?

Solving Problems

1. Read carefully to find the facts.
2. Look for the question.
3. Decide what to do.
4. Find the answer.
5. Read again. Does your answer make sense?

Sometimes there are two things to do.

Susan bought 2 pencils. How much did they cost? She also bought 1 animal. How much money did she spend in all?

$$
\begin{array}{r}
{\scriptstyle 1}\\
25 c\\
\times\ \ 2\\
\hline
50 c
\end{array}
\qquad
\begin{array}{r}
50 c\\
+39 c\\
\hline
89 c
\end{array}
$$

Susan spent 89¢ in all.

1. Jack wants 3 of the small shells at 29¢ each. How much will they cost? He also wants a plant for 89¢. How much money does he need in all?

2. Danny has one dollar. He wants to buy an animal. How much change will he get? Which size shell can Danny buy with his change?

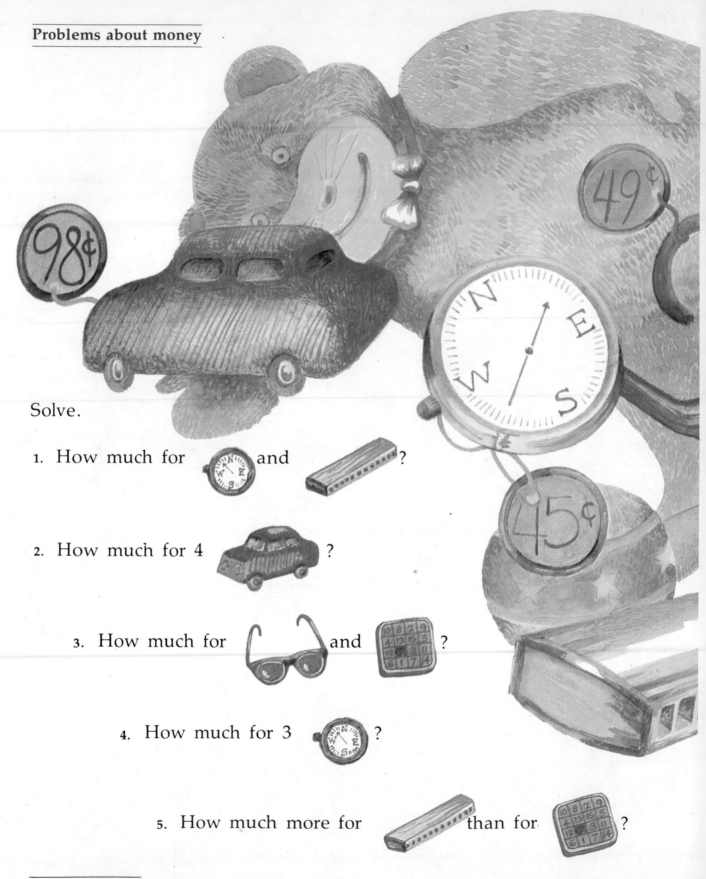

Solve.

1. How much for and ?

2. How much for 4 ?

3. How much for and ?

4. How much for 3 ?

5. How much more for than for ?

6. How much for 2 ?

How much for 1 ?
How much in all?

7. How much for 1 ?

How much for 3 ?
How much in all?

8. How much for 2 ?

How much more for 1 ?

9. How much for and ?

How much more for 2 ?

10. How much for and ?

How much for 4 ?
How much in all?

Taking pictures

Many people like to take pictures just for fun. Others take pictures of things they want to remember. Some people make a living by taking pictures. This book has many pictures. Can you tell which ones were taken with a camera?

Try these problems about taking pictures.

1. A camera was first used to take pictures in 1826. A better camera was used 13 years later. What year was that?

2. A new way to take color pictures was invented in 1942. How many years ago was that?

3. An old-time camera took 100 pictures on a roll. Some cameras today take 36 pictures on a roll. How many more pictures were on the 100-picture roll?

4. Judy's camera takes 36 pictures on a roll. How many pictures are on 4 rolls?

5. Bill's camera takes 12 pictures on each roll. Ted's camera takes 20 pictures on each roll. How many more pictures can Ted take on a roll?

6. Mike can fit 4 pictures on a page in his book of pictures. How many pages will he use for 36 pictures?

7. Linda has 3 rolls that take 20 pictures each. How many pictures is this? She has another roll that takes 36 pictures. How many pictures can she take in all?

8. Sandy has taken 12 color pictures and 20 black-and-white pictures. How many pictures is this? She wants to put 4 pictures on a page in her book of pictures. How many pages does she need?

☆ 9. Beth has a book with 24 pages. She can fit 6 pictures on a page. How many pictures can she fit in the book? Ron's book holds 72 pictures. How many more pictures does Beth's book hold?

☆ 10. Kim has 2 rolls that take 36 pictures each. How many pictures can he take? He also has 1 roll that takes 20 pictures. How many pictures can he take in all?

Practicing your skills

Add.

1.
```
  24
  32
+ 46
```

2.
```
  71
  84
+ 25
```

3.
```
  94
  75
+ 52
```

4.
```
  68
  93
+ 46
```

5.
```
  28
  17
+ 13
```

6.
```
  43
  74
+ 59
```

7.
```
  12
  45
+ 68
```

8.
```
  61
  59
+ 32
```

9.
```
  58
  37
+ 47
```

10.
```
  87
  56
+ 92
```

11.
```
  627
  957
+ 413
```

12.
```
  316
  564
+  47
```

13.
```
  482
  863
+ 375
```

14.
```
  593
  927
+ 284
```

15.
```
  114
  823
+ 596
```

Subtract.

16.
```
  76
- 19
```

17.
```
  52
- 36
```

18.
```
  63
- 38
```

19.
```
  48
- 26
```

20.
```
  91
- 58
```

21.
```
  54
- 38
```

22.
```
  66
- 45
```

23.
```
  72
- 34
```

24.
```
  83
- 59
```

25.
```
  24
- 17
```

26.
```
  182
-  54
```

27.
```
  365
- 147
```

28.
```
  473
- 298
```

29.
```
  654
- 346
```

30.
```
  796
- 534
```

31.
```
  804
- 325
```

32.
```
  414
- 258
```

33.
```
  692
- 439
```

34.
```
  305
- 188
```

35.
```
  827
- 654
```

Multiply.

1. $\begin{array}{r} 42 \\ \times\ 2 \\ \hline \end{array}$
2. $\begin{array}{r} 35 \\ \times\ 3 \\ \hline \end{array}$
3. $\begin{array}{r} 28 \\ \times\ 4 \\ \hline \end{array}$
4. $\begin{array}{r} 75 \\ \times\ 5 \\ \hline \end{array}$
5. $\begin{array}{r} 36 \\ \times\ 4 \\ \hline \end{array}$

6. $\begin{array}{r} 28 \\ \times\ 6 \\ \hline \end{array}$
7. $\begin{array}{r} 45 \\ \times\ 7 \\ \hline \end{array}$
8. $\begin{array}{r} 83 \\ \times\ 4 \\ \hline \end{array}$
9. $\begin{array}{r} 57 \\ \times\ 8 \\ \hline \end{array}$
10. $\begin{array}{r} 95 \\ \times\ 5 \\ \hline \end{array}$

☆ 11. $\begin{array}{r} 348 \\ \times\ 4 \\ \hline \end{array}$
☆ 12. $\begin{array}{r} 572 \\ \times\ 6 \\ \hline \end{array}$
☆ 13. $\begin{array}{r} 823 \\ \times\ 3 \\ \hline \end{array}$
☆ 14. $\begin{array}{r} 465 \\ \times\ 7 \\ \hline \end{array}$
☆ 15. $\begin{array}{r} 602 \\ \times\ 9 \\ \hline \end{array}$

☆ 16. $\begin{array}{r} 653 \\ \times\ 8 \\ \hline \end{array}$
☆ 17. $\begin{array}{r} 401 \\ \times\ 9 \\ \hline \end{array}$
☆ 18. $\begin{array}{r} 349 \\ \times\ 7 \\ \hline \end{array}$
☆ 19. $\begin{array}{r} 725 \\ \times\ 8 \\ \hline \end{array}$
☆ 20. $\begin{array}{r} 812 \\ \times\ 6 \\ \hline \end{array}$

Copy the puzzle.
Give the missing numbers.

Across
1. 3 × 25
3. 4 × 19
5. 3 × 74
9. 358 − 273
10. 135 − 79

Down
2. 187 + 395
4. 3 × 21
6. 171 − 145
7. 6 × 13
8. 8 × 12

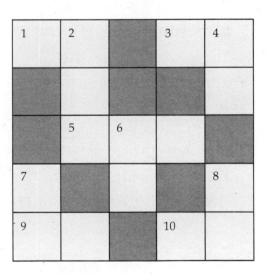

The faces of a block are numbered from 1 to 6. What is the sum of the numbers you cannot see?

Kangaroos

Kangaroos live in the grasslands of
Australia. They hop around on large,
strong back legs. The mother kangaroo
carries her young in a pouch. You can
learn more about kangaroos in these problems.

1. Baby kangaroo: 3 cm
   6 months later: 31 cm
   How much did the
   kangaroo grow?

2. Old kangaroo: 8 years
   12 months in a year
   How many months old?

3. Fast kangaroo: 64 km each hour
   How far in 3 hours?

4. Young kangaroo: 34 cm tail
   Older kangaroo: 120 cm tail
   How much longer is the tail
   of the older kangaroo?

5. 27 kangaroos in one field
   35 in another
   How many kangaroos
   all together?

6. Small kangaroo: 128 cm
   Tall kangaroo: 210 cm
   How much taller is
   the tall kangaroo?

☆ 8. Small kangaroo: 45 kg
   Large kangaroo: 19 kg more
   How many kilograms in all?

7. Baby in the pouch: 7 months
   How many days?
   (Use 30 days a month.)

☆ 9. Long kangaroo hop: 8 m
   How far in 16 hops?
   Short kangaroo hop: 3 m
   How far in 16 hops?
   What is the difference
   in total distance?

Estimation

about 6 dollars

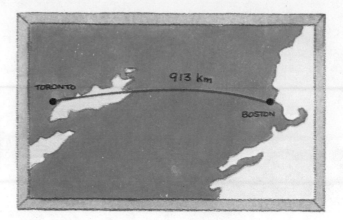

about 900 km

Give an estimate for each amount.

1.

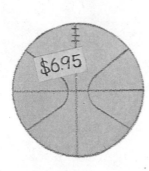

about ▊ dollars

2.

about ▊ kg

3.

about ▊ dollars

4.

about ▊ km

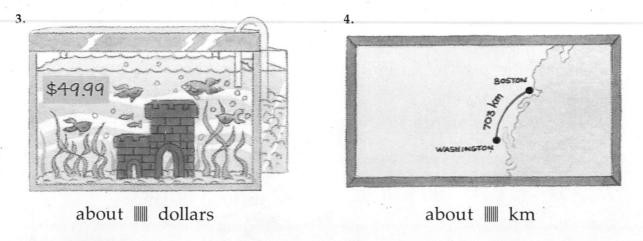

Give these estimates.

1.

About how much for the book?
About how much for 2 books?

2.

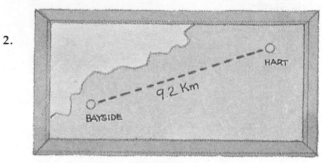

About how far from
Bayside to Hart?
About how far from
Bayside to Hart and back?

3.

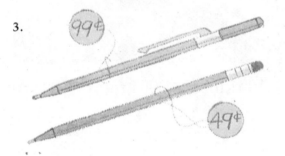

About how much for the pen?
About how much for the pencil?
About how much in all?

4.

About how much change
from a ten-dollar bill?

5.

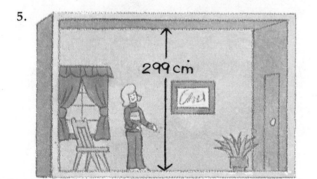

About how many meters high?

6.

About how much
for 1 tennis ball?

Answers for Self-check   1. $1.60   2. $1.44   3. $0.87; $1.36   4. B

1. Saul bought 5 pens.
   Each pen cost 32¢.
   How much did he pay?

2. How much for 4?

3. Memo pads cost 29¢ each.
   How much money will Katy
   need for 3 of them?
   She also wants 1 box
   of crayons at 49¢.
   How much will Katy pay
   for the memo pads
   and the crayons?

4. Choose the best estimate for
   the distance on the map.

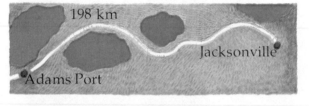

   A 100 km   B 200 km   C 300 km

Answers for Self-check—page 241

Test

1. Luisa bought 4 books.
   Each book cost 72¢.
   How much did she pay?

2. How much for 3?

3. Tablets cost 74¢ each.
   How much money will
   Glenn need for 2?
   He also wants 1 paint
   set that costs 65¢.
   What will be the
   total cost?

4. Choose the best estimate for
   the cost.

   A $2.00   B $3.00   C $4.00

What are they?

All of these
are daps.

None of these
is a dap.

Which of these
are daps?

A   B   C   D

All of these
are mots.

None of these
is a mot.

Which of these
are mots?

A   B   C   D

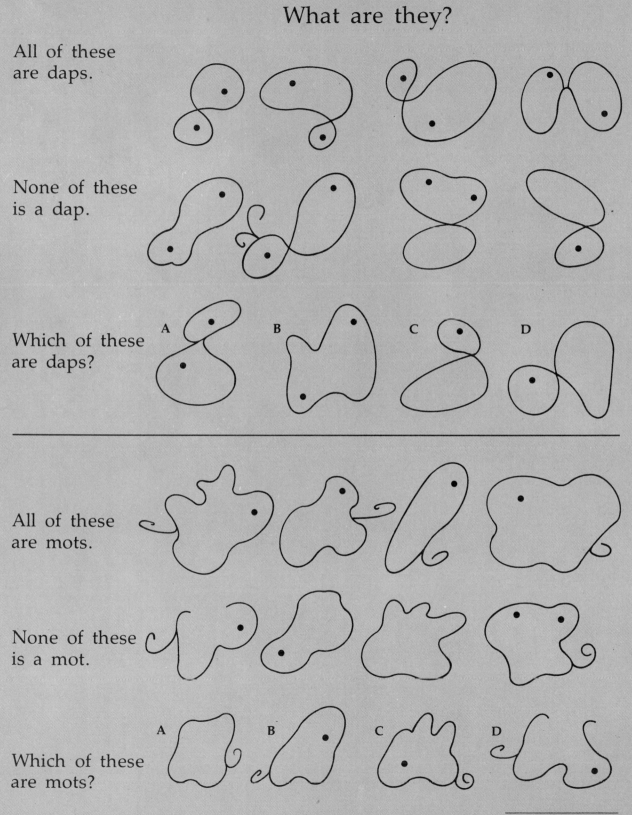

Measurement 2

Guess how many tiles it will take
to cover the table.
Can you find a way to check your guess?

This is a **centimeter unit.** ——

This is a **square centimeter unit.**

Square centimeters
can be used to
cover regions.

Give the number of square centimeters
covering each region.

1.

2.

3.

4.

5.

Counting square units

Ron's class was having an art show. They all drew pictures and made special frames. This picture and frame covers 3 square units.

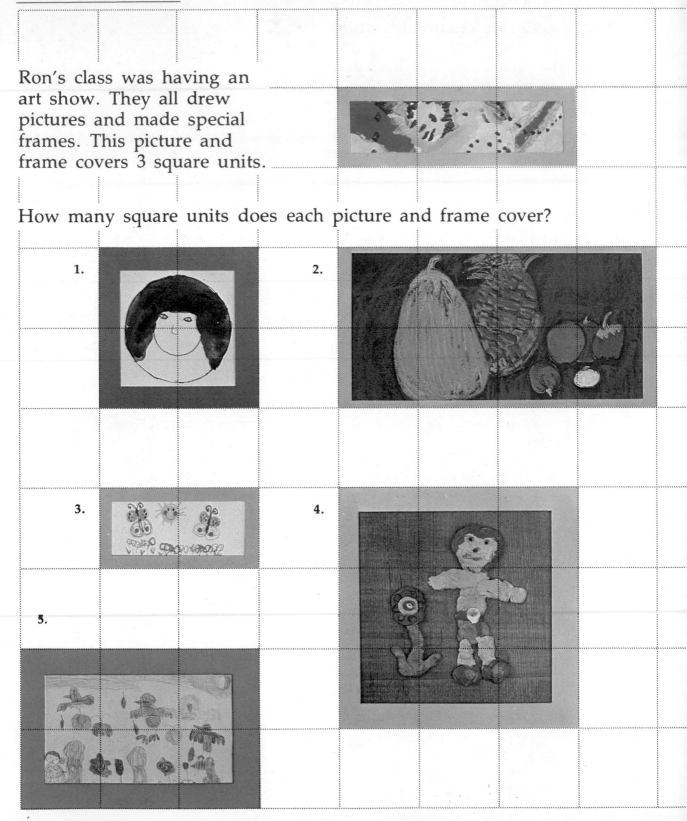

How many square units does each picture and frame cover?

1.

2.

3.

4.

5.

How many square units does each picture and frame cover?

Room 38 Art Show

6.

7.

8.

9.

10.

11.

12.

Area

You can find the **area** of some
regions by counting square units.

unit

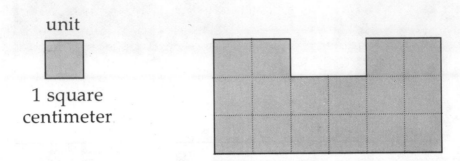

1 square
centimeter

The area is 16 square centimeters.

Find the area of each region in square centimeters.

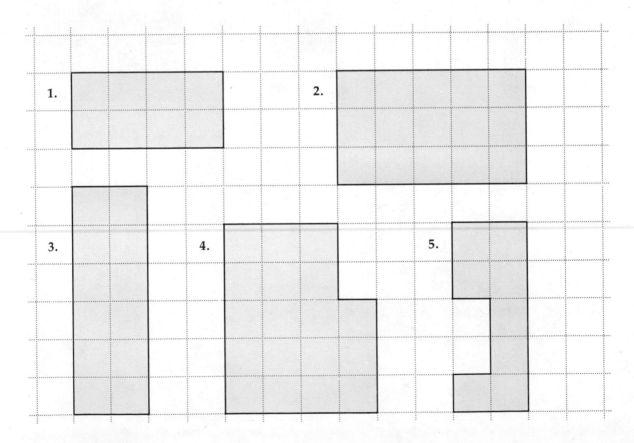

1.

2.

3.

4.

5.

Find the area of each region in square centimeters.

1.

2.

3.

4.

5.

6.

7. Use graph paper.
   Draw regions with
   these areas.

   A 15 square units
   B 12 square units
   C 10 square units
   D 20 square units

The area of
this region
is 9. Draw
a picture of
the unit.

Volume

A cube can be used as the
unit for measuring **volume**.

The box holds 6 cubes.
The volume of the box
is 6 cubic units.

Give the volume of each box.

1.

2.

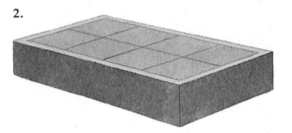

3.

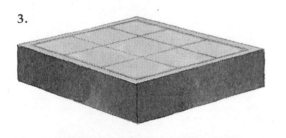

4.

Find the volume of each box.
Give the answer in cubic units.

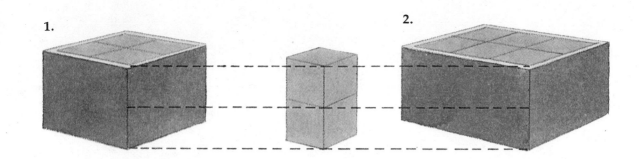

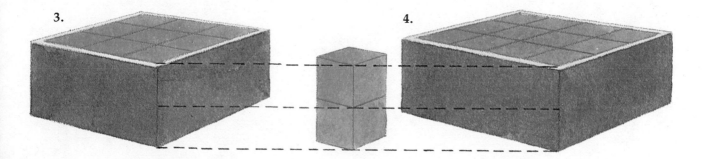

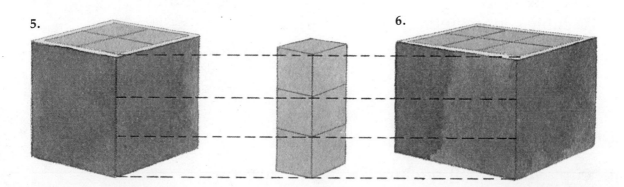

A liter box holds
1000 cubic centimeters.

It also holds 1 liter of water.

1 cubic centimeter

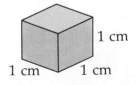

1 cm

1 cm   1 cm

Which of these holds about 1 liter?

1. cup   2. a small pitcher   3. a juice glass

1 liter holds 4 cups.

Answer **more** or **less than** a liter.

1. a water pail

2. a glass of milk

3. a paper cup

4. an aquarium

Choose the correct answer.

5. One half liter is the same as
   A 3 cups   B 2 cups   c 1 cup

6. Three cups is
   A more than 1 liter   B less than 1 liter

7. Six cups is
   A the same as 1 liter   B more than 1 liter

8. One liter is the same as
   A 5 cups   B 4 cups   c 3 cups

Answers for Self-check   1. 10 square units   2. 14 square units   3. 16 cubic units   4. **A**

Self-check

Find the area of each region.

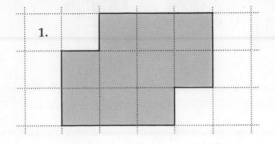

1.

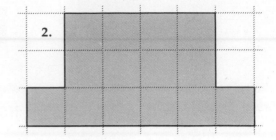

2.

3. Give the volume of the box in cubic units.

4.  4 cups

A is the same as 1 liter
B is more than 1 liter

Answers for Self-check—page 253

Test

Find the area of each region.

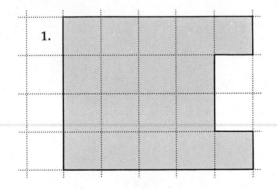

1.

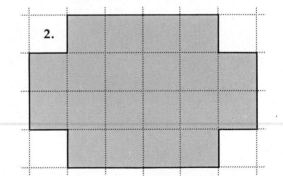

2.

3. Find the volume of the box in cubic units.

4. One half liter is the same as

A 4 cups
B 3 cups
C 2 cups

Outside Area

The cost of painting squares
this size is 2 cents. How
much will it cost to paint
this block of wood? All
the faces are like the
square below.

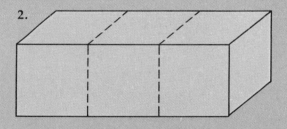

How much will it cost to paint these pieces of wood?
The dashed lines help you count squares.

1.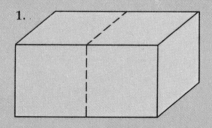

2.

3.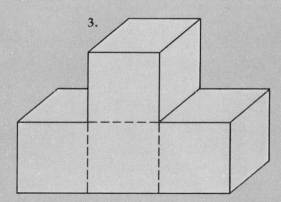

4.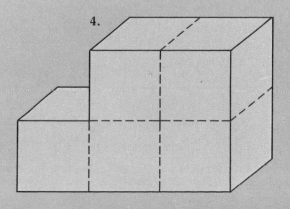

Level 15 review

Solve the equations.

1. $4 \times 10 = \square$
2. $7 \times 100 = \square$
3. $3 \times 10 = \square$

4. $6 \times 100 = \square$
5. $9 \times 10 = \square$
6. $5 \times 100 = \square$

7. $7 \times 20 = \square$
8. $6 \times 30 = \square$
9. $4 \times 90 = \square$

10. $2 \times 60 = \square$
11. $5 \times 40 = \square$
12. $3 \times 80 = \square$

13. $8 \times 70 = \square$
14. $2 \times 30 = \square$
15. $5 \times 90 = \square$

16. $3 \times 200 = \square$
17. $8 \times 400 = \square$
18. $4 \times 600 = \square$

Multiply.

19. $\begin{array}{r} 21 \\ \times\ 4 \\ \hline \end{array}$
20. $\begin{array}{r} 32 \\ \times\ 3 \\ \hline \end{array}$
21. $\begin{array}{r} 41 \\ \times\ 2 \\ \hline \end{array}$
22. $\begin{array}{r} 50 \\ \times\ 5 \\ \hline \end{array}$
23. $\begin{array}{r} 72 \\ \times\ 4 \\ \hline \end{array}$
24. $\begin{array}{r} 61 \\ \times\ 3 \\ \hline \end{array}$

25. $\begin{array}{r} 65 \\ \times\ 3 \\ \hline \end{array}$
26. $\begin{array}{r} 47 \\ \times\ 5 \\ \hline \end{array}$
27. $\begin{array}{r} 35 \\ \times\ 2 \\ \hline \end{array}$
28. $\begin{array}{r} 48 \\ \times\ 4 \\ \hline \end{array}$
29. $\begin{array}{r} 54 \\ \times\ 3 \\ \hline \end{array}$
30. $\begin{array}{r} 98 \\ \times\ 5 \\ \hline \end{array}$

31. $\begin{array}{r} 24 \\ \times\ 5 \\ \hline \end{array}$
32. $\begin{array}{r} 56 \\ \times\ 3 \\ \hline \end{array}$
33. $\begin{array}{r} 27 \\ \times\ 2 \\ \hline \end{array}$
34. $\begin{array}{r} 58 \\ \times\ 4 \\ \hline \end{array}$
35. $\begin{array}{r} 25 \\ \times\ 3 \\ \hline \end{array}$
36. $\begin{array}{r} 84 \\ \times\ 5 \\ \hline \end{array}$

37. $\begin{array}{r} 52 \\ \times\ 7 \\ \hline \end{array}$
38. $\begin{array}{r} 83 \\ \times\ 6 \\ \hline \end{array}$
39. $\begin{array}{r} 72 \\ \times\ 8 \\ \hline \end{array}$
40. $\begin{array}{r} 85 \\ \times\ 9 \\ \hline \end{array}$
41. $\begin{array}{r} 43 \\ \times\ 6 \\ \hline \end{array}$
42. $\begin{array}{r} 64 \\ \times\ 8 \\ \hline \end{array}$

43. Sara bought 2 tablets that cost 52¢ each. How much did she pay? She also bought a box of crayons for 37¢. How much did she pay in all?

44. Don has a 5 dollar bill for a tennis ball that costs $1.09. How much change will he get? Will he have enough money to buy a baseball that costs $3.95?

Fact Family Numbers and Division
Dividing
Problem Solving—Using Your Skills
Fractional Numbers
Decimals
Measurement 3

Fact Family Numbers and Division

Getting started

Choose one of these sets of cards.
Make the cards with a star.
Put the missing factor on the back.

Fact family
numbers with 6

| 6 | 12 | 18 | 24 | 30 | 36* | 42* | 48* | 54* |
| 6 ‖ | 6 ‖‖‖ | 6 ‖‖‖ | 6 ‖‖‖ | 6 ‖‖‖ | 6 ‖‖‖ | 6 ‖‖‖ | 6 ‖‖‖ | 6 ‖‖‖ |

Fact family
numbers with 7

| 7 | 14 | 21 | 28 | 35 | 42* | 49* | 56* | 63* |
| 7 ‖‖‖ | 7 ‖‖‖ | 7 ‖‖‖ | 7 ‖‖‖ | 7 ‖‖‖ | 7 ‖‖‖ | 7 ‖‖‖ | 7 ‖‖‖ | 7 ‖‖‖ |

Fact family
numbers with 8

| 8 | 16 | 24 | 32 | 40 | 48* | 56* | 64* | 72* |
| 8 ‖‖‖ | 8 ‖‖‖ | 8 ‖‖‖ | 8 ‖‖‖ | 8 ‖‖‖ | 8 ‖‖‖ | 8 ‖‖‖ | 8 ‖‖‖ | 8 ‖‖‖ |

Fact family
numbers with 9

| 9 | 18 | 27 | 36 | 45 | 54* | 63* | 72* | 81* |
| 9 ‖‖‖ | 9 ‖‖‖ | 9 ‖‖‖ | 9 ‖‖‖ | 9 ‖‖‖ | 9 ‖‖‖ | 9 ‖‖‖ | 9 ‖‖‖ | 9 ‖‖‖ |

Try to remember the missing factors.
Have a classmate check you.

Thinking about missing factors can help you find quotients.

Give each quotient.

$6 \times 7 = 42$

1. $42 \div 6 = \square$

$8 \times 7 = 56$

2. $56 \div 8 = \square$

$7 \times 7 = 49$

3. $49 \div 7 = \square$

$9 \times 8 = 72$

4. $72 \div 9 = \square$

$6 \times 8 = 48$

5. $48 \div 6 = \square$

$9 \times 6 = 54$

6. $54 \div 9 = \square$

Dividing zero.

Example:

$0 \div 6 = 0$

7. $0 \div 8 = \square$

8. $0 \div 7 = \square$

9. $0 \div 9 = \square$

Dividing by 6

The marker has landed on 48.
What is the score?

Score: Divide by 6.

$$48 \div 6 = 8$$

The quotient 8 is the score.

Think about the missing factors.
Find each one.

Find the quotients.

1. $24 \div 6 = \square$ 2. $36 \div 6 = \square$ 3. $54 \div 6 = \square$ 4. $36 \div 6 = \square$

5. $54 \div 6 = \square$ 6. $18 \div 6 = \square$ 7. $30 \div 6 = \square$ 8. $48 \div 6 = \square$

9. $6 \div 6 = \square$ 10. $42 \div 6 = \square$ 11. $12 \div 6 = \square$ 12. $6 \div 6 = \square$

13. $48 \div 6 = \square$ 14. $0 \div 6 = \square$ 15. $24 \div 6 = \square$ 16. $42 \div 6 = \square$

17. $12 \div 6 = \square$ 18. $30 \div 6 = \square$ 19. $0 \div 6 = \square$ 20. $18 \div 6 = \square$

21. $54 \div 6 = \square$ 22. $48 \div 6 = \square$ 23. $36 \div 6 = \square$ 24. $24 \div 6 = \square$

Dividing by 4, 5, or 6.

1. $20 \div 5 = \square$
2. $48 \div 6 = \square$
3. $18 \div 6 = \square$
4. $15 \div 5 = \square$

5. $36 \div 6 = \square$
6. $40 \div 5 = \square$
7. $54 \div 6 = \square$
8. $0 \div 4 = \square$

9. $12 \div 4 = \square$
10. $4 \div 4 = \square$
11. $16 \div 4 = \square$
12. $42 \div 6 = \square$

13. $6 \div 6 = \square$
14. $12 \div 6 = \square$
15. $45 \div 5 = \square$
16. $35 \div 5 = \square$

17. $30 \div 5 = \square$
18. $24 \div 4 = \square$
19. $30 \div 6 = \square$
20. $8 \div 4 = \square$

Dividing by 1, 2, 3, 4, 5, or 6.

21. $28 \div 4 = \square$
22. $18 \div 3 = \square$
23. $30 \div 5 = \square$
24. $24 \div 3 = \square$

25. $12 \div 2 = \square$
26. $4 \div 1 = \square$
27. $27 \div 3 = \square$
28. $24 \div 6 = \square$

29. $20 \div 4 = \square$
30. $5 \div 5 = \square$
31. $15 \div 3 = \square$
32. $36 \div 4 = \square$

33. $8 \div 1 = \square$
34. $12 \div 3 = \square$
35. $18 \div 2 = \square$
36. $21 \div 3 = \square$

37. $4 \div 4 = \square$
38. $10 \div 2 = \square$
39. $32 \div 4 = \square$
40. $25 \div 5 = \square$

41. Find the score.

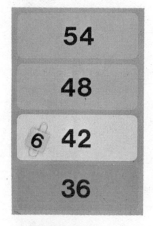

54

48

6 42

36

Divide by 6.

42. Try the divide-by-6 game with a friend. First player with 50 points wins.

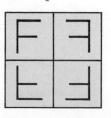

Look at this square.

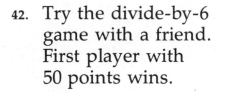

Make one just like it using P.

P | ?
? | ?

Dividing by 7

Gary spent 21 days
at camp.
How many weeks?

$$21 \div 7 = 3$$

Gary spent
3 weeks at camp.

Think about missing factors.
Find each one.

Find the quotients.

1. $35 \div 7 = \square$ 2. $49 \div 7 = \square$ 3. $28 \div 7 = \square$

4. $56 \div 7 = \square$ 5. $14 \div 7 = \square$ 6. $21 \div 7 = \square$

7. $35 \div 7 = \square$ 8. $42 \div 7 = \square$ 9. $56 \div 7 = \square$

10. $63 \div 7 = \square$ 11. $0 \div 7 = \square$

12. $49 \div 7 = \square$ 13. $7 \div 7 = \square$

14. $21 \div 7 = \square$ 15. $14 \div 7 = \square$

16. $42 \div 7 = \square$ 17. $28 \div 7 = \square$

18. $63 \div 7 = \square$ 19. $7 \div 7 = \square$

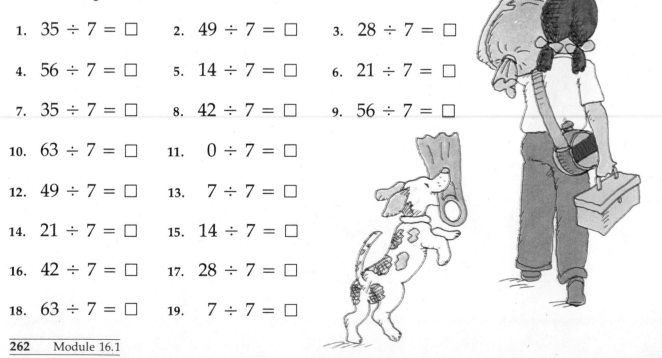

Dividing by 5, 6, or 7

1. $12 \div 6 = \square$ 2. $63 \div 7 = \square$ 3. $30 \div 5 = \square$

4. $28 \div 7 = \square$ 5. $35 \div 7 = \square$ 6. $15 \div 5 = \square$

7. $30 \div 6 = \square$ 8. $14 \div 7 = \square$ 9. $40 \div 5 = \square$

10. $24 \div 6 = \square$ 11. $35 \div 5 = \square$ 12. $18 \div 6 = \square$

13. $21 \div 7 = \square$ 14. $49 \div 7 = \square$ 15. $48 \div 6 = \square$

16. $56 \div 7 = \square$ 17. $25 \div 5 = \square$ 18. $45 \div 5 = \square$

19. $42 \div 7 = \square$ 20. $54 \div 6 = \square$

Dividing by 1, 2, 3, 4, 5, 6, or 7

21. $36 \div 6 = \square$ 22. $28 \div 4 = \square$

23. $40 \div 5 = \square$ 24. $42 \div 7 = \square$ 25. $63 \div 7 = \square$

26. $24 \div 3 = \square$ 27. $27 \div 3 = \square$ 28. $56 \div 7 = \square$ 29. $32 \div 4 = \square$

30. $7 \div 1 = \square$ 31. $45 \div 5 = \square$ 32. $48 \div 6 = \square$ 33. $35 \div 7 = \square$

34. $28 \div 7 = \square$ 35. $18 \div 2 = \square$ 36. $35 \div 5 = \square$ 37. $54 \div 6 = \square$

38. $16 \div 2 = \square$ 39. $42 \div 6 = \square$ 40. $21 \div 3 = \square$ 41. $36 \div 4 = \square$

42. School is out in 35 days. How many weeks?

43. Gail swam every day for 56 days. How many weeks?

If it's products you must find,
You'll think I'm quite a guy.
I don't cause a single change
When I just multiply.

Who am I?

Dividing by 8

Score: divide your number by 8. $56 \div 8 = 7$

Score

Think about missing factors.
Find each one.

8	16	24	32	40	48*	56*	64*	72*
8						8						8						8						8						8						8						8						8					

Find the quotients.

1. $32 \div 8 = \square$ 2. $48 \div 8 = \square$ 3. $40 \div 8 = \square$ 4. $16 \div 8 = \square$

5. $72 \div 8 = \square$ 6. $24 \div 8 = \square$ 7. $16 \div 8 = \square$ 8. $8 \div 8 = \square$

9. $24 \div 8 = \square$ 10. $0 \div 8 = \square$ 11. $56 \div 8 = \square$ 12. $64 \div 8 = \square$

13. $56 \div 8 = \square$ 14. $40 \div 8 = \square$ 15. $32 \div 8 = \square$ 16. $48 \div 8 = \square$

17. $8 \div 8 = \square$ 18. $64 \div 8 = \square$ 19. $72 \div 8 = \square$ 20. $0 \div 8 = \square$

Dividing by 6, 7, or 8

1. $36 \div 6 = \square$
2. $7 \div 7 = \square$
3. $24 \div 8 = \square$
4. $40 \div 8 = \square$

5. $48 \div 8 = \square$
6. $64 \div 8 = \square$
7. $12 \div 6 = \square$
8. $42 \div 6 = \square$

9. $21 \div 7 = \square$
10. $48 \div 6 = \square$
11. $42 \div 7 = \square$
12. $14 \div 7 = \square$

13. $24 \div 6 = \square$
14. $49 \div 7 = \square$
15. $72 \div 8 = \square$
16. $56 \div 8 = \square$

17. $32 \div 8 = \square$
18. $30 \div 6 = \square$
19. $54 \div 6 = \square$
20. $18 \div 6 = \square$

21. $35 \div 7 = \square$
22. $16 \div 8 = \square$
23. $0 \div 7 = \square$
24. $28 \div 7 = \square$

Dividing by 1, 2, 3, 4, 5, 6, 7, or 8

25. $24 \div 3 = \square$
26. $32 \div 4 = \square$
27. $45 \div 5 = \square$
28. $12 \div 3 = \square$

29. $24 \div 4 = \square$
30. $30 \div 5 = \square$
31. $36 \div 4 = \square$
32. $16 \div 8 = \square$

33. $35 \div 5 = \square$
34. $9 \div 1 = \square$
35. $24 \div 8 = \square$
36. $24 \div 6 = \square$

37. $18 \div 2 = \square$
38. $63 \div 7 = \square$
39. $56 \div 7 = \square$
40. $35 \div 7 = \square$

41. $21 \div 3 = \square$
42. $28 \div 4 = \square$
43. $12 \div 6 = \square$
44. $40 \div 5 = \square$

45.

What is the score?
Divide by 8.

☆ 46. Make a spinner and play a divide-by-8 game with a friend. 100 wins!

Think!

How many minutes will it be until the hands form a straight line?

How many minutes will it be until the hands form a square corner?

Dividing by 9

The products 81, 72, 63, 54, 45, 36 are on the faces of the cube.

Score: Divide the top number by 9.

What is the score?

$$63 \div 9 = 7$$

↑
Score

Think about missing factors.
Find each one.

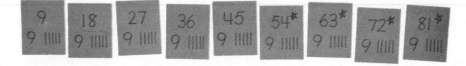

Solve.

1. $5 \times 9 = \square$

   $9 \times 5 = \square$

   $45 \div 9 = \square$

   $45 \div 5 = \square$

2. $3 \times 9 = \square$

   $9 \times 3 = \square$

   $27 \div 9 = \square$

   $27 \div 3 = \square$

3. $8 \times 9 = \square$

   $9 \times 8 = \square$

   $72 \div 9 = \square$

   $72 \div 8 = \square$

4. $6 \times 9 = \square$

   $9 \times 6 = \square$

   $54 \div 9 = \square$

   $54 \div 6 = \square$

5. $4 \times 9 = \square$

   $9 \times 4 = \square$

   $36 \div 9 = \square$

   $36 \div 4 = \square$

6. $2 \times 9 = \square$

   $9 \times 2 = \square$

   $18 \div 9 = \square$

   $18 \div 2 = \square$

7. $7 \times 9 = \square$

   $9 \times 7 = \square$

   $63 \div 7 = \square$

   $63 \div 9 = \square$

8. $1 \times 9 = \square$

   $9 \times 1 = \square$

   $9 \div 9 = \square$

   $9 \div 1 = \square$

More practice, page 336, Set B; page 338A

Dividing by 1, 2, 3, 4, 5, or 6

1. $24 \div 4 = \square$ 2. $30 \div 5 = \square$ 3. $45 \div 5 = \square$ 4. $25 \div 5 = \square$

5. $18 \div 3 = \square$ 6. $48 \div 6 = \square$ 7. $18 \div 6 = \square$ 8. $16 \div 2 = \square$

9. $36 \div 6 = \square$ 10. $16 \div 4 = \square$ 11. $4 \div 1 = \square$ 12. $20 \div 4 = \square$

13. $40 \div 5 = \square$ 14. $24 \div 6 = \square$ 15. $54 \div 6 = \square$ 16. $42 \div 6 = \square$

Dividing by 7, 8, or 9

17. $32 \div 8 = \square$ 18. $8 \div 8 = \square$ 19. $14 \div 7 = \square$ 20. $27 \div 9 = \square$

21. $56 \div 7 = \square$ 22. $24 \div 8 = \square$ 23. $16 \div 8 = \square$ 24. $81 \div 9 = \square$

25. $21 \div 7 = \square$ 26. $18 \div 9 = \square$ 27. $28 \div 7 = \square$ 28. $48 \div 8 = \square$

29. $35 \div 7 = \square$ 30. $36 \div 9 = \square$ 31. $63 \div 7 = \square$ 32. $40 \div 8 = \square$

Dividing by 1, 2, 3, 4, 5, 6, 7, 8, or 9

33. $9\overline{)45}$ 34. $4\overline{)28}$ 35. $7\overline{)49}$ 36. $6\overline{)48}$

37. $5\overline{)30}$ 38. $2\overline{)16}$ 39. $9\overline{)72}$ 40. $9\overline{)63}$

41. $1\overline{)5}$ 42. $5\overline{)35}$ 43. $8\overline{)72}$ 44. $7\overline{)42}$

45. $6\overline{)54}$ 46. $3\overline{)24}$ 47. $8\overline{)64}$ 48. $6\overline{)42}$

49. $8\overline{)56}$ 50. $9\overline{)54}$ 51. $5\overline{)40}$ 52. $7\overline{)63}$

Think!

Which is more?

$1.00 for a week
or
1¢ the first day,
2¢ the second,
4¢ the third, and
so on for a week.

Guess first; then
work it out.

Answers for Self-check   1. 5   2. 5   3. 7   4. 5   5. 4   6. 0   7. 3   8. 2   9. 2   10. 1   11. 3   12. 6
13. 7   14. 9   15. 8   16. 1   17. 4   18. 2   19. 4   20. 9   21. 6   22. 3   23. 0   24. 8   25. 6   26. 3   27. 6
28. 1

More practice, page 336, Set B

Self-check

Find the quotients.

1. $35 \div 7 = \square$ 2. $45 \div 9 = \square$ 3. $49 \div 7 = \square$ 4. $40 \div 8 = \square$

5. $24 \div 6 = \square$ 6. $0 \div 9 = \square$ 7. $27 \div 9 = \square$ 8. $16 \div 8 = \square$

9. $18 \div 9 = \square$ 10. $7 \div 7 = \square$ 11. $18 \div 6 = \square$ 12. $36 \div 6 = \square$

13. $8 \overline{)56}$ 14. $8 \overline{)72}$ 15. $7 \overline{)56}$ 16. $8 \overline{)8}$

17. $7 \overline{)28}$ 18. $6 \overline{)12}$ 19. $9 \overline{)36}$ 20. $9 \overline{)81}$

21. $9 \overline{)54}$ 22. $8 \overline{)24}$ 23. $6 \overline{)0}$ 24. $9 \overline{)72}$

25. $6 \overline{)36}$ 26. $7 \overline{)21}$ 27. $8 \overline{)48}$ 28. $7 \overline{)7}$

Answers for Self-check—page 267

Test

Find the quotients.

1. $49 \div 7 = \square$ 2. $35 \div 7 = \square$ 3. $72 \div 9 = \square$ 4. $8 \div 8 = \square$

5. $36 \div 6 = \square$ 6. $64 \div 8 = \square$ 7. $40 \div 8 = \square$ 8. $0 \div 9 = \square$

9. $63 \div 7 = \square$ 10. $30 \div 6 = \square$ 11. $36 \div 9 = \square$ 12. $72 \div 8 = \square$

13. $8 \overline{)32}$ 14. $7 \overline{)56}$ 15. $8 \overline{)48}$ 16. $9 \overline{)63}$

17. $7 \overline{)42}$ 18. $6 \overline{)54}$ 19. $6 \overline{)6}$ 20. $7 \overline{)28}$

21. $6 \overline{)30}$ 22. $9 \overline{)9}$ 23. $9 \overline{)81}$ 24. $8 \overline{)24}$

25. $9 \overline{)45}$ 26. $8 \overline{)16}$ 27. $7 \overline{)0}$ 28. $6 \overline{)42}$

Hidden Number Names

How many number names can you find?

Read: across ⟶

      down ↓

      diagonally ↘

Ten has been ringed to help you start.

Z	U	H	T	W	O	N	C
A	C	T	H	R	E	E	Q
F	I	V	E	M	Y	S	P
B	O	Z	S	N	A	R	L
G	N	Q	E	I	G	H	T
S	E	V	E	N	X	S	L
S	I	T	R	E	M	Q	O
F	O	U	R	L	V	X	D

Dividing

Getting started

How many triangles can be made with 48 straws?

How many threes in 48?
Fred subtracted 1 three each time.

48 − 3 45	45 − 3 42	42 − 3 39	39 − 3 36	36 − 3 33	33 − 3 30
30 − 3 27	27 − 3 24	24 − 3 21	21 − 3 18	18 − 3 15	15 − 3 12
12 − 3 9	9 − 3 6	6 − 3 3	3 − 3 0		

Jerry subtracted
4 threes at a time.

```
  48
−12  ← 4 threes
  36
−12  ← 4 threes
  24
−12  ← 4 threes
  12
−12  ← 4 threes
   0
```

Maria subtracted
10 threes first.

```
  48
−30  ← 10 threes
  18
−12  ← 4 threes
   6
− 6  ← 2 threes
   0
```

How many threes did each child find in 48?

Now find how many fives there are in 70.

Dividing: 1-digit quotients

31 pictures
4 on a page

How many pages
can Sandy fill?

Finding the answer

How many can be subtracted?	→	Multiply	→	Subtract

$$
\begin{array}{r} \\ 4\overline{)31} \end{array}
\qquad
\begin{array}{r} 7 \\ 4\overline{)31} \\ 28 \end{array}
\qquad
\text{divisor}\rightarrow
\begin{array}{r} 7 \leftarrow\text{quotient} \\ 4\overline{)31} \\ 28 \leftarrow \boxed{7 \text{ fours}} \\ 3 \leftarrow\text{remainder} \end{array}
$$

Sandy can fill 7 pages with 3 pictures left over.

Other examples

$$
\begin{array}{r} 4\,R1 \\ 5\overline{)21} \\ 20 \\ \hline 1 \end{array}
\qquad
\begin{array}{r} 8 \\ 3\overline{)24} \\ 24 \\ \hline 0 \end{array}
\qquad
\begin{array}{r} 8\,R2 \\ 4\overline{)34} \\ 32 \\ \hline 2 \end{array}
$$

Find the quotients and remainders.

1. $3\overline{)17}$ 2. $4\overline{)30}$ 3. $4\overline{)20}$ 4. $5\overline{)32}$

5. $2\overline{)16}$ 6. $3\overline{)25}$ 7. $5\overline{)49}$ 8. $2\overline{)15}$

Find the quotients and remainders.

1. $3\overline{)16}$ 2. $4\overline{)18}$ 3. $2\overline{)11}$ 4. $5\overline{)44}$ 5. $3\overline{)28}$

6. $4\overline{)24}$ 7. $2\overline{)17}$ 8. $3\overline{)14}$ 9. $5\overline{)23}$ 10. $4\overline{)32}$

11. $2\overline{)12}$ 12. $4\overline{)13}$ 13. $3\overline{)19}$ 14. $2\overline{)7}$ 15. $5\overline{)47}$

16. $4\overline{)36}$ 17. $2\overline{)8}$ 18. $5\overline{)27}$ 19. $3\overline{)20}$ 20. $5\overline{)34}$

21. $3\overline{)11}$ 22. $5\overline{)35}$ 23. $4\overline{)26}$ 24. $3\overline{)22}$ 25. $4\overline{)23}$

☆ 26. $8\overline{)47}$ ☆ 27. $7\overline{)53}$ ☆ 28. $9\overline{)60}$

☆ 29. $6\overline{)50}$ ☆ 30. $7\overline{)68}$ ☆ 31. $9\overline{)75}$

32. 33 pictures
5 on a page
How many
full pages?

33. 50 pictures
8 on a page
How many
full pages?

Think !

1. Pick a number.   ?
2. Add 4.   + 4
3. Multiply by 2.   × 2
4. Subtract 6.   − 6
5. Divide by 2.   ÷ 2
6. Subtract the number
   you started with.   − ?

Do you think you will
always end with 1?
Try this several times.

⊛ Dividing: 2-digit quotients

Carlos cut out 85 squares.
His strip is 5 squares wide.
How many squares long is it?

Finding the answer

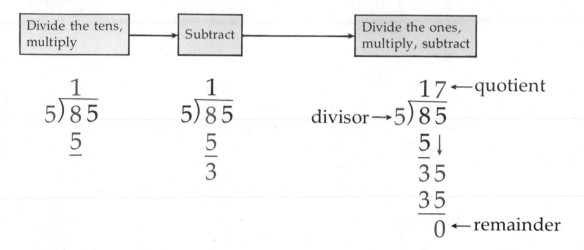

| Divide the tens, multiply | → | Subtract | → | Divide the ones, multiply, subtract |

$$\begin{array}{r} 1 \\ 5\overline{)85} \\ \underline{5} \end{array}$$

$$\begin{array}{r} 1 \\ 5\overline{)85} \\ \underline{5} \\ 3 \end{array}$$

divisor →
$$\begin{array}{r} 17 \leftarrow \text{quotient}\\ 5\overline{)85} \\ \underline{5}\!\downarrow \\ 35 \\ \underline{35} \\ 0 \leftarrow \text{remainder} \end{array}$$

The strip is 17 squares long.

Other examples

$$\begin{array}{r} 24\,\text{R2} \\ 3\overline{)74} \\ \underline{6} \\ 14 \\ \underline{12} \\ 2 \end{array}$$
$$\begin{array}{r} 45 \\ 2\overline{)90} \\ \underline{8} \\ 10 \\ \underline{10} \\ 0 \end{array}$$
$$\begin{array}{r} 21 \\ 4\overline{)84} \\ \underline{8} \\ 4 \\ \underline{4} \\ 0 \end{array}$$

Find the quotients and remainders.

1. $3\overline{)45}$ 2. $2\overline{)75}$ 3. $4\overline{)64}$ 4. $3\overline{)96}$ 5. $5\overline{)78}$

Find the quotients and remainders.

1. $3 \overline{)73}$ 2. $2 \overline{)57}$ 3. $5 \overline{)65}$ 4. $4 \overline{)50}$ 5. $3 \overline{)97}$

6. $5 \overline{)99}$ 7. $3 \overline{)49}$ 8. $2 \overline{)68}$ 9. $4 \overline{)63}$ 10. $5 \overline{)81}$

11. $2 \overline{)93}$ 12. $3 \overline{)74}$ 13. $4 \overline{)44}$ 14. $2 \overline{)63}$ 15. $5 \overline{)57}$

16. $3 \overline{)69}$ 17. $4 \overline{)70}$ 18. $2 \overline{)55}$ 19. $5 \overline{)93}$ 20. $4 \overline{)55}$

☆ 21. $7 \overline{)87}$ ☆ 22. $8 \overline{)96}$ ☆ 23. $6 \overline{)94}$ ☆ 24. $7 \overline{)99}$

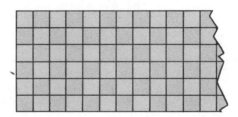

☆ 25. 6 squares wide
90 squares in all
How many
squares long?

☆ 26. Cut a strip from graph
paper so that it has
exactly 96 squares.

Study the first four equations.
Then solve the last one.
Can you check it?

$(1 \times 9) + 2 = 11$
$(12 \times 9) + 3 = 111$
$(123 \times 9) + 4 = 1111$
$(1234 \times 9) + 5 = 11\ 111$
$(12\ 345 \times 9) + 6 = \square$

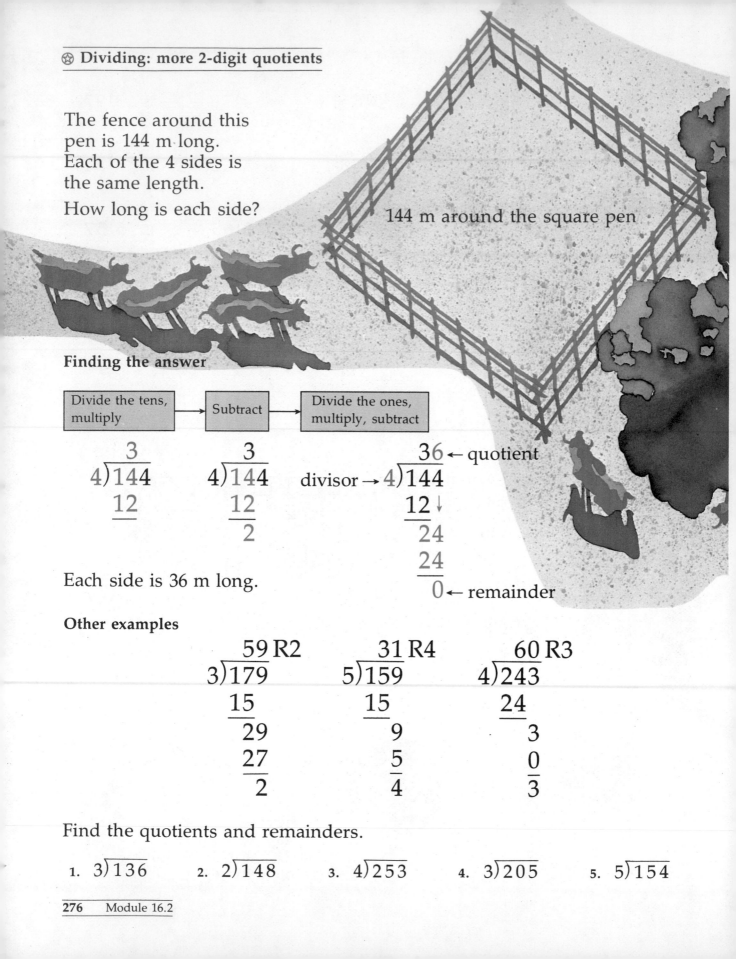

✦ Dividing: more 2-digit quotients

The fence around this
pen is 144 m long.
Each of the 4 sides is
the same length.

How long is each side?

144 m around the square pen

Finding the answer

Divide the tens, multiply	→	Subtract	→	Divide the ones, multiply, subtract

$$
\begin{array}{r}
3 \\
4)\overline{144} \\
12 \\
\end{array}
\qquad
\begin{array}{r}
3 \\
4)\overline{144} \\
12 \\
\hline
2 \\
\end{array}
\qquad
\text{divisor} \rightarrow
\begin{array}{r}
36 \leftarrow \text{quotient} \\
4)\overline{144} \\
12 \downarrow \\
\hline
24 \\
24 \\
\hline
0 \leftarrow \text{remainder}
\end{array}
$$

Each side is 36 m long.

Other examples

$$
\begin{array}{r}
59\,R2 \\
3)\overline{179} \\
15 \\
\hline
29 \\
27 \\
\hline
2 \\
\end{array}
\qquad
\begin{array}{r}
31\,R4 \\
5)\overline{159} \\
15 \\
\hline
9 \\
5 \\
\hline
4 \\
\end{array}
\qquad
\begin{array}{r}
60\,R3 \\
4)\overline{243} \\
24 \\
\hline
3 \\
0 \\
\hline
3 \\
\end{array}
$$

Find the quotients and remainders.

1. $3)\overline{136}$
2. $2)\overline{148}$
3. $4)\overline{253}$
4. $3)\overline{205}$
5. $5)\overline{154}$

Find the quotients and remainders.

1. $4\overline{)257}$ 2. $2\overline{)135}$ 3. $3\overline{)262}$ 4. $5\overline{)132}$ 5. $4\overline{)228}$

6. $5\overline{)416}$ 7. $3\overline{)203}$ 8. $4\overline{)275}$ 9. $2\overline{)128}$ 10. $3\overline{)168}$

11. $2\overline{)151}$ 12. $3\overline{)212}$ 13. $5\overline{)180}$ 14. $4\overline{)240}$ 15. $2\overline{)192}$

16. $2\overline{)199}$ 17. $5\overline{)376}$ 18. $4\overline{)222}$ 19. $5\overline{)304}$ 20. $3\overline{)234}$

☆ 21. $8\overline{)643}$ ☆ 22. $6\overline{)275}$ ☆ 23. $7\overline{)614}$ ☆ 24. $9\overline{)476}$ ☆ 25. $8\overline{)521}$

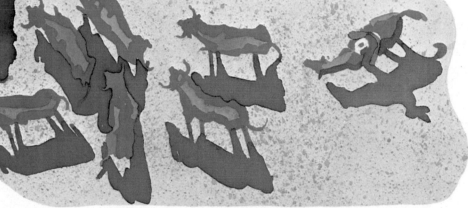

26. All sides are the same length. How long is each side?

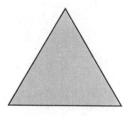

3 sides
138 m around

27. How long is each side of the square?

4 sides
236 m around

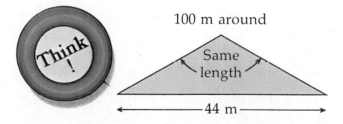

100 m around

Same length

44 m

How long are the two short sides?

⊛ Checking division

161 cookies

3 on each plate

How many plates?

How many cookies left over?

There were 53 plates and 2 cookies left over.

Jack wanted to check to see
if his answer was correct.

Finding the answer

Multiply the quotient by the divisor	→	Add the remainder to the product	→	The answer should be the number divided

$$\begin{array}{r} 53 \\ \times\ 3 \\ \hline 159 \end{array} \qquad \begin{array}{r} 53 \\ \times\ 3 \\ \hline 159 \\ +\ 2 \\ \hline 161 \end{array} \qquad 3\overline{)161}$$

same

161 matches the number divided.

Other examples

$$\begin{array}{r} 64\,R2 \\ 4\overline{)258} \\ 24 \\ \hline 18 \\ 16 \\ \hline 2 \end{array} \quad \begin{array}{r} \text{Check} \\ 64 \\ \times\ 4 \\ \hline 256 \\ +\ 2 \\ \hline 258 \end{array} \quad \begin{array}{r} 71 \\ 3\overline{)213} \\ 21 \\ \hline 3 \\ 3 \\ \hline 0 \end{array} \quad \begin{array}{r} \text{Check} \\ 71 \\ \times\ 3 \\ \hline 213 \end{array}$$

Check each of these. One of them is wrong.

1. $3\overline{)76}$ 25 R1

2. $4\overline{)138}$ 34 R2

3. $5\overline{)265}$ 53

4. $3\overline{)261}$ 87 R2

Check each of these. Which ones are correct?

1.
$$
\begin{array}{r}
49 \\
3\overline{)147} \\
12 \\
\hline
27 \\
27 \\
\hline
0
\end{array}
$$

2.
$$
\begin{array}{r}
65\,R3 \\
5\overline{)328} \\
30 \\
\hline
28 \\
25 \\
\hline
3
\end{array}
$$

3.
$$
\begin{array}{r}
64\,R3 \\
4\overline{)259} \\
24 \\
\hline
19 \\
16 \\
\hline
3
\end{array}
$$

4.
$$
\begin{array}{r}
71 \\
2\overline{)147} \\
14 \\
\hline
7 \\
7 \\
\hline
0
\end{array}
$$

5.
$$
\begin{array}{r}
12\,R1 \\
4\overline{)59} \\
4 \\
\hline
9 \\
8 \\
\hline
1
\end{array}
$$

6.
$$
\begin{array}{r}
67 \\
2\overline{)134} \\
12 \\
\hline
14 \\
14 \\
\hline
0
\end{array}
$$

7.
$$
\begin{array}{r}
75\,R4 \\
5\overline{)389} \\
35 \\
\hline
29 \\
25 \\
\hline
4
\end{array}
$$

8.
$$
\begin{array}{r}
69 \\
3\overline{)207} \\
18 \\
\hline
27 \\
27 \\
\hline
0
\end{array}
$$

Find the quotients and remainders. Check your work.

9. $5\overline{)275}$ 10. $3\overline{)164}$ 11. $2\overline{)93}$ 12. $4\overline{)276}$

13. $5\overline{)428}$ 14. $3\overline{)198}$ 15. $2\overline{)75}$ 16. $4\overline{)295}$

17. A large can holds 130 plums. How many bowls are needed to serve 4 plums in a bowl?

18. A box holds 105 apples. How many bags are needed if each bag holds 5 apples?

Think!

Study the pattern. Then copy the equations, giving the missing numbers.

$1 \times 9 = 10 - 1$
$2 \times 9 = 20 - 2$
$3 \times 9 = 30 - 3$
$4 \times 9 = 40 - 4$
$5 \times 9 = \text{▥} - \text{▥}$
$8 \times 9 = \text{▥} - \text{▥}$
$13 \times 9 = \text{▥} - \text{▥}$

Answers for Self-check   1. 5 R3   2. 4 R2   3. 7 R2   4. 6 R2   5. 9 R1   6. 15 R1   7. 23   8. 20   9. 49
10. 13 R2   11. 80 R2   12. 62 R1   13. 70 R3   14. 85 R1   15. 62 R3

Self-check

Find the quotients and remainders.

1. $4\overline{)23}$ 2. $3\overline{)14}$ 3. $5\overline{)37}$ 4. $4\overline{)26}$ 5. $3\overline{)28}$

6. $5\overline{)76}$ 7. $4\overline{)92}$ 8. $3\overline{)60}$ 9. $2\overline{)98}$ 10. $5\overline{)67}$

11. $3\overline{)242}$ 12. $4\overline{)249}$ 13. $5\overline{)353}$ 14. $2\overline{)171}$ 15. $4\overline{)251}$

Answers for Self-check—page 279

Test

Find the quotients and remainders.

1. $3\overline{)20}$ 2. $5\overline{)24}$ 3. $4\overline{)26}$ 4. $4\overline{)23}$ 5. $5\overline{)49}$

6. $3\overline{)44}$ 7. $2\overline{)75}$ 8. $5\overline{)60}$ 9. $4\overline{)81}$ 10. $3\overline{)72}$

11. $2\overline{)135}$ 12. $4\overline{)270}$ 13. $5\overline{)363}$ 14. $3\overline{)127}$ 15. $2\overline{)156}$

Finding the Pattern

The last card in each row is turned down.
Can you tell what number is hidden?

Example:

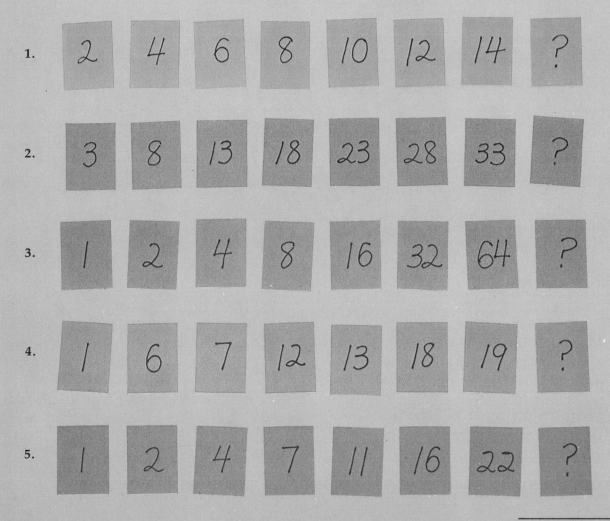

1. 2 4 6 8 10 12 14 ?

2. 3 8 13 18 23 28 33 ?

3. 1 2 4 8 16 32 64 ?

4. 1 6 7 12 13 18 19 ?

5. 1 2 4 7 11 16 22 ?

Using Your Skills

Getting started

1. How many grams would there be in each of 8 equal servings of the corn flakes?

2. How many grams are there of the nature cereal and the wheat flakes together?

3. What other problems can you solve?

Solving Problems

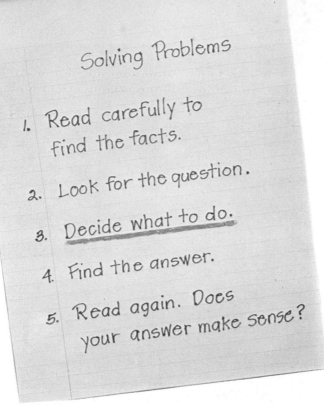

1. Read carefully to find the facts.

2. Look for the question.

3. Decide what to do.

4. Find the answer.

5. Read again. Does your answer make sense?

A large box holds 350 g.
A smaller box holds 175 g less.
How many grams are there
in the smaller box?
How many grams will there be
in each of 7 equal servings from
the smaller box?

$$350 \text{ g} - 175 \text{ g} = 175 \text{ g}$$

```
     25 g
  7)175
    14
    ‾‾
     35
     35
     ‾‾
      0
```

There are 175 g in the
smaller box.
There will be 25 g in
each of 7 equal servings.

Solve these problems.

1. The Brown family has taken
   4 equal servings of bran
   flakes. Each was a 35 g
   serving. How many grams
   of bran flakes did they
   use? How many grams of
   bran flakes are left in
   the 335 g package?

2. Joey eats a 240 g box of corn
   flakes in 6 days. How much
   does he eat each day?
   Anna eats 38 g of corn flakes
   each day. How much more
   does Joey eat than Anna?

Animals, trees, birds, and insects grow old. You'll find some of their ages in these problems.

1. An old cat: 15 years old
   An old turtle: 10 times as old
   How old is an old turtle?

2. An old rabbit: 6 years old
   An old goose: 11 times as old
   How old is an old goose?

3. An old bear: 35 years old
   An old camel: 28 years old
   How much older is an old bear than an old camel?

5. A spruce tree: 243 years old now
   Lives 339 more years.
   How old then?

4. An old reindeer: 12 years old
   An old whale: 6 times as old
   How old is an old whale?

6. An old eagle: 46 years old
   An old elm tree: 7 times as old
   How old is an old elm tree?

7. An old elephant: 61 years old
   An old cow: 24 years old
   How much older is an old elephant than an old cow?

8. An old butterfly: 56 days old
   An old housefly: 42 days old
   How many days older is the old butterfly?

1. 60 minutes in 1 hour
   How many minutes in 8 hours?
   How many minutes in 8 hours
   and 35 minutes?

2. 28 brown chairs
   47 tan chairs
   How many chairs?
   Placed them in 5 equal rows.
   How many in each row?

3. 12 pages of Indian head pennies
   9 on a page
   How many pennies?
   Put 15 more pennies in the book.
   How many pennies in all?

4. Bought eight 13¢ stamps.
   Cost how much?
   Then bought nine 20¢ stamps.
   Cost how much in all?

5. Total trip: 835 km
   Drove 182 km on Friday.
   How far yet to go?
   Drove 496 km on Saturday.
   How far to go now?

6. Had 39 pictures.
   Gave away 3.
   How many left?
   Put 4 on each page
   of a picture book.
   How many pages
   are needed?

7. Bought 7 peaches
   at 12¢ each. How much?
   Also bought 9 pears
   at 16¢ each. How much
   for the peaches and
   pears together?

Bicycles

On the first bicycle, the pedals were near the front wheel. Some early bicycles had a large front wheel and a small back wheel. The wheels on most bicycles today are the same size. Try some of these problems about bicycles.

1. First bicycle with pedals: 1839
   The word "bicycle": 26 years later
   When was that?

2. First bicycle with pedals: 1839
   First modern bicycle: 1893
   How many years apart?

3. Bicycle without pedals: 1816
   Bicycle with pedals: 1839
   How many years apart?

4. Some old bicycles:
Back wheel: 29 cm high
Front wheel: 5 times that high
How high was the front wheel?

5. Bicycle length:
Many bicycles: about 150 cm long
Longest bicycle: 10 times that long
How long was the longest bicycle?

6. Front wheels:
New bicycle: 67 cm high
Old bicycle: 83 cm higher
How high was the
old bicycle wheel?

7. United States road race: 80 km
Road race in Canada: 274 km
How much farther is the race in Canada?

☆ 8. Riding fast:
New bicycle: 140 km in 4 hours
How many kilometers in 1 hour?
Early bicycle: 12 km in 1 hour
How many more kilometers in
1 hour for the new bicycle?

Practicing your skills

Add.

1. 217
    + 938

2. 363
    + 496

3. 357
    + 247

4. 852
    + 265

5. 193
    + 831

6. 421
    387
    + 535

7. 274
    529
    + 412

8. 928
    215
    + 504

9. 279
    328
    + 397

10. 457
    658
    + 260

11. 688
    816
    + 467

12. 395
    774
    + 876

13. 469
    816
    + 925

14. 146
    119
    + 684

15. 861
    942
    + 574

Find the total amounts.

16. $ 1.21
    + 2.35

17. $ 4.85
    + 3.46

18. $ 2.04
    + 0.59

19. $ 3.99
    + 8.00

20. $ 5.46
    + 6.07

21. $ 11.68
    1.15
    + 12.45

22. $ 3.49
    5.01
    + 8.56

23. $ 18.42
    7.51
    + 12.73

24. $ 7.80
    0.96
    + 3.21

25. $ 2.53
    4.10
    + 7.09

Subtract.

26. 714
    − 356

27. 115
    − 86

28. 709
    − 24

29. 831
    − 605

30. 762
    − 413

31. 540
    − 325

32. 461
    − 293

33. 802
    − 453

34. 795
    − 680

35. 628
    − 379

Find the differences in the amounts.

1. $ 8.52
  − 6.47

2. $ 6.15
  − 3.47

3. $ 4.20
  − 1.98

4. $ 7.11
  − 2.34

5. $ 5.09
  − 2.14

6. $ 7.65
  − 2.78

7. $ 9.31
  − 7.63

8. $ 8.42
  − 6.50

9. $ 6.79
  − 3.99

10. $ 9.08
  − 8.75

Multiply.

11. $\begin{array}{r} 47 \\ \times\ 4 \end{array}$

12. $\begin{array}{r} 29 \\ \times\ 3 \end{array}$

13. $\begin{array}{r} 13 \\ \times\ 5 \end{array}$

14. $\begin{array}{r} 52 \\ \times\ 4 \end{array}$

15. $\begin{array}{r} 67 \\ \times\ 5 \end{array}$

16. $\begin{array}{r} 88 \\ \times\ 4 \end{array}$

17. $\begin{array}{r} 31 \\ \times\ 3 \end{array}$

18. $\begin{array}{r} 54 \\ \times\ 5 \end{array}$

19. $\begin{array}{r} 69 \\ \times\ 4 \end{array}$

20. $\begin{array}{r} 74 \\ \times\ 3 \end{array}$

21. $\begin{array}{r} 51 \\ \times\ 7 \end{array}$

22. $\begin{array}{r} 46 \\ \times\ 8 \end{array}$

23. $\begin{array}{r} 38 \\ \times\ 7 \end{array}$

24. $\begin{array}{r} 75 \\ \times\ 9 \end{array}$

25. $\begin{array}{r} 92 \\ \times\ 6 \end{array}$

Divide.

26. $4\overline{)25}$

27. $3\overline{)19}$

☆ 28. $5\overline{)60}$

☆ 29. $2\overline{)48}$

☆ 30. $3\overline{)43}$

☆ 31. $2\overline{)104}$

☆ 32. $5\overline{)258}$

☆ 33. $4\overline{)316}$

☆ 34. $3\overline{)215}$

☆ 35. $5\overline{)462}$

Jim and Ida together have a mass of 41 kg.
Jim, Ida, and Jeff together have a mass of 67 kg.
What is Jeff's mass?

Maybe you like to watch T.V. Many
people are needed to bring you the
shows you like best. The pictures
below show just a few T.V. jobs.
These are the people you do not see
when you watch T.V.

1. The first part of a T.V.
   circus show takes
   28 minutes. The second
   part takes 27 minutes.
   How many minutes in all?

2. A movie was 108 minutes
   long. It was shown on T.V.
   in 4 equal parts. How long
   was each part?

3. A T.V. news show was on
   for 26 minutes each night.
   It was on 5 nights a week.
   What was the total number of
   minutes it showed in a week?

4. One game show played for
   25 minutes. Another played
   for 26 minutes. Ads for soap
   were on for 7 minutes. How
   many minutes was this in all?

5. A T.V. worker had a board 230 cm long. The board was cut to be 87 cm shorter. How long was the board after the cut?

6. Another T.V. worker wrote at a desk for 7 hours. He made $84. How much did he make in 1 hour?

7. A camera person worked 23 days in May. She worked 8 hours each day. How many hours in May did she work?

☆ 8. A T.V. star came to get ready for a show at 2:07 p.m. The show started at 2:30 p.m. How much time did the star have to get ready?

☆ 9. A nearby T.V. station is on for 18 hours a day, 7 days a week. How many hours is it on in a week? In 2 weeks?

Answers for Self-check   1. 90   2. 118   3. 54   4. 124; 31

1. An old cat: 15 years old
   An old man: 6 times as old
   How old is the old man?

2. Sports show: 109 minutes
   Ads for cars: 9 minutes
   How many minutes in all?

3. Gary had 270 marbles and
   5 bags. He put the same
   number of marbles in
   each bag. How many
   marbles did he put
   in each bag?

4. A country school has 56 girls
   and 68 boys. How many
   children is this? There are
   4 classes of equal size. How
   many children are in each class?

Answers for Self-check—page 291

⊛ Test

1. 92 pictures
   4 on a page
   How many pages?

2. Game show:
   28 minutes each day
   5 days a week
   How many minutes a week?

3. Jill rode 39 km in 3 hours.
   About how many kilometers
   did she ride each hour?

4. Room 12 has 35 children.
   Room 14 has 29 children.
   How many children in all?
   When they go on a field
   trip, 4 children fit in a car.
   How many cars are needed?

How Many Squares?

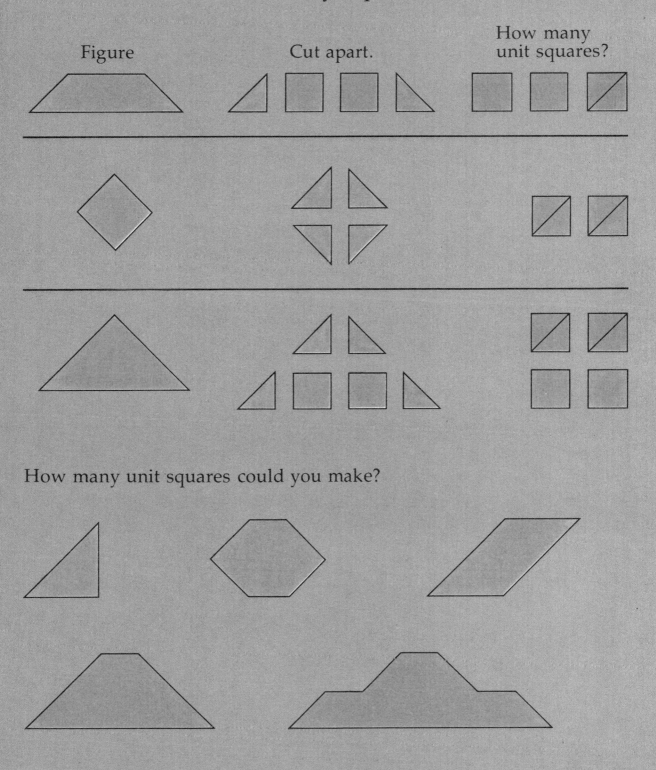

Figure	Cut apart.	How many unit squares?

How many unit squares could you make?

Fractional Numbers

Getting started

Share the food equally.

Trace the outline of each picture. Show on your paper how they would share the food.

Give the missing numbers.

We see:	We think:	We write:	We say:
	Each piece is 1 of 2 equal parts.	$\frac{1}{2}$	one half
	Each piece is 1 of ‖‖ equal parts.	$\frac{1}{3}$	one third
	Each piece is 1 of ‖‖ equal parts.	$\frac{1}{‖‖}$	one fourth
	Each piece is 1 of ‖‖ equal parts.	$\frac{1}{‖‖}$	one tenth

Parts of a whole

Larry and his friends ate 3 pieces of a pie.

What part of a pie did they eat?

pieces eaten 3

pieces in all 4

fraction $\frac{3}{4}$

three fourths

They ate $\frac{3}{4}$ (three fourths) of a pie.

Choose the fraction for the lighter piece.
The folds show equal parts.

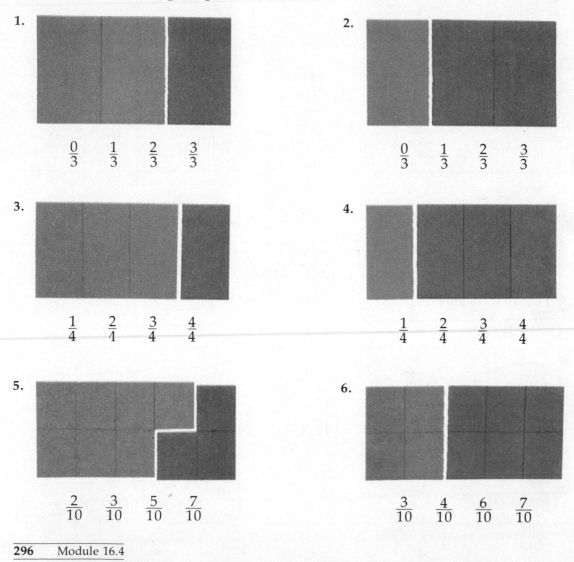

1.

$\frac{0}{3}$ $\frac{1}{3}$ $\frac{2}{3}$ $\frac{3}{3}$

2.

$\frac{0}{3}$ $\frac{1}{3}$ $\frac{2}{3}$ $\frac{3}{3}$

3.

$\frac{1}{4}$ $\frac{2}{4}$ $\frac{3}{4}$ $\frac{4}{4}$

4.

$\frac{1}{4}$ $\frac{2}{4}$ $\frac{3}{4}$ $\frac{4}{4}$

5.

$\frac{2}{10}$ $\frac{3}{10}$ $\frac{5}{10}$ $\frac{7}{10}$

6.

$\frac{3}{10}$ $\frac{4}{10}$ $\frac{6}{10}$ $\frac{7}{10}$

Give a fraction for each part.

1.

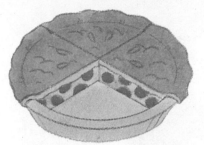

What part is missing?

2.

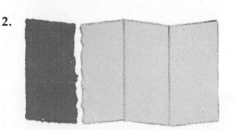

What part is red?

3.

What part is broken?

4.

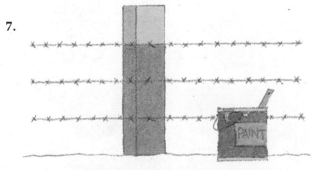

What part has not been sliced?

5.

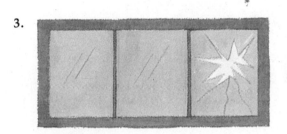

What part is missing?

6.

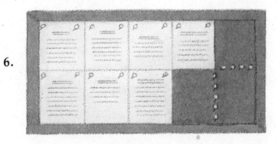

What part is covered?

7.

What part is painted?

8.

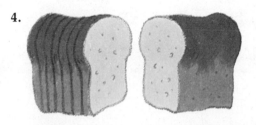

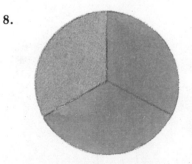

What part is green?

Parts of a set

Lisa made the green kite. There are 3 kites in all.
What fraction of the kites did she make?

1 green kite

3 kites in all

$\frac{1}{3}$ one third

Lisa made $\frac{1}{3}$
(one third)
of the kites.

Which fraction tells the part of the set that is green?

1.

$\frac{1}{2}$ $\frac{1}{3}$ $\frac{1}{4}$ $\frac{1}{5}$

2.

$\frac{2}{3}$ $\frac{2}{4}$ $\frac{2}{5}$ $\frac{2}{8}$

3.

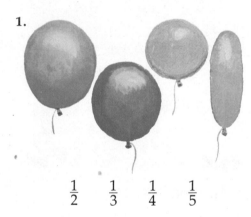

$\frac{1}{2}$ $\frac{1}{3}$ $\frac{1}{4}$ $\frac{1}{5}$

4.

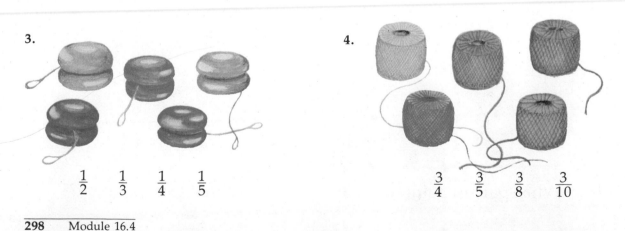

$\frac{3}{4}$ $\frac{3}{5}$ $\frac{3}{8}$ $\frac{3}{10}$

Give a fraction for the part of each picture that is named.

1.

the red car

2.

the green hat

3.

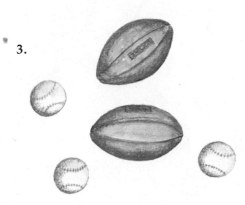

the baseballs

4.

the tops

5.

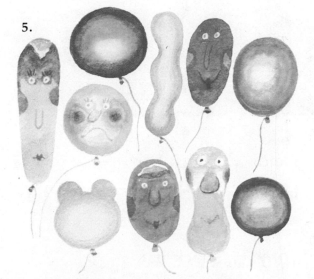

the balloons with faces

6.

the balls with stripes

Tenths

Karen ate $\frac{3}{10}$ of her snack bar.

Mel ate $\frac{1}{2}$ of his snack bar.

That is the same as $\frac{5}{10}$

Who ate more?

Mel ate $\frac{5}{10}$.   Karen ate $\frac{3}{10}$.

Mel ate more.

In each problem, tell who ate more.

1. Rosa: $\frac{1}{2}$ snack bar

    Jeff: $\frac{7}{10}$ snack bar

2. Heidi: $\frac{5}{10}$ snack bar

    Hans: $\frac{3}{10}$ snack bar

5. Joe: $\frac{1}{2}$ snack bar

    Sarah: $\frac{6}{10}$ snack bar

4. Tony: $\frac{3}{10}$ snack bar

    Bonnie: $\frac{1}{2}$ snack bar

Each stack has 10 cubes.
Give a fraction that tells
how much of each stack is blue.

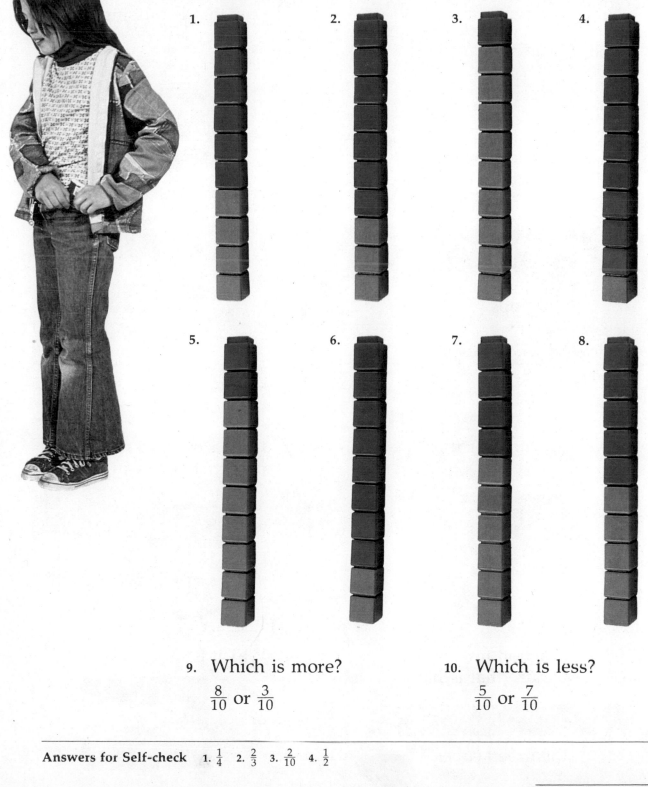

1.   2.   3.   4.

5.   6.   7.   8.

9. **Which is more?**

$\frac{8}{10}$ or $\frac{3}{10}$

10. **Which is less?**

$\frac{5}{10}$ or $\frac{7}{10}$

Answers for Self-check   1. $\frac{1}{4}$ 2. $\frac{2}{3}$ 3. $\frac{2}{10}$ 4. $\frac{1}{2}$

1. Give a fraction for the lighter piece.

2. Give a fraction for the part that is missing.

3. Give a fraction for the part of the picture that is named.

the tops

4. Which is more?

$\frac{3}{10}$

or

$\frac{1}{2}$

Answers for Self-check—page 301

Test

1. Give a fraction for the lighter piece.

2. Give a fraction for the part that is missing.

3. Give a fraction for the part of the picture that is named.

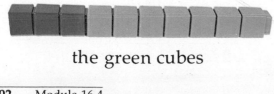

the green cubes

4. Which is more?

$\frac{6}{10}$

or

$\frac{1}{2}$

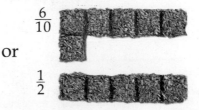

Making Symmetrical Figures

Trace this figure on a piece of paper.
Fold the paper on the red line. Cut out the
shape. (Do not cut on the fold.)

Finish the drawing.

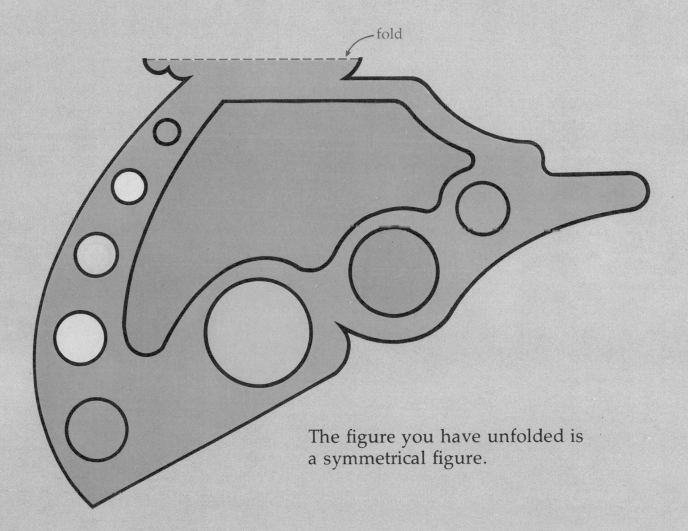

fold

The figure you have unfolded is
a symmetrical figure.

A is a symmetrical letter. What other letters are symmetrical?

⊛ Decimals

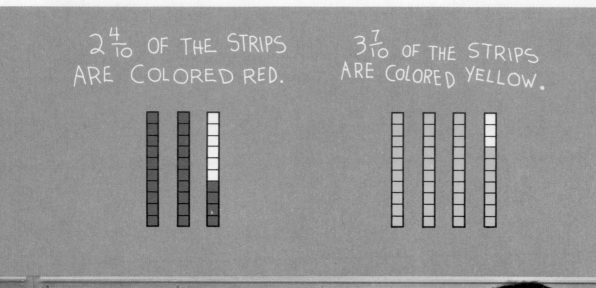

$2\frac{4}{10}$ OF THE STRIPS ARE COLORED RED.

$3\frac{7}{10}$ OF THE STRIPS ARE COLORED YELLOW.

Getting started

How would you show $5\frac{3}{10}$ with graph paper strips?

Give the missing decimals.

We see:	We write:		We say:
	fractions	decimals	
	$4\frac{2}{10}$	4.2	four and two tenths
	$5\frac{4}{10}$	5.4	five and four tenths
	$2\frac{7}{10}$	2.7	two and seven tenths
	$3\frac{5}{10}$		three and five tenths
	$4\frac{1}{10}$		four and one tenth

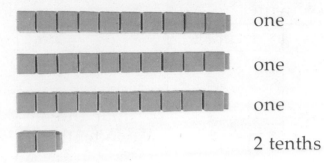

one
one
one
2 tenths

Each row of 10 cubes can be thought of as one. Each cube is then 1 tenth.

We write: 3.2
We say: 3 and 2 tenths

Give a decimal for each picture.

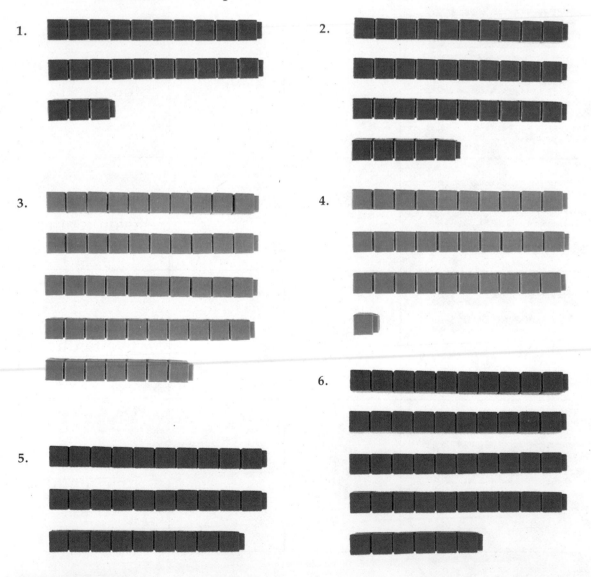

1.

2.

3.

4.

5.

6.

Give a decimal for each picture.

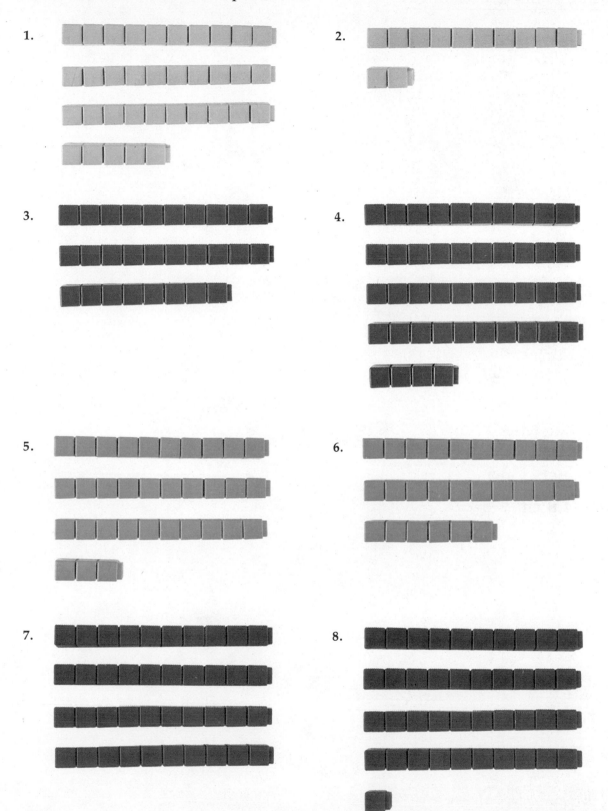

1.

2.

3.

4.

5.

6.

7.

8.

This centimeter ruler shows tenths.

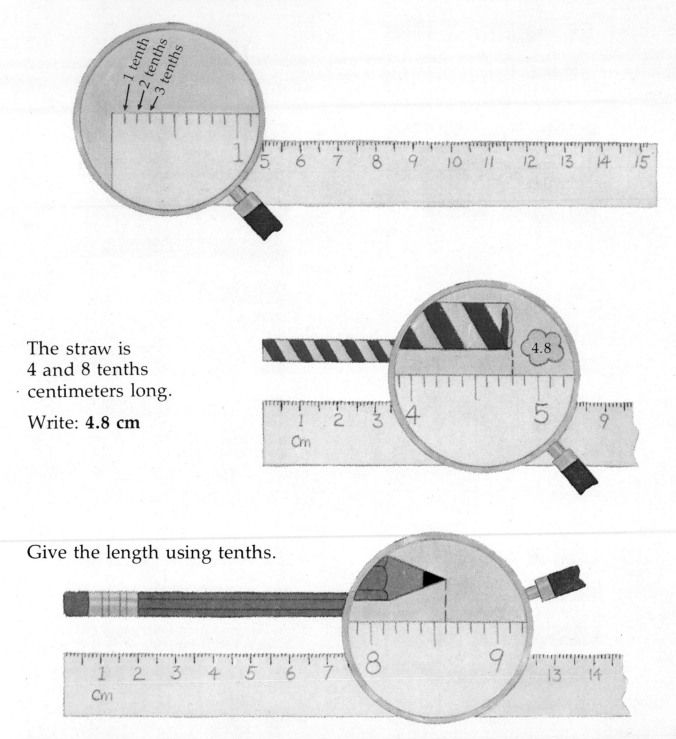

The straw is
4 and 8 tenths
centimeters long.

Write: **4.8 cm**

Give the length using tenths.

Give each length using tenths:

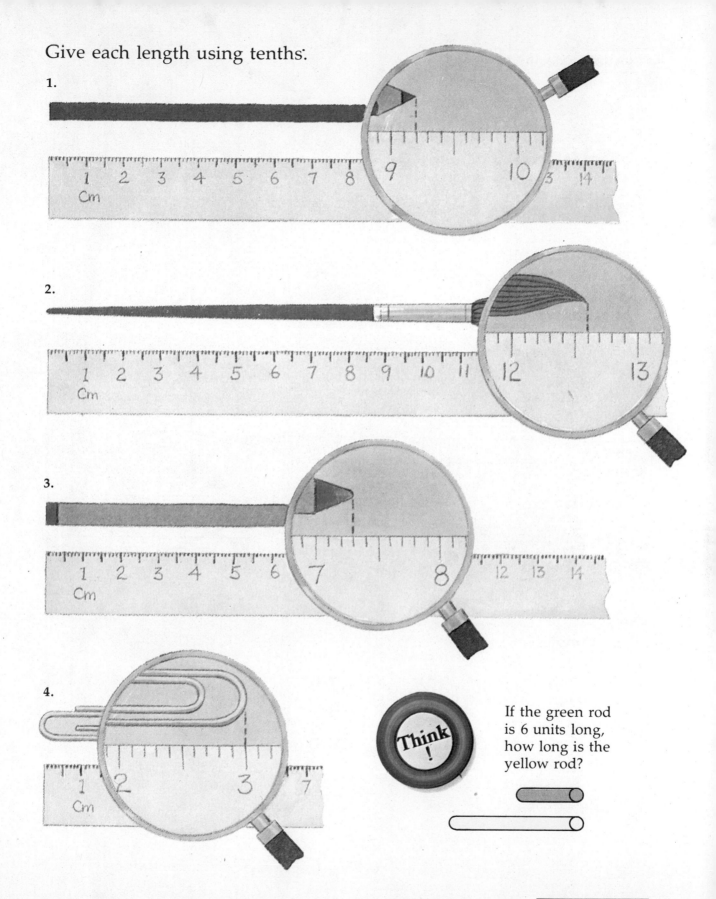

1.

2.

3.

4.

Think!

If the green rod is 6 units long, how long is the yellow rod?

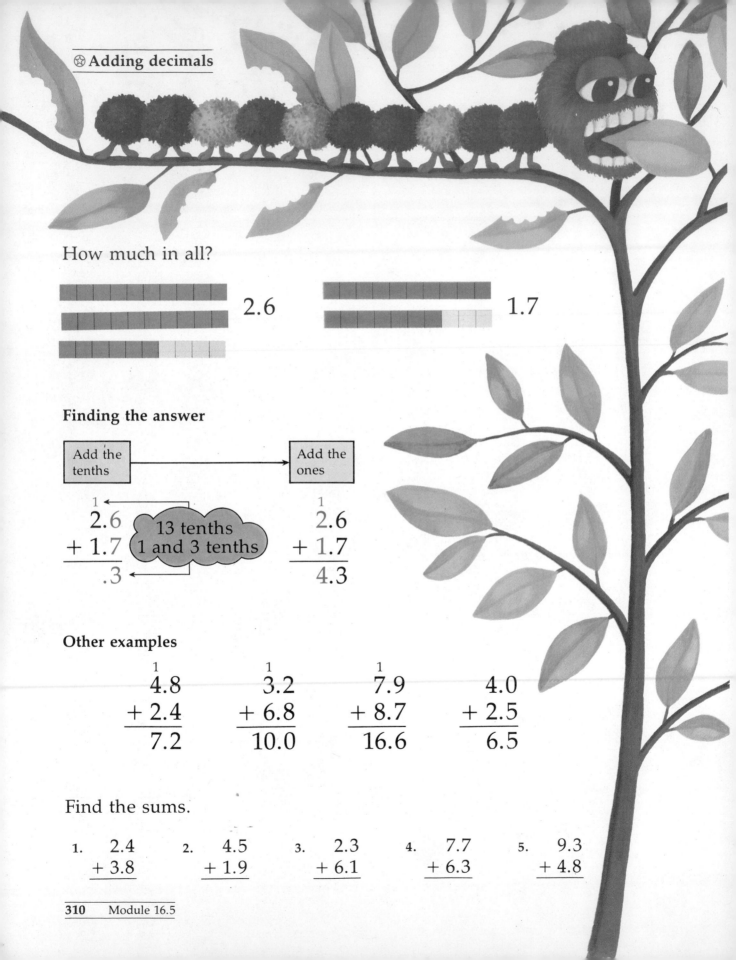

⊛ Adding decimals

How much in all?

2.6

1.7

Finding the answer

Add the tenths	→	Add the ones

$$\begin{array}{r} \overset{1}{2.6} \\ + 1.7 \\ \hline .3 \end{array}$$

13 tenths
1 and 3 tenths

$$\begin{array}{r} \overset{1}{2.6} \\ + 1.7 \\ \hline 4.3 \end{array}$$

Other examples

$$\begin{array}{r} \overset{1}{4.8} \\ + 2.4 \\ \hline 7.2 \end{array} \qquad \begin{array}{r} \overset{1}{3.2} \\ + 6.8 \\ \hline 10.0 \end{array} \qquad \begin{array}{r} \overset{1}{7.9} \\ + 8.7 \\ \hline 16.6 \end{array} \qquad \begin{array}{r} 4.0 \\ + 2.5 \\ \hline 6.5 \end{array}$$

Find the sums.

1. $\begin{array}{r} 2.4 \\ + 3.8 \end{array}$ 2. $\begin{array}{r} 4.5 \\ + 1.9 \end{array}$ 3. $\begin{array}{r} 2.3 \\ + 6.1 \end{array}$ 4. $\begin{array}{r} 7.7 \\ + 6.3 \end{array}$ 5. $\begin{array}{r} 9.3 \\ + 4.8 \end{array}$

How far from Fremont to Clay to Baker?

$$\begin{array}{r} \overset{1}{}6.5 \text{ km} \\ +\ 3.7 \text{ km} \\ \hline 10.2 \text{ km} \end{array}$$

The distance from Fremont to Clay to Baker is 10.2 km.

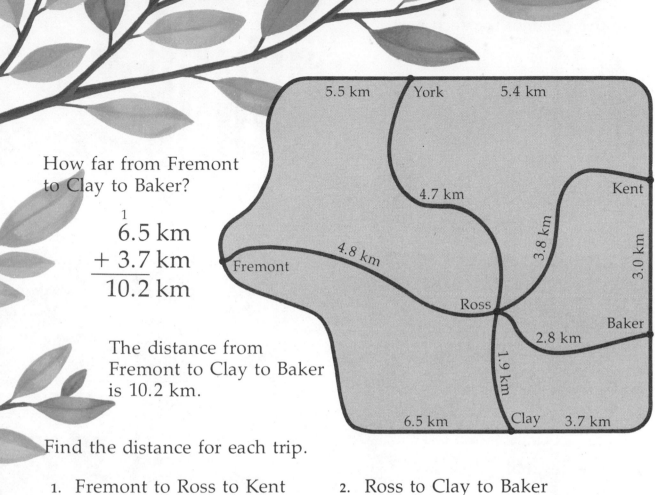

5.5 km York 5.4 km

4.7 km Kent

3.8 km

3.0 km

Fremont 4.8 km

Ross Baker

2.8 km

1.9 km

6.5 km Clay 3.7 km

Find the distance for each trip.

1. Fremont to Ross to Kent
2. Ross to Clay to Baker
3. Kent to Ross to Clay
4. Fremont to York to Kent
5. Clay to Baker to Kent
6. York to Kent to Baker
7. York to Fremont to Clay
☆ 8. Fremont to York to Kent to Baker

☆ 9. Baker to Ross to York to Kent

☆ 10. Baker to Clay to Ross to Fremont

Think!

A train that is 1 kilometer long is traveling 1 kilometer every 3 minutes. How long does it take this train to pass through a 2-kilometer tunnel?

Answers for Self-check   1. 4.3   2. 9.2   3. 1.8   4. 6.5   5. 14.0

Give the decimal for each part.

1.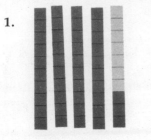

2.

3. Give the length using tenths.

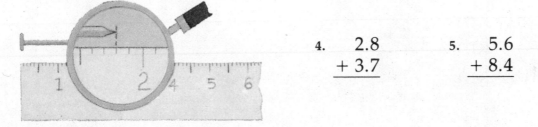

4. 2.8
  + 3.7

5. 5.6
  + 8.4

Answers for Self-check—page 311

✪ Test

Give the decimal.

1.

2.

3. Give the length using tenths.

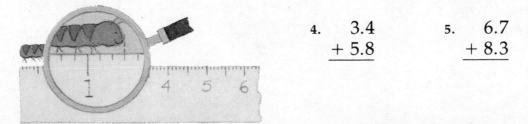

4. 3.4
  + 5.8

5. 6.7
  + 8.3

For fun

Nomograph

This is a nomograph.
It helps you find
sums. The yellow
strip shows the sum
of 46 and 37.

$$\begin{array}{r} 46 \\ + 37 \\ \hline 83 \end{array}$$

See if you can use
the nomograph to
find these sums.

1. $\begin{array}{r} 45 \\ + 39 \\ \hline \end{array}$

2. $\begin{array}{r} 39 \\ + 53 \\ \hline \end{array}$

3. $\begin{array}{r} 47 \\ + 54 \\ \hline \end{array}$

4. $\begin{array}{r} 54 \\ + 36 \\ \hline \end{array}$

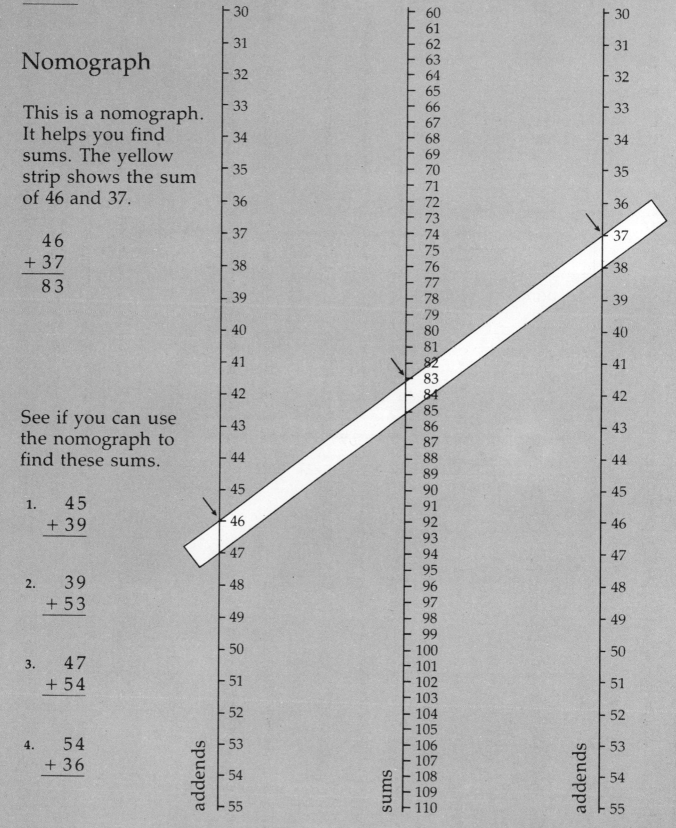

Measurement 3

inch unit

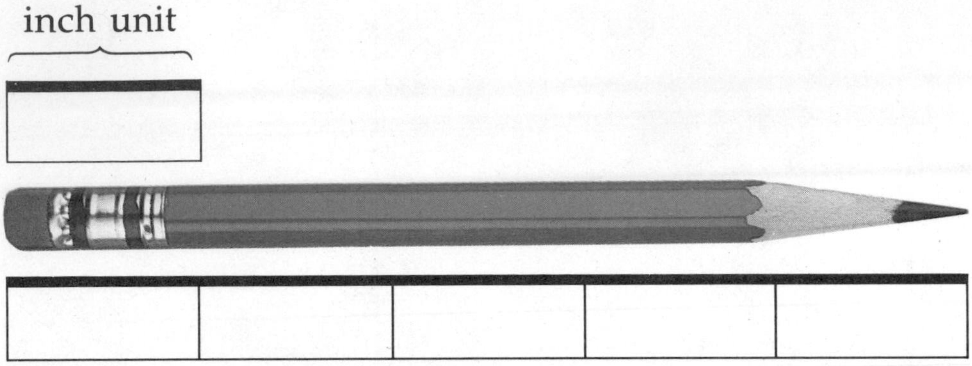

The pencil is 5 inches long.

Give the number of inches for each.

1.

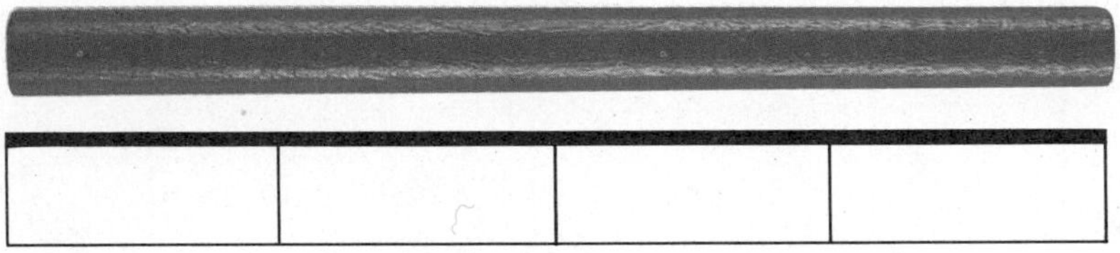

2.

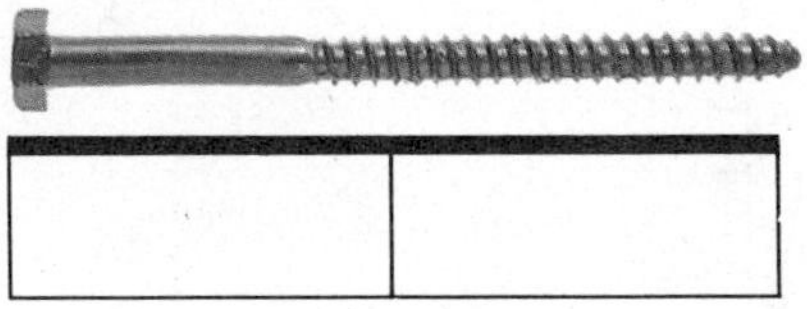

3.

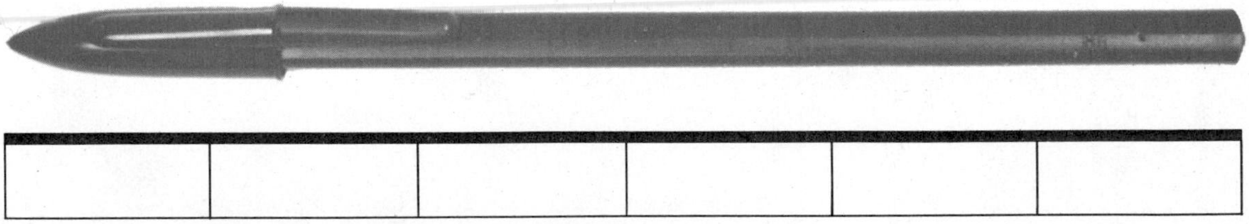

4.

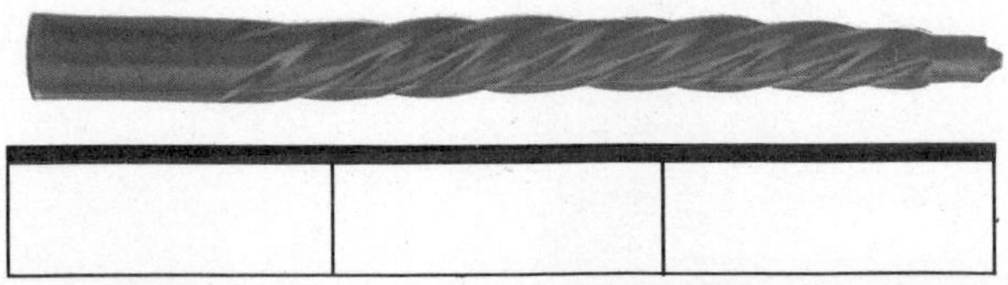

Find each length. Use your inch ruler.

1.

2.

3.

4.

5.

6.

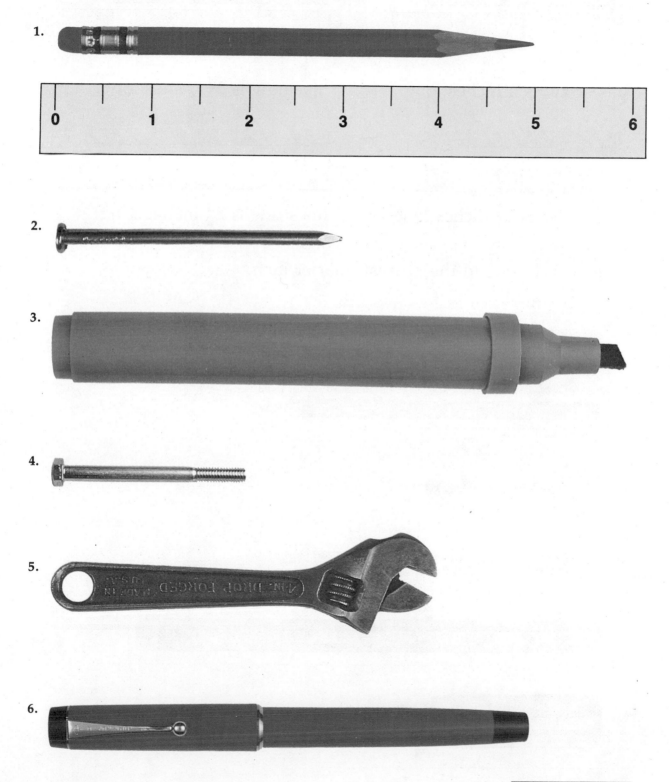

Measuring to quarter inches

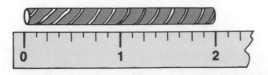

This straw is 2 inches long.

This straw is $2\frac{1}{4}$ inches long.

$\frac{1}{4}$ $\frac{1}{2}$ $\frac{3}{4}$

This straw is $1\frac{3}{4}$ inches long.

This straw is $2\frac{1}{2}$ inches long.

Give each length to the nearest quarter inch.

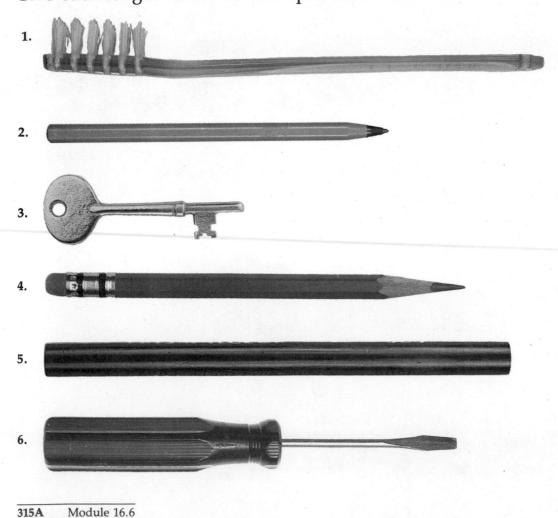

1.

2.

3.

4.

5.

6.

The leaf is about $4\frac{3}{4}$ inches long.

The pencil is about $2\frac{1}{2}$ inches long.

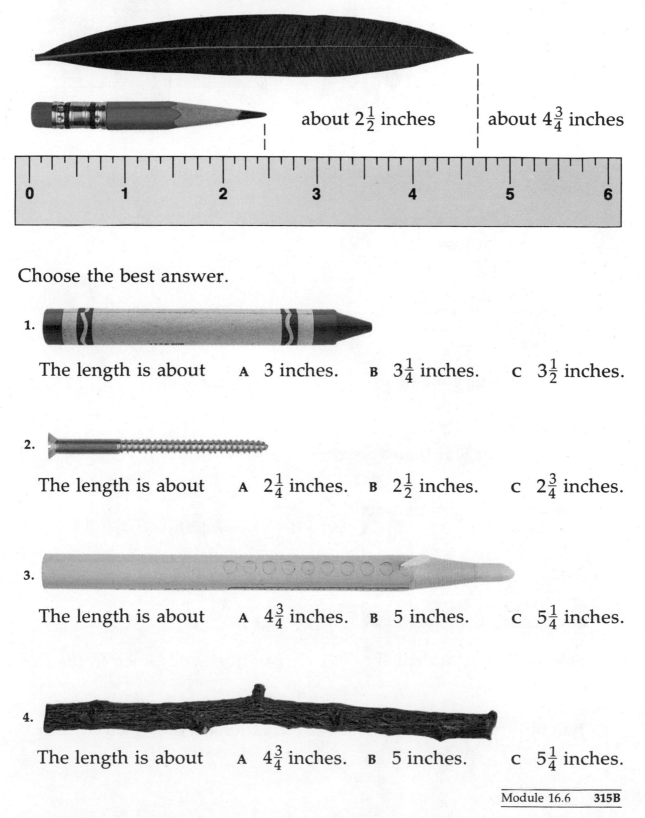

about $2\frac{1}{2}$ inches   about $4\frac{3}{4}$ inches

Choose the best answer.

1. The length is about   A 3 inches.   B $3\frac{1}{4}$ inches.   C $3\frac{1}{2}$ inches.

2. The length is about   A $2\frac{1}{4}$ inches.   B $2\frac{1}{2}$ inches.   C $2\frac{3}{4}$ inches.

3. The length is about   A $4\frac{3}{4}$ inches.   B 5 inches.   C $5\frac{1}{4}$ inches.

4. The length is about   A $4\frac{3}{4}$ inches.   B 5 inches.   C $5\frac{1}{4}$ inches.

Larger units for length

foot   yard

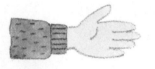

1 inch

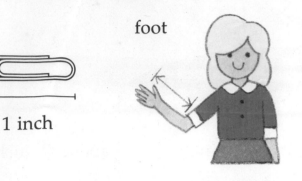

12 inches   3 feet or 36 inches

Answer **more** or **less** than 1 foot.

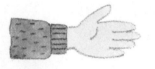

1. width of your hand   2. your waist

Answer **more** or **less** than 1 yard.

3. how high you can reach   4. from your knee to the floor

5. height of your desk   6. length of a shelf in your
                                  classroom

A mile is 1760 yards.
A mile is 5280 feet.

Answer **more** or **less** than 1 mile.

1. height of a very tall mountain   2. length of a football field

Choose **inches**, **feet**, **yards**, or **miles**
to complete each sentence.

3. A door is about 8 ___?___ high.

4. A chalkboard eraser is about 5 ___?___ long.

5. A railroad train may be 1 ___?___ long.

6. A person who is 6 ft tall is 2 ___?___ tall.

7. A new pencil is about 8 ___?___ long.

8. A school room was 35 ___?___ long.

9. A 747 jet plane may fly 6 ___?___ high.

10. A football field is 100 ___?___ long.

11. A 25¢ coin is about 1 ___?___ across.

12. A car might travel 50 ___?___ in one hour.

13. Your little finger is about 2 ___?___ long.

14. A doorway is about 1 ___?___ wide.

Area and volume

Square inch unit

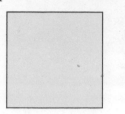

The area of
this figure is
4 square inches.

Give the area of each figure.

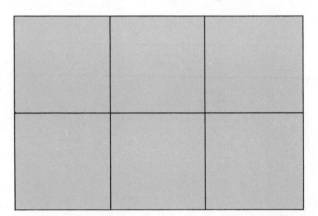

1. The area of this figure is |||| square inches.

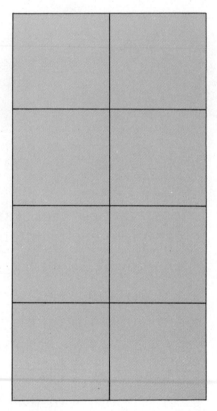

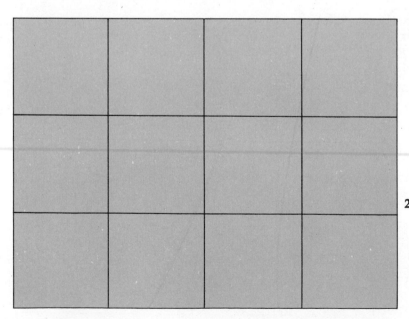

2. The area of this figure
is |||| square inches.

3. The area of this figure is |||| square inches.

Think of each 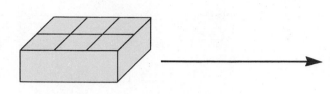 as 1 cubic inch.

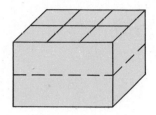

This box holds
6 cubic inches.

1. This box holds
||||| cubic inches.

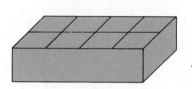

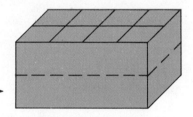

2. This box holds
||||| cubic inches.

3. This box holds
||||| cubic inches.

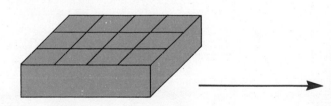

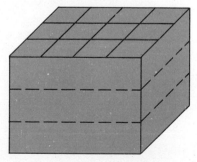

4. This box holds
||||| cubic inches.

5. This box holds
||||| cubic inches.

Liquid measure

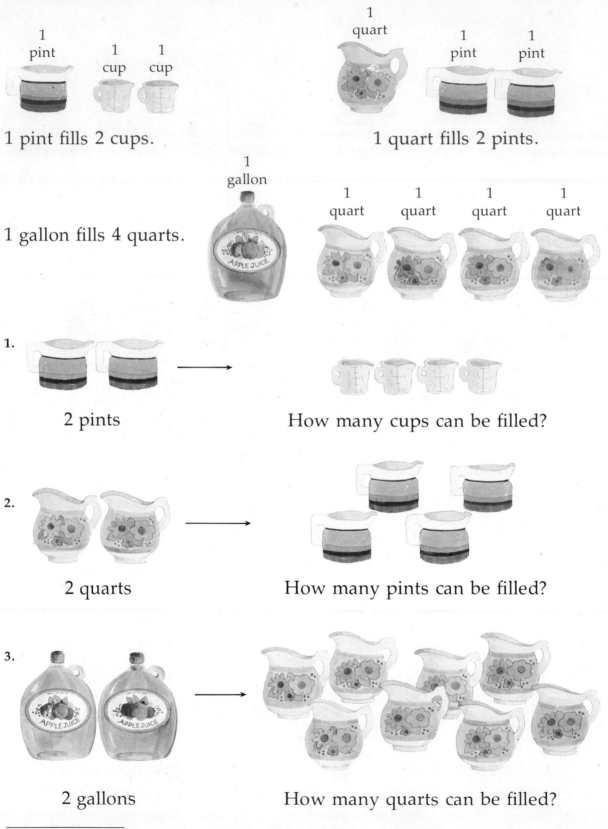

1 pint fills 2 cups.

1 quart fills 2 pints.

1 gallon fills 4 quarts.

1. 2 pints   How many cups can be filled?

2. 2 quarts   How many pints can be filled?

3. 2 gallons   How many quarts can be filled?

Which is more?

4.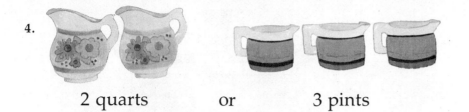

    2 quarts   or   3 pints

5.

    2 pints   or   5 cups

6.

    1 gallon   or   3 quarts

Answer **more** or **less** than a quart.

7.

    3 pints

8.

    6 cups

9.

    1 gallon

10.

    3 cups

Weight—pounds

1 pint of water

A pint of water weighs
about one pound.

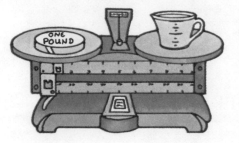

1. Which of these weighs less than 1 pound?

    A   B   C

2. Which of these weighs about 1 pound?

    A   B   C

3. Which of these weighs about 10 pounds?

    A   B   C

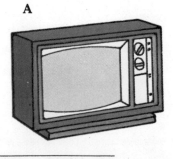 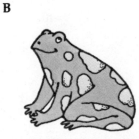 

Give an estimate for each amount.

The boy weighs about 100 pounds.

1.

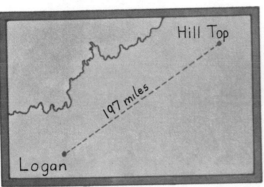

The distance from Logan to Hill Top is about ▥ miles.

2.

The room is about ▥ inches high.

3.

The football player weighs about ▥ pounds.

4.

The tank car can hold about ▥ gallons.

Telling time—15- and 5-minute intervals

2:30
two thirty

1:45
one forty-five

6:15
six fifteen

Give each time.

1.

2.

3.

4.

5.

6

7.

8.

9.

10:40
ten forty

1:25
one twenty-five

Give each time.

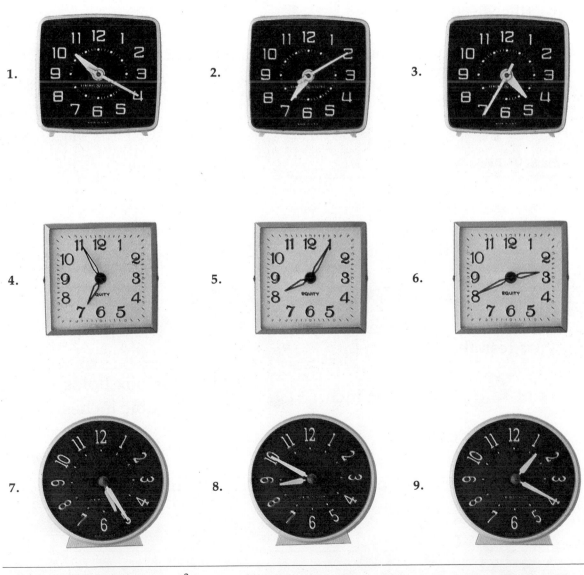

1.   2.   3.

4.   5.   6.

7.   8.   9.

Self-check

Give the length to the nearest quarter inch.

1.

2. Is the height of your classroom door **more** or **less** than 1 yard?

3. Think of ☐ as 1 square inch.

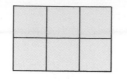

The area of this figure is ‖‖ square inches.

4. 1 pint fills ‖‖ cups.

5. Which one is about 1 pound?

6. Give the time.

A  B

Answers for Self-check—page 320B

Test

Give the length to the nearest quarter inch.

1.

2. Is the width of your shoe **more** or **less** than 1 foot?

3. Think of as 1 cubic inch.

This box holds ‖‖ cubic inches.

4. 1 quart fills ‖‖ cups.

5. Which one is about 1 pound?

6. Give the time.

A  B

Calendar Coloring

Make a copy of the calendar.

MAY						
Sunday	Monday	Tuesday	Wednesday	Thursday	Friday	Saturday
	1	2	3	4	5	6
7	8	9	10	11	12	13
14	15	16	17	18	19	20
21	22	23	24	25	26	27
28	29	30	31			

Color.

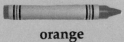

red	**orange**	**blue**
Monday, May 1	Third Tuesday	Fourth Friday
Third Monday	Monday, May 8	May 12
First Wednesday	Second Wednesday	Third Friday
May 17	Fourth Monday	May 5
Fifth Wednesday	May 24	
Monday, May 29		

Level 16 review

Find the quotients.

1. $49 \div 7 = \square$ 2. $45 \div 5 = \square$ 3. $32 \div 8 = \square$ 4. $18 \div 9 = \square$

5. $72 \div 8 = \square$ 6. $36 \div 4 = \square$ 7. $28 \div 4 = \square$ 8. $63 \div 7 = \square$

Find the quotients and remainders.

9. $5\overline{)26}$ 10. $4\overline{)22}$ 11. $3\overline{)19}$ 12. $5\overline{)32}$ 13. $5\overline{)48}$

14. $5\overline{)65}$ 15. $4\overline{)81}$ 16. $5\overline{)72}$ 17. $3\overline{)46}$ 18. $4\overline{)58}$

19. $3\overline{)241}$ 20. $5\overline{)402}$ 21. $4\overline{)295}$ 22. $2\overline{)178}$ 23. $5\overline{)372}$

24. Brenda traveled 24 km in 2 hours. How many kilometers did she travel in 1 hour?

25. Fred has 72 pictures. He put 4 pictures on some pages of his book. How many pages did he use?

Add.

26. $\begin{array}{r} 9.2 \\ + 4.1 \\ \hline \end{array}$ 27. $\begin{array}{r} 6.3 \\ + 7.2 \\ \hline \end{array}$ 28. $\begin{array}{r} 8.5 \\ + 6.8 \\ \hline \end{array}$ 29. $\begin{array}{r} 4.3 \\ + 2.7 \\ \hline \end{array}$ 30. $\begin{array}{r} 7.5 \\ + 6.6 \\ \hline \end{array}$

31. $\begin{array}{r} 5.7 \\ + 8.2 \\ \hline \end{array}$ 32. $\begin{array}{r} 6.8 \\ + 9.7 \\ \hline \end{array}$ 33. $\begin{array}{r} 2.8 \\ + 3.2 \\ \hline \end{array}$ 34. $\begin{array}{r} 5.1 \\ + 4.9 \\ \hline \end{array}$ 35. $\begin{array}{r} 7.8 \\ + 6.8 \\ \hline \end{array}$

Appendix

More Practice

Add.

1. $\begin{array}{r} 2 \\ +3 \\ \hline \end{array}$ 2. $\begin{array}{r} 3 \\ +1 \\ \hline \end{array}$ 3. $\begin{array}{r} 1 \\ +1 \\ \hline \end{array}$ 4. $\begin{array}{r} 0 \\ +3 \\ \hline \end{array}$ 5. $\begin{array}{r} 2 \\ +2 \\ \hline \end{array}$ 6. $\begin{array}{r} 4 \\ +1 \\ \hline \end{array}$ 7. $\begin{array}{r} 2 \\ +1 \\ \hline \end{array}$

8. $\begin{array}{r} 5 \\ +1 \\ \hline \end{array}$ 9. $\begin{array}{r} 1 \\ +2 \\ \hline \end{array}$ 10. $\begin{array}{r} 3 \\ +2 \\ \hline \end{array}$ 11. $\begin{array}{r} 1 \\ +4 \\ \hline \end{array}$ 12. $\begin{array}{r} 3 \\ +3 \\ \hline \end{array}$ 13. $\begin{array}{r} 2 \\ +4 \\ \hline \end{array}$ 14. $\begin{array}{r} 4 \\ +0 \\ \hline \end{array}$

15. $\begin{array}{r} 5 \\ +3 \\ \hline \end{array}$ 16. $\begin{array}{r} 4 \\ +3 \\ \hline \end{array}$ 17. $\begin{array}{r} 8 \\ +1 \\ \hline \end{array}$ 18. $\begin{array}{r} 6 \\ +2 \\ \hline \end{array}$ 19. $\begin{array}{r} 1 \\ +9 \\ \hline \end{array}$ 20. $\begin{array}{r} 3 \\ +6 \\ \hline \end{array}$ 21. $\begin{array}{r} 5 \\ +4 \\ \hline \end{array}$

22. $\begin{array}{r} 7 \\ +2 \\ \hline \end{array}$ 23. $\begin{array}{r} 2 \\ +5 \\ \hline \end{array}$ 24. $\begin{array}{r} 4 \\ +4 \\ \hline \end{array}$ 25. $\begin{array}{r} 1 \\ +6 \\ \hline \end{array}$ 26. $\begin{array}{r} 5 \\ +5 \\ \hline \end{array}$ 27. $\begin{array}{r} 1 \\ +8 \\ \hline \end{array}$ 28. $\begin{array}{r} 3 \\ +7 \\ \hline \end{array}$

29. $\begin{array}{r} 2 \\ +8 \\ \hline \end{array}$ 30. $\begin{array}{r} 7 \\ +3 \\ \hline \end{array}$ 31. $\begin{array}{r} 2 \\ +6 \\ \hline \end{array}$ 32. $\begin{array}{r} 6 \\ +3 \\ \hline \end{array}$ 33. $\begin{array}{r} 3 \\ +5 \\ \hline \end{array}$ 34. $\begin{array}{r} 4 \\ +6 \\ \hline \end{array}$ 35. $\begin{array}{r} 7 \\ +1 \\ \hline \end{array}$

Subtract.

1. $\begin{array}{r} 5 \\ -3 \\ \hline \end{array}$ 2. $\begin{array}{r} 2 \\ -1 \\ \hline \end{array}$ 3. $\begin{array}{r} 4 \\ -4 \\ \hline \end{array}$ 4. $\begin{array}{r} 6 \\ -3 \\ \hline \end{array}$ 5. $\begin{array}{r} 7 \\ -2 \\ \hline \end{array}$ 6. $\begin{array}{r} 3 \\ -1 \\ \hline \end{array}$ 7. $\begin{array}{r} 2 \\ -2 \\ \hline \end{array}$

8. $\begin{array}{r} 4 \\ -0 \\ \hline \end{array}$ 9. $\begin{array}{r} 3 \\ -2 \\ \hline \end{array}$ 10. $\begin{array}{r} 6 \\ -4 \\ \hline \end{array}$ 11. $\begin{array}{r} 8 \\ -4 \\ \hline \end{array}$ 12. $\begin{array}{r} 10 \\ -5 \\ \hline \end{array}$ 13. $\begin{array}{r} 9 \\ -2 \\ \hline \end{array}$ 14. $\begin{array}{r} 7 \\ -5 \\ \hline \end{array}$

15. $\begin{array}{r} 8 \\ -2 \\ \hline \end{array}$ 16. $\begin{array}{r} 7 \\ -4 \\ \hline \end{array}$ 17. $\begin{array}{r} 10 \\ -6 \\ \hline \end{array}$ 18. $\begin{array}{r} 4 \\ -3 \\ \hline \end{array}$ 19. $\begin{array}{r} 9 \\ -4 \\ \hline \end{array}$ 20. $\begin{array}{r} 6 \\ -5 \\ \hline \end{array}$ 21. $\begin{array}{r} 8 \\ -6 \\ \hline \end{array}$

22. $\begin{array}{r} 10 \\ -2 \\ \hline \end{array}$ 23. $\begin{array}{r} 4 \\ -2 \\ \hline \end{array}$ 24. $\begin{array}{r} 9 \\ -3 \\ \hline \end{array}$ 25. $\begin{array}{r} 5 \\ -4 \\ \hline \end{array}$ 26. $\begin{array}{r} 3 \\ -3 \\ \hline \end{array}$ 27. $\begin{array}{r} 9 \\ -6 \\ \hline \end{array}$ 28. $\begin{array}{r} 7 \\ -3 \\ \hline \end{array}$

29. $\begin{array}{r} 9 \\ -5 \\ \hline \end{array}$ 30. $\begin{array}{r} 7 \\ -1 \\ \hline \end{array}$ 31. $\begin{array}{r} 10 \\ -3 \\ \hline \end{array}$ 32. $\begin{array}{r} 8 \\ -3 \\ \hline \end{array}$ 33. $\begin{array}{r} 9 \\ -7 \\ \hline \end{array}$ 34. $\begin{array}{r} 7 \\ -6 \\ \hline \end{array}$ 35. $\begin{array}{r} 5 \\ -2 \\ \hline \end{array}$

Add.

1.   4
    + 7

2.   6
    + 6

3.   7
    + 6

4.   3
    + 9

5.   5
    + 8

6.   9
    + 2

7.   8
    + 4

8.   5
    + 7

9.   8
    + 6

10.   4
    + 8

11.   6
    + 7

12.   9
    + 3

13.   5
    + 6

14.   4
    + 9

15.   7
    + 7

16.   2
    + 9

17.   9
    + 5

18.   3
    + 8

19.   7
    + 5

20.   6
    + 8

21.   6
    + 5

22.   8
    + 3

23.   6
    + 9

24.   7
    + 4

25.   9
    + 4

26.   8
    + 8

27.   7
    + 8

28.   9
    + 7

29.   9
    + 8

30.   7
    + 9

31.   8
    + 5

32.   9
    + 9

33.   5
    + 9

34.   9
    + 6

35.   8
    + 9

Subtract.

1.   11
    − 3

2.   14
    − 7

3.   12
    − 4

4.   16
    − 7

5.   13
    − 5

6.   12
    − 5

7.   11
    − 6

8.   15
    − 6

9.   13
    − 8

10.   11
    − 4

11.   12
    − 6

12.   14
    − 6

13.   15
    − 8

14.   13
    − 4

15.   12
    − 8

16.   16
    − 9

17.   13
    − 7

18.   15
    − 7

19.   11
    − 7

20.   17
    − 8

21.   14
    − 8

22.   13
    − 9

23.   11
    − 2

24.   15
    − 9

25.   12
    − 7

26.   16
    − 8

27.   14
    − 5

28.   11
    − 5

29.   17
    − 9

30.   11
    − 8

31.   18
    − 9

32.   14
    − 9

33.   13
    − 6

34.   11
    − 9

35.   12
    − 3

Add.

1. $\begin{array}{r} 32 \\ +24 \\ \hline \end{array}$
2. $\begin{array}{r} 45 \\ +34 \\ \hline \end{array}$
3. $\begin{array}{r} 64 \\ +23 \\ \hline \end{array}$
4. $\begin{array}{r} 52 \\ +36 \\ \hline \end{array}$
5. $\begin{array}{r} 91 \\ +25 \\ \hline \end{array}$
6. $\begin{array}{r} 32 \\ +63 \\ \hline \end{array}$

7. $\begin{array}{r} 75 \\ +12 \\ \hline \end{array}$
8. $\begin{array}{r} 86 \\ +11 \\ \hline \end{array}$
9. $\begin{array}{r} 48 \\ +51 \\ \hline \end{array}$
10. $\begin{array}{r} 66 \\ +43 \\ \hline \end{array}$
11. $\begin{array}{r} 37 \\ +52 \\ \hline \end{array}$
12. $\begin{array}{r} 24 \\ +44 \\ \hline \end{array}$

13. $\begin{array}{r} 23 \\ +54 \\ \hline \end{array}$
14. $\begin{array}{r} 51 \\ +67 \\ \hline \end{array}$
15. $\begin{array}{r} 92 \\ +36 \\ \hline \end{array}$
16. $\begin{array}{r} 72 \\ +25 \\ \hline \end{array}$
17. $\begin{array}{r} 84 \\ +65 \\ \hline \end{array}$
18. $\begin{array}{r} 65 \\ +13 \\ \hline \end{array}$

19. $\begin{array}{r} 46 \\ +23 \\ \hline \end{array}$
20. $\begin{array}{r} 12 \\ +87 \\ \hline \end{array}$
21. $\begin{array}{r} 25 \\ +33 \\ \hline \end{array}$
22. $\begin{array}{r} 65 \\ +74 \\ \hline \end{array}$
23. $\begin{array}{r} 73 \\ +53 \\ \hline \end{array}$
24. $\begin{array}{r} 82 \\ +36 \\ \hline \end{array}$

25. $\begin{array}{r} 328 \\ +431 \\ \hline \end{array}$
26. $\begin{array}{r} 704 \\ +235 \\ \hline \end{array}$
27. $\begin{array}{r} 403 \\ +261 \\ \hline \end{array}$
28. $\begin{array}{r} 224 \\ +641 \\ \hline \end{array}$
29. $\begin{array}{r} 562 \\ +123 \\ \hline \end{array}$
30. $\begin{array}{r} 852 \\ +36 \\ \hline \end{array}$

31. $\begin{array}{r} 331 \\ +254 \\ \hline \end{array}$
32. $\begin{array}{r} 806 \\ +352 \\ \hline \end{array}$
33. $\begin{array}{r} 523 \\ +263 \\ \hline \end{array}$
34. $\begin{array}{r} 34 \\ +634 \\ \hline \end{array}$
35. $\begin{array}{r} 421 \\ +356 \\ \hline \end{array}$
36. $\begin{array}{r} 342 \\ +625 \\ \hline \end{array}$

37. $\begin{array}{r} 245 \\ +433 \\ \hline \end{array}$
38. $\begin{array}{r} 654 \\ +32 \\ \hline \end{array}$
39. $\begin{array}{r} 162 \\ +535 \\ \hline \end{array}$
40. $\begin{array}{r} 328 \\ +641 \\ \hline \end{array}$
41. $\begin{array}{r} 231 \\ +756 \\ \hline \end{array}$
42. $\begin{array}{r} 716 \\ +143 \\ \hline \end{array}$

43. $\begin{array}{r} 134 \\ +824 \\ \hline \end{array}$
44. $\begin{array}{r} 46 \\ +452 \\ \hline \end{array}$
45. $\begin{array}{r} 534 \\ +222 \\ \hline \end{array}$
46. $\begin{array}{r} 831 \\ +146 \\ \hline \end{array}$
47. $\begin{array}{r} 713 \\ +56 \\ \hline \end{array}$
48. $\begin{array}{r} 652 \\ +345 \\ \hline \end{array}$

49. $\begin{array}{r} 627 \\ +542 \\ \hline \end{array}$
50. $\begin{array}{r} 451 \\ +734 \\ \hline \end{array}$
51. $\begin{array}{r} 261 \\ +325 \\ \hline \end{array}$
52. $\begin{array}{r} 725 \\ +63 \\ \hline \end{array}$
53. $\begin{array}{r} 924 \\ +352 \\ \hline \end{array}$
54. $\begin{array}{r} 451 \\ +823 \\ \hline \end{array}$

55. $\begin{array}{r} 366 \\ +521 \\ \hline \end{array}$
56. $\begin{array}{r} 283 \\ +915 \\ \hline \end{array}$
57. $\begin{array}{r} 826 \\ +322 \\ \hline \end{array}$
58. $\begin{array}{r} 743 \\ +546 \\ \hline \end{array}$
59. $\begin{array}{r} 631 \\ +423 \\ \hline \end{array}$
60. $\begin{array}{r} 564 \\ +622 \\ \hline \end{array}$

Add.

1. 36
  +24

2. 56
  +15

3. 25
  +37

4. 43
  +17

5. 18
  +35

6. 26
  +47

7. 48
  +34

8. 19
  +52

9. 38
  +28

10. 75
  +16

11. 29
  +45

12. 25
  +65

13. 17
  +55

14. 49
  +23

15. 54
  +39

16. 37
  +46

17. 18
  +76

18. 67
  +28

19. 53
  +28

20. 15
  +65

21. 48
  +12

22. 27
  +13

23. 44
  +27

24. 56
  +36

25. 49
  +47

26. 73
  +18

27. 68
  +29

28. 37
  +27

29. 35
  +38

30. 59
  +28

31. 94
  +29

32. 59
  +86

33. 37
  +95

34. 57
  +84

35. 76
  +58

36. 88
  +25

37. 37
  +68

38. 22
  +99

39. 74
  +27

40. 85
  +38

41. 57
  +77

42. 26
  +85

43. 87
  +24

44. 44
  +78

45. 39
  +82

46. 73
  +58

47. 66
  +56

48. 89
  +43

49. 65
  +68

50. 77
  +57

51. 75
  +67

52. 28
  +86

53. 93
  +17

54. 48
  +62

55. 47
  +98

56. 86
  +57

57. 94
  +99

58. 98
  +68

59. 35
  +79

60. 85
  +86

Add.

1. 142
+328

2. 256
+467

3. 543
+368

4. 448
+376

5. 559
+162

6. 383
+359

7. 235
+576

8. 357
+228

9. 453
+329

10. 537
+444

11. 806
+146

12. 728
+225

13. 154
+529

14. 265
+607

15. 735
+148

16. 628
+334

17. 384
+356

18. 457
+538

19. 346
+765

20. 468
+575

21. 835
+286

22. 728
+476

23. 647
+827

24. 737
+689

25. 562
+758

26. 636
+885

27. 483
+958

28. 618
+568

29. 934
+366

30. 329
+585

31. 857
+555

32. 746
+679

33. 478
+846

34. 862
+759

35. 583
+947

36. 675
+845

37. 667
+654

38. 396
+877

39. 587
+653

40. 684
+768

41. 843
+978

42. 458
+379

43. 646
+874

44. 967
+448

45. 726
+599

46. 748
+975

47. 967
+685

48. 586
+847

Add.

1.	24 43 +18	2.	56 31 +22	3.	46 29 +32	4.	36 44 +19	5.	62 33 +45	6.	75 24 +31

7.	17 56 +34	8.	42 56 +28	9.	36 17 +47	10.	60 48 +33	11.	52 26 +19	12.	21 64 +57

13.	83 25 +18	14.	34 92 +10	15.	72 43 +26	16.	36 85 +21	17.	64 35 +44	18.	17 18 +94

19.	234 347 +105	20.	452 186 +325	21.	354 562 +193	22.	157 632 +338	23.	531 265 +478	24.	327 605 +448

25.	620 238 +275	26.	576 432 +188	27.	703 328 +266	28.	453 826 +139	29.	364 921 +109	30.	468 236 +824

31.	428 736 +225	32.	634 528 +365	33.	834 268 +472	34.	906 475 +688	35.	539 465 +722	36.	724 168 +243

37.	523 645 +238	38.	147 736 +254	39.	325 824 +366	40.	438 264 +527	41.	615 133 +728	42.	286 357 +640

43.	876 230 +467	44.	308 964 +275	45.	567 326 +743	46.	736 253 +626	47.	921 376 +164	48.	407 625 +348

Subtract.

1.	2.	3.	4.	5.	6.
36 − 15	21 − 10	45 − 32	56 − 23	18 − 7	47 − 23

7.	8.	9.	10.	11.	12.
78 − 43	86 − 12	64 − 52	48 − 42	97 − 35	55 − 13

13.	14.	15.	16.	17.	18.
356 − 221	648 − 436	256 − 32	468 − 343	575 − 421	657 − 212

19.	20.	21.	22.	23.	24.
747 − 324	503 − 402	865 − 523	958 − 632	625 − 614	769 − 233

Subtract.

1.	2.	3.	4.	5.	6.
31 − 18	64 − 28	43 − 36	25 − 16	56 − 38	72 − 49

7.	8.	9.	10.	11.	12.
73 − 28	82 − 35	54 − 17	60 − 43	75 − 57	45 − 19

13.	14.	15.	16.	17.	18.
46 − 17	32 − 28	65 − 38	72 − 47	81 − 36	94 − 55

19.	20.	21.	22.	23.	24.
53 − 27	44 − 26	87 − 48	61 − 14	52 − 36	78 − 59

Subtract.

1. $\begin{array}{r} 48 \\ -19 \\ \hline \end{array}$
2. $\begin{array}{r} 22 \\ -15 \\ \hline \end{array}$
3. $\begin{array}{r} 61 \\ -42 \\ \hline \end{array}$
4. $\begin{array}{r} 37 \\ -28 \\ \hline \end{array}$
5. $\begin{array}{r} 44 \\ -35 \\ \hline \end{array}$
6. $\begin{array}{r} 86 \\ -38 \\ \hline \end{array}$

7. $\begin{array}{r} 23 \\ -19 \\ \hline \end{array}$
8. $\begin{array}{r} 42 \\ -17 \\ \hline \end{array}$
9. $\begin{array}{r} 73 \\ -47 \\ \hline \end{array}$
10. $\begin{array}{r} 64 \\ -25 \\ \hline \end{array}$
11. $\begin{array}{r} 81 \\ -52 \\ \hline \end{array}$
12. $\begin{array}{r} 73 \\ -29 \\ \hline \end{array}$

13. $\begin{array}{r} 68 \\ -19 \\ \hline \end{array}$
14. $\begin{array}{r} 35 \\ -15 \\ \hline \end{array}$
15. $\begin{array}{r} 19 \\ -12 \\ \hline \end{array}$
16. $\begin{array}{r} 27 \\ -18 \\ \hline \end{array}$
17. $\begin{array}{r} 46 \\ -19 \\ \hline \end{array}$
18. $\begin{array}{r} 78 \\ -63 \\ \hline \end{array}$

19. $\begin{array}{r} 93 \\ -45 \\ \hline \end{array}$
20. $\begin{array}{r} 62 \\ -19 \\ \hline \end{array}$
21. $\begin{array}{r} 56 \\ -47 \\ \hline \end{array}$
22. $\begin{array}{r} 49 \\ -29 \\ \hline \end{array}$
23. $\begin{array}{r} 64 \\ -18 \\ \hline \end{array}$
24. $\begin{array}{r} 27 \\ -14 \\ \hline \end{array}$

25. $\begin{array}{r} 43 \\ -26 \\ \hline \end{array}$
26. $\begin{array}{r} 86 \\ -26 \\ \hline \end{array}$
27. $\begin{array}{r} 63 \\ -59 \\ \hline \end{array}$
28. $\begin{array}{r} 98 \\ -49 \\ \hline \end{array}$
29. $\begin{array}{r} 47 \\ -19 \\ \hline \end{array}$
30. $\begin{array}{r} 21 \\ -17 \\ \hline \end{array}$

31. $\begin{array}{r} 60 \\ -33 \\ \hline \end{array}$
32. $\begin{array}{r} 33 \\ -26 \\ \hline \end{array}$
33. $\begin{array}{r} 49 \\ -38 \\ \hline \end{array}$
34. $\begin{array}{r} 84 \\ -76 \\ \hline \end{array}$
35. $\begin{array}{r} 75 \\ -28 \\ \hline \end{array}$
36. $\begin{array}{r} 31 \\ -23 \\ \hline \end{array}$

37. $\begin{array}{r} 52 \\ -15 \\ \hline \end{array}$
38. $\begin{array}{r} 72 \\ -39 \\ \hline \end{array}$
39. $\begin{array}{r} 85 \\ -58 \\ \hline \end{array}$
40. $\begin{array}{r} 50 \\ -24 \\ \hline \end{array}$
41. $\begin{array}{r} 38 \\ -19 \\ \hline \end{array}$
42. $\begin{array}{r} 55 \\ -27 \\ \hline \end{array}$

43. $\begin{array}{r} 36 \\ -29 \\ \hline \end{array}$
44. $\begin{array}{r} 82 \\ -65 \\ \hline \end{array}$
45. $\begin{array}{r} 95 \\ -77 \\ \hline \end{array}$
46. $\begin{array}{r} 25 \\ -23 \\ \hline \end{array}$
47. $\begin{array}{r} 74 \\ -35 \\ \hline \end{array}$
48. $\begin{array}{r} 88 \\ -39 \\ \hline \end{array}$

49. $\begin{array}{r} 74 \\ -25 \\ \hline \end{array}$
50. $\begin{array}{r} 39 \\ -19 \\ \hline \end{array}$
51. $\begin{array}{r} 24 \\ -16 \\ \hline \end{array}$
52. $\begin{array}{r} 44 \\ -38 \\ \hline \end{array}$
53. $\begin{array}{r} 92 \\ -47 \\ \hline \end{array}$
54. $\begin{array}{r} 72 \\ -55 \\ \hline \end{array}$

55. $\begin{array}{r} 28 \\ -19 \\ \hline \end{array}$
56. $\begin{array}{r} 41 \\ -23 \\ \hline \end{array}$
57. $\begin{array}{r} 53 \\ -36 \\ \hline \end{array}$
58. $\begin{array}{r} 32 \\ -24 \\ \hline \end{array}$
59. $\begin{array}{r} 86 \\ -35 \\ \hline \end{array}$
60. $\begin{array}{r} 67 \\ -48 \\ \hline \end{array}$

Subtract.

1. 112
  − 85

2. 191
  − 93

3. 126
  − 57

4. 148
  − 69

5. 166
  − 78

6. 145
  − 49

7. 143
  − 95

8. 124
  − 65

9. 155
  − 76

10. 140
  − 87

11. 131
  − 56

12. 118
  − 29

13. 131
  − 35

14. 134
  − 77

15. 138
  − 48

16. 135
  − 54

17. 117
  − 88

18. 122
  − 56

19. 115
  − 28

20. 120
  − 45

21. 153
  − 56

22. 172
  − 83

23. 126
  − 99

24. 138
  − 99

25. 152
  − 88

26. 161
  − 74

27. 122
  − 77

28. 144
  − 58

29. 153
  − 85

30. 170
  − 76

31. 129
  − 59

32. 151
  − 69

33. 164
  − 72

34. 125
  − 88

35. 112
  − 94

36. 122
  − 37

37. 114
  − 45

38. 146
  − 67

39. 175
  − 89

40. 139
  − 40

41. 156
  − 98

42. 160
  − 79

43. 187
  − 88

44. 133
  − 65

45. 116
  − 87

46. 152
  − 65

47. 127
  − 38

48. 159
  − 69

49. 190
  − 98

50. 154
  − 75

51. 128
  − 39

52. 163
  − 84

53. 171
  − 82

54. 132
  − 55

55. 111
  − 22

56. 165
  − 77

57. 130
  − 41

58. 181
  − 87

59. 176
  − 97

60. 123
  − 78

Set A   For use after page 73

Subtract.

1. $\begin{array}{r} 31 \\ -15 \\ \hline \end{array}$	2. $\begin{array}{r} 63 \\ -27 \\ \hline \end{array}$	3. $\begin{array}{r} 42 \\ -38 \\ \hline \end{array}$	4. $\begin{array}{r} 54 \\ -17 \\ \hline \end{array}$	5. $\begin{array}{r} 71 \\ -24 \\ \hline \end{array}$	6. $\begin{array}{r} 32 \\ -25 \\ \hline \end{array}$
7. $\begin{array}{r} 44 \\ -26 \\ \hline \end{array}$	8. $\begin{array}{r} 72 \\ -34 \\ \hline \end{array}$	9. $\begin{array}{r} 36 \\ -19 \\ \hline \end{array}$	10. $\begin{array}{r} 54 \\ -15 \\ \hline \end{array}$	11. $\begin{array}{r} 65 \\ -48 \\ \hline \end{array}$	12. $\begin{array}{r} 81 \\ -57 \\ \hline \end{array}$
13. $\begin{array}{r} 53 \\ -26 \\ \hline \end{array}$	14. $\begin{array}{r} 91 \\ -33 \\ \hline \end{array}$	15. $\begin{array}{r} 75 \\ -46 \\ \hline \end{array}$	16. $\begin{array}{r} 63 \\ -29 \\ \hline \end{array}$	17. $\begin{array}{r} 42 \\ -17 \\ \hline \end{array}$	18. $\begin{array}{r} 64 \\ -38 \\ \hline \end{array}$
19. $\begin{array}{r} 62 \\ -29 \\ \hline \end{array}$	20. $\begin{array}{r} 97 \\ -86 \\ \hline \end{array}$	21. $\begin{array}{r} 82 \\ -36 \\ \hline \end{array}$	22. $\begin{array}{r} 43 \\ -25 \\ \hline \end{array}$	23. $\begin{array}{r} 57 \\ -33 \\ \hline \end{array}$	24. $\begin{array}{r} 95 \\ -47 \\ \hline \end{array}$

Set B   For use after page 75

Subtract.

1. $\begin{array}{r} 451 \\ -\ 26 \\ \hline \end{array}$	2. $\begin{array}{r} 514 \\ -\ 82 \\ \hline \end{array}$	3. $\begin{array}{r} 362 \\ -\ 37 \\ \hline \end{array}$	4. $\begin{array}{r} 748 \\ -\ 94 \\ \hline \end{array}$	5. $\begin{array}{r} 634 \\ -\ 52 \\ \hline \end{array}$	6. $\begin{array}{r} 852 \\ -\ 36 \\ \hline \end{array}$
7. $\begin{array}{r} 212 \\ -\ 41 \\ \hline \end{array}$	8. $\begin{array}{r} 471 \\ -\ 90 \\ \hline \end{array}$	9. $\begin{array}{r} 366 \\ -\ 84 \\ \hline \end{array}$	10. $\begin{array}{r} 557 \\ -\ 48 \\ \hline \end{array}$	11. $\begin{array}{r} 439 \\ -\ 56 \\ \hline \end{array}$	12. $\begin{array}{r} 694 \\ -\ 56 \\ \hline \end{array}$
13. $\begin{array}{r} 333 \\ -\ 91 \\ \hline \end{array}$	14. $\begin{array}{r} 522 \\ -\ 31 \\ \hline \end{array}$	15. $\begin{array}{r} 265 \\ -\ 83 \\ \hline \end{array}$	16. $\begin{array}{r} 416 \\ -\ 17 \\ \hline \end{array}$	17. $\begin{array}{r} 619 \\ -\ 67 \\ \hline \end{array}$	18. $\begin{array}{r} 382 \\ -\ 65 \\ \hline \end{array}$
19. $\begin{array}{r} 257 \\ -\ 49 \\ \hline \end{array}$	20. $\begin{array}{r} 747 \\ -\ 53 \\ \hline \end{array}$	21. $\begin{array}{r} 662 \\ -\ 71 \\ \hline \end{array}$	22. $\begin{array}{r} 835 \\ -\ 63 \\ \hline \end{array}$	23. $\begin{array}{r} 281 \\ -\ 53 \\ \hline \end{array}$	24. $\begin{array}{r} 565 \\ -\ 49 \\ \hline \end{array}$

Subtract.

1. 156
− 38

2. 477
−258

3. 249
− 71

4. 596
− 37

5. 334
−183

6. 676
− 39

7. 331
−116

8. 789
− 94

9. 552
−391

10. 183
− 46

11. 421
−217

12. 861
− 56

13. 915
−663

14. 444
− 35

15. 222
− 18

16. 625
−313

17. 969
−778

18. 325
− 62

19. 114
− 43

20. 531
− 26

21. 817
−535

22. 970
− 25

23. 263
− 36

24. 774
−347

25. 217
− 56

26. 688
−249

27. 379
−194

28. 729
− 58

29. 942
−821

30. 845
− 62

31. 798
−369

32. 490
− 38

33. 954
−733

34. 643
−452

35. 564
−193

36. 179
− 94

37. 591
−286

38. 145
− 82

39. 713
−222

40. 921
− 73

41. 827
−694

42. 943
−560

43. 343
− 51

44. 967
−148

45. 622
−372

46. 295
− 87

47. 762
−471

48. 451
−226

331A   More practice

Subtract.

1. 721
    -316

2. 536
    -162

3. 439
    -275

4. 265
    -191

5. 554
    -325

6. 826
    -651

7. 383
    -157

8. 973
    -566

9. 450
    -127

10. 887
    -249

11. 356
    -129

12. 668
    -572

13. 435
    -292

14. 674
    -419

15. 230
    -119

16. 932
    -671

17. 528
    -319

18. 445
    -317

19. 615
    -209

20. 960
    -548

21. 781
    -390

22. 333
    -181

23. 918
    -209

24. 378
    -186

25. 557
    -229

26. 455
    -364

27. 892
    -456

28. 434
    -225

29. 641
    -480

30. 894
    -176

31. 880
    -661

32. 927
    -435

33. 991
    -743

34. 512
    -108

35. 738
    -273

36. 447
    -318

37. 676
    -592

38. 252
    -137

39. 463
    -119

40. 948
    -264

41. 740
    -560

42. 386
    -157

43. 896
    -358

44. 790
    -136

45. 551
    -380

46. 575
    -492

47. 972
    -619

48. 858
    -462

Subtract.

1. 325
   −162

2. 561
   −237

3. 732
   −241

4. 624
   −352

5. 416
   −253

6. 362
   −138

7. 263
   −146

8. 455
   −237

9. 348
   −175

10. 573
    −281

11. 864
    −336

12. 725
    −231

13. 514
    −163

14. 256
    −117

15. 738
    −254

16. 365
    −138

17. 627
    −272

18. 438
    −163

19. 869
    −383

20. 475
    −226

21. 257
    −129

22. 946
    −385

23. 772
    −324

24. 581
    −236

Subtract.

1. 321
   −156

2. 536
   −258

3. 754
   −387

4. 427
   −168

5. 683
   −296

6. 514
   −385

7. 213
   −158

8. 862
   −394

9. 544
   −289

10. 933
    −477

11. 372
    −198

12. 783
    −484

13. 645
    −378

14. 418
    −269

15. 867
    −479

16. 756
    −277

17. 971
    −387

18. 623
    −376

19. 731
    −484

20. 525
    −187

21. 942
    −265

22. 654
    −468

23. 863
    −167

24. 421
    −296

Subtract.

1. 332
   −164

2. 556
   −299

3. 830
   − 75

4. 965
   −686

5. 384
   − 98

6. 763
   −456

7. 777
   −389

8. 582
   −295

9. 235
   − 68

10. 939
   −250

11. 244
   −165

12. 828
   −579

13. 250
   − 66

14. 754
   −288

15. 374
   −299

16. 538
   −179

17. 224
   −156

18. 951
   −293

19. 422
   −135

20. 646
   −188

21. 320
   − 65

22. 215
   − 37

23. 848
   −389

24. 561
   −277

25. 660
   −178

26. 458
   −379

27. 285
   − 98

28. 976
   −284

29. 391
   −283

30. 231
   −155

31. 833
   −555

32. 449
   −269

33. 314
   −158

34. 618
   −279

35. 225
   −167

36. 734
   −257

37. 817
   −639

38. 910
   −355

39. 321
   −177

40. 441
   −278

41. 652
   −394

42. 519
   −249

43. 212
   − 88

44. 323
   − 57

45. 416
   −228

46. 626
   −197

47. 945
   −376

48. 872
   − 94

Subtract.

1. 360
    -125

2. 206
    -145

3. 500
    -263

4. 704
    -386

5. 420
    -172

6. 603
    -258

7. 440
    -226

8. 305
    -149

9. 900
    -327

10. 830
    -461

11. 701
    -278

12. 400
    -134

13. 703
    -346

14. 507
    -289

15. 602
    -318

16. 300
    -195

17. 908
    -471

18. 802
    -257

19. 650
    -287

20. 403
    -277

21. 740
    -268

22. 550
    -186

23. 600
    -419

24. 970
    -342

Subtract.

1. 523
    -368

2. 637
    -282

3. 824
    -516

4. 305
    -132

5. 290
    -126

6. 713
    -277

7. 815
    -138

8. 265
    -132

9. 451
    -227

10. 742
    -124

11. 514
    -319

12. 304
    -143

13. 900
    -654

14. 850
    -263

15. 728
    -353

16. 503
    -259

17. 467
    -328

18. 940
    -284

19. 753
    -397

20. 336
    -148

21. 402
    -245

22. 971
    -268

23. 630
    -276

24. 853
    -448

Multiply.

1. $1 \times 3 = \square$ 2. $0 \times 4 = \square$ 3. $2 \times 6 = \square$ 4. $4 \times 2 = \square$

5. $0 \times 7 = \square$ 6. $3 \times 2 = \square$ 7. $0 \times 6 = \square$ 8. $3 \times 6 = \square$

9. $3 \times 5 = \square$ 10. $1 \times 7 = \square$ 11. $3 \times 3 = \square$ 12. $0 \times 1 = \square$

13. $4 \times 1 = \square$ 14. $1 \times 8 = \square$ 15. $0 \times 2 = \square$ 16. $2 \times 7 = \square$

17. $4 \times 5 = \square$ 18. $2 \times 3 = \square$ 19. $4 \times 8 = \square$ 20. $0 \times 0 = \square$

21. $1 \times 6 = \square$ 22. $4 \times 3 = \square$ 23. $2 \times 1 = \square$ 24. $3 \times 7 = \square$

25. $1 \times 9 = \square$ 26. $5 \times 7 = \square$ 27. $4 \times 6 = \square$ 28. $0 \times 5 = \square$

29. $\begin{array}{r} 3 \\ \times 0 \\ \hline \end{array}$ 30. $\begin{array}{r} 8 \\ \times 2 \\ \hline \end{array}$ 31. $\begin{array}{r} 1 \\ \times 5 \\ \hline \end{array}$ 32. $\begin{array}{r} 9 \\ \times 0 \\ \hline \end{array}$ 33. $\begin{array}{r} 4 \\ \times 3 \\ \hline \end{array}$ 34. $\begin{array}{r} 8 \\ \times 0 \\ \hline \end{array}$ 35. $\begin{array}{r} 5 \\ \times 5 \\ \hline \end{array}$

36. $\begin{array}{r} 8 \\ \times 3 \\ \hline \end{array}$ 37. $\begin{array}{r} 4 \\ \times 1 \\ \hline \end{array}$ 38. $\begin{array}{r} 6 \\ \times 5 \\ \hline \end{array}$ 39. $\begin{array}{r} 2 \\ \times 1 \\ \hline \end{array}$ 40. $\begin{array}{r} 0 \\ \times 5 \\ \hline \end{array}$ 41. $\begin{array}{r} 1 \\ \times 1 \\ \hline \end{array}$ 42. $\begin{array}{r} 9 \\ \times 2 \\ \hline \end{array}$

43. $\begin{array}{r} 5 \\ \times 2 \\ \hline \end{array}$ 44. $\begin{array}{r} 9 \\ \times 4 \\ \hline \end{array}$ 45. $\begin{array}{r} 1 \\ \times 3 \\ \hline \end{array}$ 46. $\begin{array}{r} 8 \\ \times 5 \\ \hline \end{array}$ 47. $\begin{array}{r} 9 \\ \times 3 \\ \hline \end{array}$ 48. $\begin{array}{r} 5 \\ \times 1 \\ \hline \end{array}$ 49. $\begin{array}{r} 0 \\ \times 4 \\ \hline \end{array}$

50. $\begin{array}{r} 4 \\ \times 5 \\ \hline \end{array}$ 51. $\begin{array}{r} 0 \\ \times 2 \\ \hline \end{array}$ 52. $\begin{array}{r} 7 \\ \times 4 \\ \hline \end{array}$ 53. $\begin{array}{r} 4 \\ \times 2 \\ \hline \end{array}$ 54. $\begin{array}{r} 4 \\ \times 4 \\ \hline \end{array}$ 55. $\begin{array}{r} 9 \\ \times 5 \\ \hline \end{array}$ 56. $\begin{array}{r} 0 \\ \times 1 \\ \hline \end{array}$

57. $\begin{array}{r} 2 \\ \times 2 \\ \hline \end{array}$ 58. $\begin{array}{r} 1 \\ \times 4 \\ \hline \end{array}$ 59. $\begin{array}{r} 3 \\ \times 2 \\ \hline \end{array}$ 60. $\begin{array}{r} 0 \\ \times 3 \\ \hline \end{array}$ 61. $\begin{array}{r} 2 \\ \times 5 \\ \hline \end{array}$ 62. $\begin{array}{r} 3 \\ \times 3 \\ \hline \end{array}$ 63. $\begin{array}{r} 3 \\ \times 5 \\ \hline \end{array}$

Multiply.

1. $7 \times 2 = \square$ 2. $9 \times 1 = \square$ 3. $6 \times 2 = \square$ 4. $8 \times 0 = \square$

5. $6 \times 5 = \square$ 6. $9 \times 2 = \square$ 7. $7 \times 1 = \square$ 8. $6 \times 6 = \square$

9. $8 \times 5 = \square$ 10. $9 \times 6 = \square$ 11. $7 \times 5 = \square$ 12. $8 \times 2 = \square$

13. $7 \times 6 = \square$ 14. $9 \times 0 = \square$ 15. $6 \times 8 = \square$ 16. $8 \times 1 = \square$

17. $6 \times 3 = \square$ 18. $9 \times 5 = \square$ 19. $7 \times 7 = \square$ 20. $8 \times 6 = \square$

21. 3×7 22. 1×6 23. 7×8 24. 9×8 25. 3×9 26. 4×6 27. 7×9

28. 9×6 29. 3×8 30. 8×9 31. 4×7 32. 8×8 33. 8×7 34. 4×9

35. 5×6 36. 9×7 37. 7×6 38. 4×8 39. 9×9 40. 0×7 41. 6×8

42. 7×7 43. 0×6 44. 5×8 45. 6×6 46. 2×8 47. 4×7 48. 5×7

49. 9×7 50. 8×6 51. 2×7 52. 4×6 53. 5×9 54. 4×8 55. 8×8

56. 2×9 57. 3×6 58. 6×9 59. 9×9 60. 8×6 61. 4×9 62. 7×6

Multiply.

	A	B	C	D	E	F	G	H	I	J
1.	2 ×6	5 ×8	1 ×1	4 ×0	5 ×1	0 ×9	4 ×4	5 ×7	3 ×2	3 ×9
2.	2 ×9	0 ×0	2 ×8	1 ×0	3 ×6	0 ×8	1 ×2	4 ×7	2 ×5	5 ×0
3.	2 ×7	1 ×3	2 ×0	3 ×1	5 ×6	4 ×8	2 ×1	0 ×6	1 ×4	1 ×7
4.	2 ×2	0 ×2	1 ×6	5 ×3	1 ×5	0 ×3	5 ×9	3 ×7	4 ×9	3 ×3
5.	4 ×3	0 ×5	2 ×3	5 ×4	5 ×2	1 ×9	0 ×4	5 ×5	4 ×1	3 ×0
6.	1 ×8	4 ×5	3 ×8	0 ×7	2 ×4	3 ×5	3 ×4	4 ×2	4 ×6	0 ×1
7.	9 ×5	8 ×9	9 ×0	7 ×4	6 ×1	9 ×2	7 ×3	7 ×9	6 ×6	9 ×4
8.	9 ×9	8 ×3	6 ×0	8 ×7	9 ×1	7 ×8	8 ×4	9 ×6	6 ×7	9 ×8
9.	9 ×7	8 ×2	7 ×6	6 ×4	7 ×7	7 ×1	8 ×5	6 ×3	8 ×1	6 ×2
10.	6 ×9	7 ×5	8 ×0	6 ×5	7 ×2	6 ×8	8 ×8	9 ×3	7 ×0	8 ×6

Divide.

1. $4 \div 2 = \square$ 2. $9 \div 1 = \square$ 3. $8 \div 2 = \square$ 4. $18 \div 3 = \square$

5. $10 \div 5 = \square$ 6. $21 \div 3 = \square$ 7. $3 \div 1 = \square$ 8. $5 \div 5 = \square$

9. $16 \div 2 = \square$ 10. $0 \div 3 = \square$ 11. $20 \div 5 = \square$ 12. $9 \div 3 = \square$

13. $4 \div 4 = \square$ 14. $24 \div 4 = \square$ 15. $32 \div 4 = \square$ 16. $24 \div 3 = \square$

17. $2\overline{)18}$ 18. $3\overline{)6}$ 19. $5\overline{)25}$ 20. $2\overline{)14}$ 21. $5\overline{)35}$

22. $1\overline{)8}$ 23. $4\overline{)28}$ 24. $4\overline{)16}$ 25. $2\overline{)10}$ 26. $3\overline{)27}$

27. $5\overline{)30}$ 28. $4\overline{)20}$ 29. $2\overline{)12}$ 30. $3\overline{)15}$ 31. $4\overline{)36}$

32. $1\overline{)7}$ 33. $4\overline{)12}$ 34. $5\overline{)40}$ 35. $1\overline{)5}$ 36. $5\overline{)45}$

Divide.

1. $7 \div 7 = \square$ 2. $12 \div 6 = \square$ 3. $27 \div 9 = \square$ 4. $14 \div 7 = \square$

5. $0 \div 8 = \square$ 6. $24 \div 6 = \square$ 7. $16 \div 8 = \square$ 8. $21 \div 7 = \square$

9. $42 \div 6 = \square$ 10. $35 \div 7 = \square$ 11. $40 \div 8 = \square$ 12. $63 \div 7 = \square$

13. $48 \div 8 = \square$ 14. $56 \div 8 = \square$ 15. $72 \div 8 = \square$ 16. $64 \div 8 = \square$

17. $7\overline{)56}$ 18. $9\overline{)54}$ 19. $6\overline{)48}$ 20. $7\overline{)49}$ 21. $8\overline{)24}$

22. $6\overline{)36}$ 23. $7\overline{)42}$ 24. $6\overline{)0}$ 25. $9\overline{)63}$ 26. $8\overline{)32}$

27. $7\overline{)28}$ 28. $6\overline{)18}$ 29. $9\overline{)81}$ 30. $6\overline{)30}$ 31. $9\overline{)72}$

32. $7\overline{)56}$ 33. $6\overline{)54}$ 34. $9\overline{)36}$ 35. $8\overline{)48}$ 36. $9\overline{)45}$

Multiply.

1. 23 × 3	2. 41 × 2	3. 54 × 2	4. 31 × 5	5. 60 × 4	6. 14 × 2
7. 70 × 3	8. 52 × 2	9. 22 × 4	10. 43 × 2	11. 11 × 6	12. 72 × 4
13. 31 × 3	14. 62 × 3	15. 91 × 4	16. 83 × 2	17. 51 × 3	18. 42 × 3
19. 82 × 4	20. 21 × 6	21. 70 × 8	22. 34 × 2	23. 93 × 3	24. 53 × 2

Set B   For use after page 221

Multiply.

1. 36 × 2	2. 84 × 7	3. 29 × 4	4. 64 × 5	5. 76 × 4	6. 57 × 6
7. 97 × 3	8. 68 × 2	9. 35 × 5	10. 87 × 2	11. 48 × 6	12. 73 × 9
13. 78 × 5	14. 49 × 6	15. 93 × 4	16. 54 × 8	17. 38 × 7	18. 89 × 5
19. 15 × 7	20. 46 × 3	21. 74 × 4	22. 25 × 6	23. 58 × 3	24. 77 × 5
25. 86 × 6	26. 34 × 3	27. 55 × 8	28. 92 × 9	29. 47 × 7	30. 79 × 8
31. 45 × 4	32. 67 × 6	33. 83 × 8	34. 28 × 7	35. 56 × 3	36. 88 × 8

Multiply.

1.	42 × 5	2.	77 × 3	3.	40 × 6	4.	56 × 7	5.	34 × 8	6.	65 × 6
7.	28 × 9	8.	54 × 9	9.	35 × 2	10.	82 × 3	11.	39 × 5	12.	24 × 7
13.	75 × 8	14.	26 × 3	15.	44 × 4	16.	45 × 3	17.	53 × 7	18.	70 × 9
19.	86 × 9	20.	69 × 8	21.	55 × 6	22.	16 × 7	23.	38 × 3	24.	63 × 4
25.	18 × 7	26.	95 × 2	27.	21 × 5	28.	66 × 4	29.	88 × 7	30.	97 × 6

Multiply.

1.	75¢ × 3	2.	15¢ × 6	3.	19¢ × 4	4.	69¢ × 5	5.	50¢ × 8	6.	62¢ × 2
7.	33¢ × 4	8.	98¢ × 3	9.	64¢ × 6	10.	40¢ × 9	11.	84¢ × 7	12.	99¢ × 5
13.	20¢ × 8	14.	67¢ × 7	15.	89¢ × 4	16.	25¢ × 9	17.	10¢ × 6	18.	83¢ × 3
19.	47¢ × 6	20.	72¢ × 5	21.	58¢ × 4	22.	44¢ × 7	23.	51¢ × 8	24.	88¢ × 2
25.	49¢ × 9	26.	92¢ × 3	27.	74¢ × 8	28.	90¢ × 7	29.	93¢ × 5	30.	68¢ × 6

Multiply.

1. 341 × 3	2. 536 × 2	3. 871 × 5	4. 713 × 4	5. 221 × 6	6. 625 × 3
7. 416 × 4	8. 614 × 5	9. 139 × 2	10. 513 × 7	11. 926 × 3	12. 328 × 2
13. 715 × 6	14. 527 × 3	15. 414 × 7	16. 324 × 4	17. 637 × 2	18. 563 × 3
19. 231 × 8	20. 881 × 4	21. 953 × 2	22. 651 × 3	23. 416 × 6	24. 742 × 4

Set B   For use after page 227

Multiply.

1. 435 × 6	2. 267 × 4	3. 548 × 5	4. 735 × 3	5. 368 × 2	6. 476 × 8
7. 647 × 3	8. 895 × 2	9. 128 × 7	10. 949 × 4	11. 248 × 6	12. 568 × 3
13. 927 × 5	14. 776 × 2	15. 424 × 8	16. 635 × 5	17. 586 × 4	18. 857 × 5
19. 394 × 5	20. 838 × 6	21. 557 × 7	22. 783 × 4	23. 479 × 6	24. 626 × 7
25. 463 × 9	26. 655 × 7	27. 386 × 5	28. 237 × 9	29. 824 × 6	30. 953 × 5
31. 726 × 8	32. 593 × 4	33. 829 × 5	34. 474 × 3	35. 668 × 7	36. 392 × 8

Divide.

	A	B	C	D	E	F	G	H	I
1.	5)0̄	1)3̄	5)4̄0̄	4)2̄8̄	2)1̄8̄	3)2̄1̄	2)2̄	2)8̄	3)6̄
2.	4)4̄	5)3̄0̄	3)1̄2̄	4)2̄0̄	5)2̄5̄	1)0̄	3)3̄	1)6̄	2)0̄
3.	2)1̄6̄	5)2̄0̄	1)1̄	4)0̄	4)2̄4̄	3)9̄	2)6̄	1)9̄	3)2̄7̄
4.	2)1̄2̄	5)3̄5̄	3)1̄5̄	5)5̄	2)1̄4̄	3)1̄8̄	3)0̄	4)3̄6̄	5)1̄5̄
5.	1)4̄	5)4̄5̄	4)8̄	3)2̄4̄	5)1̄0̄	1)5̄	4)1̄2̄	1)8̄	2)4̄
6.	4)1̄6̄	4)3̄2̄	1)2̄	2)1̄0̄	1)7̄	9)7̄2̄	6)3̄0̄	9)9̄	6)1̄8̄
7.	6)0̄	9)5̄4̄	8)4̄0̄	7)2̄1̄	9)4̄5̄	6)4̄2̄	9)0̄	7)4̄2̄	8)8̄
8.	6)1̄2̄	9)8̄1̄	7)0̄	7)5̄6̄	6)2̄4̄	6)6̄	7)7̄	8)2̄4̄	7)6̄3̄
9.	6)4̄8̄	8)6̄4̄	6)3̄6̄	7)1̄4̄	9)3̄6̄	8)1̄6̄	7)3̄5̄	8)5̄6̄	9)6̄3̄
10.	6)5̄4̄	8)0̄	7)2̄8̄	7)4̄9̄	8)3̄2̄	9)2̄7̄	8)7̄2̄	9)1̄8̄	8)4̄8̄

Find the quotients and remainders.

1. $4\overline{)17}$ 2. $3\overline{)26}$ 3. $6\overline{)45}$ 4. $2\overline{)13}$ 5. $5\overline{)38}$

6. $3\overline{)19}$ 7. $7\overline{)31}$ 8. $2\overline{)17}$ 9. $6\overline{)34}$ 10. $4\overline{)25}$

11. $8\overline{)44}$ 12. $5\overline{)18}$ 13. $9\overline{)58}$ 14. $7\overline{)65}$ 15. $2\overline{)15}$

16. $9\overline{)76}$ 17. $6\overline{)38}$ 18. $3\overline{)23}$ 19. $5\overline{)48}$ 20. $4\overline{)33}$

21. $5\overline{)13}$ 22. $7\overline{)51}$ 23. $4\overline{)22}$ 24. $6\overline{)52}$ 25. $3\overline{)29}$

26. $3\overline{)14}$ 27. $4\overline{)37}$ 28. $5\overline{)28}$ 29. $9\overline{)24}$ 30. $8\overline{)59}$

31. $7\overline{)68}$ 32. $6\overline{)47}$ 33. $4\overline{)30}$ 34. $2\overline{)19}$ 35. $5\overline{)23}$

Find the quotients and remainders.

1. $5\overline{)243}$ 2. $7\overline{)381}$ 3. $6\overline{)493}$ 4. $8\overline{)571}$ 5. $4\overline{)367}$

6. $7\overline{)170}$ 7. $4\overline{)215}$ 8. $2\overline{)131}$ 9. $3\overline{)140}$ 10. $6\overline{)231}$

11. $5\overline{)313}$ 12. $8\overline{)350}$ 13. $3\overline{)176}$ 14. $4\overline{)306}$ 15. $2\overline{)169}$

16. $6\overline{)151}$ 17. $2\overline{)147}$ 18. $7\overline{)451}$ 19. $3\overline{)247}$ 20. $8\overline{)450}$

21. $9\overline{)327}$ 22. $4\overline{)194}$ 23. $5\overline{)463}$ 24. $6\overline{)430}$ 25. $7\overline{)267}$

26. $6\overline{)346}$ 27. $2\overline{)139}$ 28. $7\overline{)516}$ 29. $5\overline{)412}$ 30. $3\overline{)199}$

31. $7\overline{)395}$ 32. $5\overline{)341}$ 33. $4\overline{)310}$ 34. $3\overline{)257}$ 35. $6\overline{)404}$

Find the quotients and remainders. Check your answers.

1. 3)127 2. 5)367 3. 2)113 4. 6)232 5. 4)261

6. 7)256 7. 6)265 8. 3)217 9. 5)317 10. 2)163

11. 6)327 12. 4)182 13. 5)413 14. 8)274 15. 3)193

16. 4)294 17. 9)238 18. 7)290 19. 6)331 20. 4)329

21. 2)135 22. 5)267 23. 3)254 24. 7)199 25. 8)349

26. 9)346 27. 4)261 28. 6)435 29. 5)196 30. 3)283

31. 3)281 32. 8)435 33. 4)153 34. 7)471 35. 9)416

36. 7)333 37. 6)435 38. 5)408 39. 3)233 40. 4)381

41. 3)115 42. 8)674 43. 4)226 44. 6)385 45. 7)502

46. 5)467 47. 2)153 48. 3)170 49. 7)668 50. 4)193

51. 9)473 52. 6)495 53. 5)332 54. 2)99 55. 7)263

56. 8)732 57. 3)203 58. 7)589 59. 4)301 60. 6)572

61. 7)445 62. 6)177 63. 5)282 64. 3)289 65. 8)506

66. 4)233 67. 5)413 68. 7)331 69. 9)258 70. 6)237

Solve.

1. Wendy swam 8 laps before lunch and 7 laps before dinner. How many laps did Wendy swim in all?

2. Jim's volleyball team won 12 games. Stan's team won 6 games. How many more games did Jim's team win?

3. Vicki ran 4 km on Monday, 6 km on Tuesday, and 3 km on Wednesday. How far did Vicki run in all?

4. There are 6 people in the morning tennis class. There are 5 people in the afternoon class. How many people are in tennis classes?
Three people decided not to take any more lessons. Now how many are taking lessons?

5. Carl caught 4 trout and 2 bass. How many fish did he catch?
Carl threw 3 of the fish back. How many did he take home?

6. Sarah has 8 yellow ping pong balls and 6 white ping pong balls. How many ping pong balls does she have?
Two of the balls are cracked. How many are not cracked?

Solve.

1. Janice collected 65 stamps for her stamp album. Her brother gave her another 46 stamps. How many stamps does she have for her album?

2. Ted bought 12 model airplanes and 21 model boats last year. How many models did he buy?
If Ted has built 9 of these models, how many more does he have left to build?

3. Frannie collected 40 nickels and 35 pennies for her coin collection. How many coins did she have?
Frannie's coin album only held 50 coins. How many extra coins did she have?

4. Kirk had 247 baseball cards. John had 98 baseball cards. How many more cards did Kirk have?

5. Dan had 98 clear marbles, 42 steel marbles, and 21 cats-eye marbles. How many marbles did he have in all?

6. Diane had 18 antique brown bottles. She had 15 antique clear bottles. How many bottles did she have in her collection?
She had caps for 7 of the bottles. How many bottles still need caps?

Solve.

1. This summer 68 boys and 55 girls went to camp. How many went to camp altogether?

2. There are 12 rowboats and 22 sailboats on the lake. Five boats are white and the rest are blue. How many blue boats are on the lake?

3. The cook ordered 186 L of regular milk and 66 L of low-fat milk for the trip. At the end of the week 25 L of milk were left over. How much milk did the campers drink?

4. Sue found 45 pretty stones at the lake. Kimberly found 70. How many more stones did Kimberly find?

5. Last night 15 campfires were lit. During the night 8 fires went out. Three more fires were lit in the morning for cooking breakfast. How many fires were burning at breakfast time?

6. Mr. Page took 25 children on a hike. After 5 km, 5 children went back to camp. After 10 km, 5 more children went back. The rest of the children finished the hike. How many children finished the hike?

Solve.

1. There were 29 students in the third grade class. Five students moved away, and 6 new students entered the class. Now how many students are in the third grade class?

2. There are 3 third grade classes at Lincoln School. There are 25 students in one room, 29 in another, and 31 in another. How many students are in third grade at Lincoln School?

3. There are 175 students at school. At lunch 50 students ate pizza, 29 had soup, and the rest ate sandwiches. How many students ate sandwiches?

4. There are 32 students in Mr. Neal's class. All but 18 students are in clubs. How many are in clubs?

5. One day 72 children rode the bus to school. Twenty students got on at the first bus stop and 31 got on at the second stop. The rest got on at the third stop. How many got on the bus at the third stop?

6. There were 65 students in the school play. There were 24 students helping with costumes. There were 18 more students building scenery. The rest of the students were actors. How many were actors?

Multiply or divide.

1. Rose bought 4 cartons of juice. Each carton holds 6 cans. How many cans of juice did Rose buy?

2. Tina bought 3 cartons of eggs. Each carton holds 12 eggs. How many eggs did Tina buy?

3. Jimmy put 3 tomatoes in each package. Altogether he put 24 tomatoes in packages. How many packages did he make?

4. Plastic cups are sold in packages of 8. How many cups would you get in 9 packages?

5. There are 45 grocery carts in 5 rows. Each row has the same number of carts. How many carts are in each row?

6. There were 24 hot dog rolls at the picnic. Each person took 3 rolls and there were none left over. How many people were at the picnic?

Multiply or divide.

1. There are 4 glasses on each table. There are 24 tables in the restaurant. How many glasses are on all of the tables?

2. The waiter put 128 packages of crackers in baskets. He put 4 packages in each basket. How many baskets did he fill?

3. Jeremy worked 40 hours at the restaurant last week. He worked 8 hours each day. How many days did he work?

4. Napkins are placed in piles of 5. How many piles can you make if you have 173 napkins?

5. The chef cuts each pie into 6 pieces. One day the restaurant sold 32 pies. How many pieces of pie were sold?

6. The dishwasher can hold 45 plates. On Saturday, the dishwasher was filled with plates 9 different times. How many plates were washed?

Solve.

1. There are 14 adult elephants and 8 baby elephants in the circus. How many elephants are in the circus?

2. Tickets for rides are sold in sets of 3. Mr. James bought 16 sets for his family. How many tickets did he buy?

3. Each child is given 2 balloons at the circus. If 174 balloons were given away, how many children went to the circus?

4. There were 335 people at the afternoon show. There were 428 at the evening show. How many more people went to the evening show?

5. Each row of seats in the magic show can hold 35 people. If there are 8 rows of seats, how many people can watch the magic show?

6. An elephant eats about 150 pounds of food each day. About how much does it eat in one week?

Solve.

1. The farmer had 20 cows and 12 bulls. How many cattle did the farmer have?

2. Jim had 144 chickens. He put the same number of chickens in each of his 6 chicken houses. How many chickens did he put in each house?

3. A cow eats about 42 pounds of food in one day. How much food does a cow eat in a week?

4. Carol's horse weighs 535 kg and her pony weighs 285 kg. How much more does her horse weigh?

5. The Barretts have 450 sheep and 350 pigs on their ranch. How many more sheep do the Barretts have?

6. Mrs. Ames's truck can hold about 24 bales of hay. How many bales in 7 truck loads?

Table of Measures

Metric System		English System	

Length

Metric System		English System	
1 centimeter (cm)	{10 millimeters (mm)		
1 decimeter (dm)	{100 millimeters (mm) {10 centimeters (cm)	1 foot (ft)	{12 inches (in.)
1 meter (m)	{1000 millimeters (mm) {100 centimeters (cm) {10 decimeters (dm)	1 yard (yd)	{36 inches (in.) {3 feet (ft)
		1 mile (mi)	{5280 feet (ft) {1760 yards (yd)
1 kilometer (km)	{1000 meters (m)		

Area

Metric System		English System	
1 square meter (m²)	{100 square decimeters (dm²) 10 000 square centimeters (cm²)	1 square foot (ft²)	{144 square inches (in.²)

Volume

Metric System		English System	
1 cubic decimeter (dm³)	{1000 cubic centimeters (cm³) 1 liter (L)	1 cubic foot (ft³)	{1728 cubic inches (in.³)

Capacity

Metric System		English System	
		1 cup (c)	{8 fluid ounces (fl oz)
1 teaspoon	{5 milliliters (mL)	1 pint (pt)	{16 fluid ounces (fl oz) {2 cups (c)
1 tablespoon	{12.5 milliliters (mL)	1 quart (qt)	{32 fluid ounces (fl oz) {4 cups (c) {2 pints (pt)
1 liter (L)	{1000 milliliters (mL) 1000 cubic centimeters (cm³) 1 cubic decimeter (dm³) 4 metric cups	1 gallon (gal)	{128 fluid ounces (fl oz) 16 cups (c) 8 pints (pt) 4 quarts (qt)

Mass

Metric System		English System	
1 gram (g)	{1000 milligrams (mg)	1 pound (lb)	{16 ounces (oz)
1 kilogram (kg)	{1000 grams (g)		

Time

Metric System		English System	
1 minute (min)	{60 seconds (s)	1 year (yr)	{365 days 52 weeks 12 months
1 hour (h)	{60 minutes (min)		
1 day (d)	{24 hours (h)		
1 week (w)	{7 days (d)	1 decade	{10 years
1 month (mo)	{about 4 weeks	1 century	{100 years

Glossary

acute angle   An angle with a measure of less than 90 degrees.

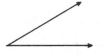

addend   Any one of a set of numbers to be added. In the equation 4 + 5 = 9, the numbers 4 and 5 are addends.

addition   An operation that combines a first number and a second number to give exactly one number called a sum.

angle   Two rays from a single point.

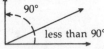

area   The measure of a region as compared to a given unit, usually a square region.

associative (grouping) principle   When adding (or multiplying) three or more numbers, the grouping of the addends (or factors) can be changed and the sum (or product) is the same.

 Examples: 2 + (8 + 6) = (2 + 8) + 6
      3 × (4 × 2) = (3 × 4) × 2

average   The average of a set of numbers is the quotient resulting when the sum of the numbers in the set is divided by the number of addends.

centimeter   A unit of length. One centimeter is 0.01 meter.

1 centimeter

circle   The set of all points in a plane which are a specified distance from a given point called the center.

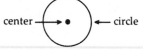

commutative (order) principle   When adding (or multiplying) two or more numbers, the order of the addends (or factors) can be changed and the sum (or product) is the same.

 Examples: 4 + 5 = 5 + 4
      2 × 3 = 3 × 2

compass   A device for drawing models of a circle.

congruent figures   Figures that have the same size and shape.

congruent triangles

coordinates   Number pairs used in graphing.

coordinate axes   Two number lines intersecting at right angles at 0.

count   To name numbers in regular succession.

cube   A rectangular prism (box) such that all faces are squares.

denominator   The number indicated by the numeral below the line in a fraction symbol.

 Example: $\dfrac{1}{3}$ ◄─── denominator

diameter   A segment that joins two points on a circle and passes through the center of the circle.

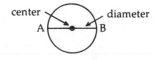

difference   The number obtained by subtracting one number from another.

 Example: 48
      − 25
      ‾‾‾‾
      23 ◄─── difference

digits   The basic Hindu-Arabic symbols used to write numerals. In the base-ten system, the digits are 0, 1, 2, 3, 4, 5, 6, 7, 8, and 9.

distributive (multiplication-addition) principle   This principle is sometimes described in terms of "breaking apart" a number before multiplying.

 Example: 6 × (20 + 4) = (6 × 20) + (6 × 4)

dividend   The number to be divided in a division problem.

 Example: 4
      7)33 ◄─── dividend
      − 28
      ‾‾‾‾
      5

division   An operation that is the inverse of multiplication.

divisor   The number by which the dividend is divided.

 Example: 4
    divisor ──► 7)33
        − 28
        ‾‾‾‾
        5

edge   An edge of a space figure is one of the segments making up any one of the faces of the figure.

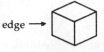

equality (equals or =)   A mathematical relation of being exactly the same.

equation   A mathematical sentence involving the use of the equality symbol.

Examples: $5 + 4 = 9$
$7 + \square = 8$
$n + 3 = 7$

equivalent fractions   Two fractions are equivalent when it can be shown that they each can be used to represent the same amount of a given object. Two fractions are equivalent if these two products are the same:

equivalent sets   Two sets that may be placed in a one-to-one correspondence.

estimate   To find an approximation for a given number. (Sometimes a sum, a product, etc.)

even numbers   The whole-number multiples of 2 $(0,2,4,6,8,10,12, \ldots)$

face   The face of a given space figure is any one of the plane geometric figures making up the space figure.

face →

factor (see multiplication)   In the equation $6 \times 7 = 42$, 6 and 7 are factors of 42.

fraction   A symbol for a fractional number such as $\frac{2}{3}, \frac{3}{4},$ or $\frac{1}{2}$.

fractional number   The one number we think about for each set of equivalent fractions. For the set $\frac{1}{2}, \frac{2}{4}, \frac{3}{6}, \frac{4}{8}, \ldots$ we think of one number, often expressed as one half or $\frac{1}{2}$.

graph   (1) A set of points associated with a given set of numbers or set of number pairs. (2) A picture used to illustrate a given collection of data. The data might be pictured in the form of a bar graph, a circle graph, a line graph, or a pictograph. (3) To draw the graph of.

greater than (>)   One of the two basic inequality relations.

Example: $6 > 5$, read 6 is greater than 5

hexagon   A polygon which has six sides.

improper fraction   A fraction in which the numerator is greater than or equal to the denominator.

Examples: $\frac{8}{5}, \frac{9}{6}, \frac{12}{3}, \frac{7}{7},$ etc.

inequality (>, ≠, <)   In arithmetic, a relation indicating that the two numbers are not equal.

kilogram   A unit of mass in the metric system. 1 kilogram is 1000 grams.

kilometer   A unit of length in the metric system. 1 kilometer is 1000 meters.

length   A number indicating the measure of one line segment with respect to another line segment called the unit.

less than (<)   One of the two basic inequality relations.

Example: $5 < 6$, read 5 is less than 6

line   A line is a straight path (formed by a set of points) that goes on and on in two directions.

line segment   See segment.

liter (cubic decimeter)   The basic unit of capacity in the metric system. 1 liter is 1000 milliliters.

lowest terms   A fraction is in lowest terms if the numerator and denominator of the fraction have no common factor greater than 1.

Examples: $\frac{3}{4}, \frac{5}{8}, \frac{11}{16}$

measure   (1) A number indicating the relation between a given object and a suitable unit. (2) The process of finding the number described above.

meter   The basic unit of length in the metric system. 1 meter is 100 centimeters.

minus (−)   Used to indicate the subtraction operation, as in $7 - 3 = 4$, read 7 minus 3 equals 4.

mixed numerals   Symbols such as $2\frac{1}{2}$ and $3\frac{1}{4}$

multiple   A first number is a multiple of a second number if there is a whole number that multiplies by the second number to give the first number.

Example: 24 is a multiple of 6 since $4 \times 6 = 24$.

multiplication   An operation that combines two numbers, called factors, to give one number called the product.

number line   A line with a subset of its points matched with a subset of the real numbers.

$$0 \ 1 \ 2 \ 3 \ 4 \ 5 \ 6 \ 7 \ 8 \ 9$$

numeral   A symbol for a number.

numerator   The number indicated by the numeral above the line in a fraction symbol.

Example: $\frac{3}{4}$ ← numerator

obtuse angle   An angle with a measure greater than 90°.

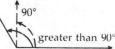

octagon   A polygon which has eight sides.

odd number   Any whole number that is not even.

Examples: 1, 3, 5, 7, 9, 11, 13, . . .

one principle (for multiplication)   Any number multiplied by 1 is that same number. One is the identity element for multiplication. $1 \times 8 = 8$

parallel lines Two lines which lie in the same plane and do not intersect.

pentagon A polygon which has five sides.

perimeter The sum of the lengths of the sides of a given polygon.

place value The value given to the place a digit occupies in a numeral.

Example:

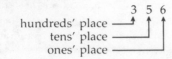

plus (+) Used to indicate the addition operation, as in 4 + 3 = 7, read 4 plus 3 equals 7.

polygon A closed geometric figure made up of line segments.

prime number A number greater than 1 whose only factors are itself and 1.

Examples: 2, 3, 5, 7, 11, 13, etc.

product The result of the multiplication operation. In the equation 6 × 7 = 42, 42 is the product of 6 and 7.

quadrilateral A polygon which has four sides.

quotient The number (other than the remainder) that is the result of the division operation.

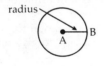

Examples: 45 ÷ 9 = 5

radius (1) Any segment from the center to a point on the circle. (2) The distance from the center to any point on the circle.

ray A ray is a part of a line consisting of a point and the part of the line on one side of the point.

rectangle A quadrilateral which has four right angles.

regrouping A method of handling place value symbols in adding or subtracting numbers.

Example:

remainder The number less than the divisor that remains after the division process is completed.

Example:

right angle An angle that has the measure of 90°.

right triangle A triangle that has one right angle.

Roman numerals Numerals used by the Romans, primarily to record numbers rather than for computing.

Examples: I, V, X, L, C, D, and M are symbols for 1, 5, 10, 50, 100, 500, and 1000 respectively.

segment Two points on a line and all the points on the line that are between the two points.

set undefined; usually thought of as a group or collection.

similar figures Two figures that have the same shape.

skip count To count by multiples of a given number.

Example: 0, 5, 10, 15, . . . (counting by fives)

solve To find the number or numbers which, when substituted for the variable or place holder, make a given equation true.

square A quadrilateral that has four right angles and four sides that are the same length.

subtraction An operation related to addition as illustrated:

$$7 + 8 = 15 \begin{cases} 15 - 8 = 7 \\ 15 - 7 = 8 \end{cases}$$

sum The number obtained by adding any set of numbers.

Example:

symmetric figure A figure that can be folded in half so that the two halves match.

times (×) Used to indicate the multiplication operation, as in 3 × 4 = 12, read 3 times 4 equals 12.

triangle A polygon which has three sides.

triangular pyramid A four-sided space figure that has triangular regions for all faces.

triangular pyramid

unit An amount or quantity adopted as a standard of measurement.

vertex The point that the two rays of an angle have in common.

vertex

volume The measure, obtained using an appropriate unit (usually a cube), of the interior region of a space figure.

whole number Any number in the set: 0, 1, 2, 3, 4, 5, 6, 7, 8, 9, 10, 11, 12, 13, 14, ...

zero principle (for addition) Any number added to zero is that same number. 0 + 5 = 5

Index

A

Addends, and sums, 3
Addition
  algorithm, 60, 62
  and multiplication, 112-13
  column addition, 20-21
  decimals, 310-311
  doubles, 13-14
  facts to 10, 2-5
  facts to 18, 12-15
  looking for tens, 21
  money, 88-89
  more than 2 addends with regrouping, 64-65
  practice of facts for speed, 18
  three 2-digit numbers without regrouping, 59
  trading ten sticks, 56-57
  2- and 3-digit addition without regrouping, 58-59
  2-digit addition with regrouping, 60-61
  3-digit addition with regrouping, 62-63
Algorithm
  addition, 60, 62
  division, 272, 274, 276
  multiplication, 220, 224, 226
  subtraction, 72, 74, 76-78
Area
  counting square units, 246-249, 317A
  rectangle, 221
  square centimeter unit, 245
  square inch, 317A
Attribute pieces, 154-155

C

Center, 41
Centimeter
  measuring, 96-97
  measuring to nearest centimeter, 98-99
  square, 245
  unit, 245
Cents, see **Money**
Checking division, 278-279
Circles
  center, 41
  drawing, 40-41
  inside, 43
Column addition
  more than 2 addends with regrouping, 64-65
  sums to 18, 20-21
  2-digit numbers without regrouping, 59

Comparing numbers, 90-91

Comparing numbers, 90-91
Compass, 41
Congruent figures, 158-159
Coordinate geometry, 115
Corner, 35
Counting
  counting square units for area, 246-247
  counting to 99, 49
  counting 3-digit numbers, 51
Cube, pattern for, 34
Cubic unit, 250, 317B
cup, 318A-318B

D

Decimals
  adding, 310-311
  reading and writing, 305-307
  tenths of a centimeter, 308-309
Difference, 3
Division
  algorithm, 272, 274, 276
  and sets, 166-167
  checking, 278-279
  dividing by 1, 2, or 3, 176-177
  dividing by 4, 178
  dividing by 1, 2, 3, or 4, 179
  dividing by 5, 180
  dividing by 1, 2, 3, 4, or 5, 181
  dividing by 6, 260
  dividing by 4, 5, or 6, 261
  dividing by 1, 2, 3, 4, 5, or 6, 261
  dividing by 7, 262
  dividing by 5, 6, or 7, 263
  dividing by 1, 2, 3, 4, 5, 6, or 7, 263
  dividing by 8, 264
  dividing by 6, 7, or 8, 265
  dividing by 1, 2, 3, 4, 5, 6, 7, or 8, 265
  dividing by 9, 266
  dividing by 1, 2, 3, 4, 5, 6, 7, 8, or 9, 267
  fact family equations, 183, 258
  missing factors and division, 174-175, 259
  new sign for division, 182
  quotient, 168-169
  subtraction in dividing, 170-171, 271
  1-digit quotients, 272-273
  2-digit quotients, 274-277
Dollar sign, 88
Doubles, 13-14

E

Edge, 35
Equations
    addition, 2, 13, 15, 19
    division, 166-167, 171
    multiplication, 119, 123, 131, 133, 135, 137
    subtraction, 2, 19
Estimation, 240-241, 319B

F

Faces, 35
Fact families
    addition and subtraction to 10, 8-9
    addition and subtraction to 18, 16-17
    multiplication and division, 176, 178, 180, 183-184, 258
Factors, 150-151
    factors and products, 110-111
    factors of 10 and 100, 210-211
    missing factors and division, 174-175, 259
Facts
    addition to 10, 2-5
    addition to 18, 12-15
    division, 176-267
    multiplication, 118-137
    subtraction to 10, 6-7
Foot, 316A-316B
Fourths, 295-296
Fractional numbers
    more and less in tenths, 301
    parts of a set, 298-299
    parts of a whole, 296-297
    reading and writing, 294-295
    symmetry, 303
    tenths, 300-301

G

Gallon, 318A-318B
Games
    counters, 11
    Toss the Number Cubes (addition), 23
    Guess My Rule (addition and subtraction to 18), 30
    Guess My Number (addition and subtraction to 18), 31
    One-Ten-Hundred Game, 55
    Magic Squares, 67
    Card Game, drawing digits to make subtraction problems, 81
    Downhill Race (multiplication), 121
    Score Line Games (multiplication), 121

    Score Line Games (multiplication), 125
    Number Name Game, 127, 269
    Breaking a Code, 141, 215
    Horseshoe Game, 153
    Hidden Shapes, 185
    Roman Numeral Puzzle, 205
    Cover the Strip Game, 197
Geometry
    attribute pieces, 154-155
    circles, 40-41
    congruent figures, 158-159
    coordinate, 115
    corner, 35
    edge, 35
    face, 35
    hidden shapes, 185
    pattern for a cube, 34
    point, 35
    segment, 35
    shapes, 36-37
    similar figure, 156-157
    square, 35
Graphs
    reading and making bar graphs, 198, 200-201
    reading picture graphs, 199, 202-203

H

Halves, 293-295
Hundreds, 50-51

I

Inch
    measuring, 314A-315B
    square, 317A
    cubic, 317B
Inequalities
    tenths, 301
    whole numbers, 90-91
Inside and outside, 43

K

Kilometer, 100-101

L

Length, 96-101
Liquid measure
    cup, quart, pint, and gallon, 318A-318B
    liter and cups, 252-253
Liter, 252-253

M

Magic Squares, 67
Measurement
  area (counting units), 248-249, 317A
  area (square inches), 317A
  calendar, 321B
  centimeter units, 96-97, 245
  compare length of line segments on
    geoboard, 103
  counting square units, 246-247, 317A
  cubic unit, 250, 317B
  cup and liter, 252-253
  half hour and quarter hour, 320A
  inch ruler, 314B-315B
  kilometer, 100-101
  larger units for length (foot, yard,
    mile), 316A-316B
  liquid measure (cup, pint, quart,
    gallon), 318A-318B
  measure to nearest centimeter, 98-99
  measuring to the nearest $\frac{1}{2}$ and $\frac{1}{4}$ inches,
    315A-315B
  square centimeter unit, 245
  tenths of a centimeter, 308-309
  volume, 250-251, 317B
  5-minute intervals on clock, 320B
Meter, 100-101
Mile, 316B
Missing factors and division, 174-175, 259
Money
  adding and subtracting, 88-89
  multiplication, 222-223
Multiplication
  algorithm, 220, 224, 226
  and addition, 112-113
  factors and products, 110-111
  0, 1, and 2 facts, 118-119
  money, 222-223
  multiplying by 3, 120-121
  multiplying by 4, 122-123
  multiplying by 5, 124-125
  multiplying by 6, 130-131
  multiplying by 7, 132-133
  multiplying by 8, 134-135
  multiplying by 9, 136-137
  multiplication triangles, 195
  multiplication wheels, 139
  practice for speed (facts to 9), 138
  sets, 108-109
  special products, 210-213
  tables, 119, 123, 139
  using cubes, 107
  2- and 3-digit x a 1-digit without
    regrouping, 218-219
  1-digit x a 2-digit with regrouping,
    220-221
  1-digit x a 3-digit with regrouping, 224-227

N

Nomograph, 313
Numbers
  comparing, 90-91
  pair and graphing, 115
  prime, 151
  puzzle, 237
Numerals
  2-digit (counting & writing), 48-49
  3-digit (counting & writing), 50-51
  4-digit (writing) 52-53

P

Pairs, number and graphing, 115
Parallelogram, 185
Patterns, 281
Perimeter, 277
Pint, 318A-318B
Place value
  2-digit numbers, 48-49
  3-digit numbers, 50-51
  grouping by tens (ten sticks), 46-52
  inequalities, 90-91
  thousands, 52-53
Point, 35
Practice wheels (addition and multiplication),
194
Practicing your skills
  addition and subtraction algorithms, 146-147
  addition, subtraction, and multiplication,
    236-237
Prime numbers, 151
Problem Solving—Using Your Skills
  addition and subtraction to 18, 26-29
  addition and subtraction of 2- and
    3-digit numbers, 84-87, 144-145,
    148-149, 188-189, 192-193, 234-235,
    238-239, 284-287, 291-292
  adding and subtracting money, 88-89
  division facts, 188-189, 192-193
  dividing, 284-287, 291-292
  estimation, 240-241
  multiplication (basic facts), 144-145,
    148-149, 188-189, 192-193
  multiplication of money, 223, 232-233
  multiplication with regrouping, 234-235,
    238-239, 284-287, 291-292
Problem Solving Bonus, 341-348
Products
  and factors, 110-111
  estimating, 240-241

Q

Quart, 318A-318B
Quotients
  finding, 168-169
  and missing factors, 174-175, 259
  subtracting to find, 170-171, 271

R

Reconstruction problems, 191
Rectangles, 36-37, 221
Regrouping
  addition of 2- and 3-digit numbers, 60-63
  more than two addends, 64-65
  subtraction of 2-digit numbers, 72-73
  subtraction of 3-digit numbers, 74-77
Remainders in division, 272
Ruler
  centimeter, 96-99
  inch, 315A-316B

S

Segment
  line, 35
  and shapes, 38-39
Sets
  and division, 166-167
  multiplication, 108-109
  parts of, 298-299
Similar figures, 156-157
Special products, 210-213
Square
  centimeter, 245
  counting units, 246-249, 317A
  inch, 317A
  shape, 35-37
Subtraction
  algorithm, 72, 74, 76-78
  difference, 3
  and division, 170-171, 271
  facts to 10, 6-7
  money, 88-89
  practice of facts for speed, 18
  trading ten-sticks, 68-69
  2- and 3-digit without regrouping, 70-71
  2-digit with regrouping, 72-73
  3-digit with regrouping, 74-77
  zeros in, 78-79
Symmetry, 303

T

Tables
  addition, 5, 19
  multiplication, 119, 123, 139
  subtraction, 7, 19
Ten-sticks
  addition, 56-57
  place value, 46-48
  subtraction, 68-69
Tenths
  fractions, 300-301
  of a centimeter, 308-309
Thousands, 52-53
Time
  five-minute intervals, 320B
  half hour and quarter hour, 320A
Trading ten-sticks
  2- and 3-digit addition, 56-57
  subtraction, 68-69
Triangle, 36-37

V

Volume
  by counting cubic units, 250-251, 317B
  liquid measure, 252-253, 318A-318B

Y

Yard, 316A-316B

Z

Zero, in subtraction, 78-79